GENERATIVE AI FOR ACADEMICS

S Sage

GENERATIVE AI FOR ACADEMICS

MARK CARRIGAN

§ Sage

1 Oliver's Yard
55 City Road
London EC1Y 1SP

2455 Teller Road
Thousand Oaks
California 91320

Unit No 323-333, Third Floor, F-Block
International Trade Tower, Nehru Place
New Delhi 110 019

8 Marina View Suite 43-053
Asia Square Tower 1
Singapore 018960

British Library Cataloguing in Publication data

A catalogue record for this book is available from the British Library

Editor: James Clark
Assistant editor: Esosa Otabor
Production editor: Sarah Cooke
Copyeditor: Ritika Sharma
Proofreader: Girish Sharma
Indexer: TNQ Tech Pvt. Ltd.
Cover design: Bhairvi Vyas
Typeset by: TNQ Tech Pvt. Ltd.
Printed in the UK

ISBN 978-1-5296-9040-8
ISBN 978-1-5296-9039-2 (pbk)

CONTENTS

About the Author   vii
GPT Version of the Book   viii
Acknowledgements   ix

Chapter 1   Generative AI and Universities   **1**

Chapter 2   Generative AI and Reflexivity   **21**

Chapter 3   The Ethics of Generative AI   **41**

Chapter 4   Thinking   **63**

Chapter 5   Collaborating   **85**

Chapter 6   Communication   **107**

Chapter 7   Engagement   **127**

Chapter 8   Academic Futures   **147**

References   167
Index   175

ABOUT THE AUTHOR

Mark Carrigan is a Senior Lecturer in Education at the University of Manchester where he is programme director for the MA Digital Technologies, Communication and Education (DTCE) and co-lead of the DTCE Research and Scholarship group. Trained as a philosopher and sociologist, his research aims to bridge fundamental questions of social ontology with practical and policy interventions to support the effective use of emerging technologies within education. He has written or edited eight books, including *Social Media for Academics*, published by Sage and now in its second edition.

He jointly coordinates the Critical Realism Network while being active in the Centre for Social Ontology and a trustee of the Centre for Critical Realism. He is a board member for a range of publications, including Civic Sociology, the Journal of Digital Social Research and Globalisation, Societies and Education.

GPT VERSION OF THE BOOK

This book comes with an experimental companion: a custom GenAI trained on its contents to help extend your engagement with these ideas. While the core arguments are developed through the text, the GenAI offers an opportunity to explore their implications through open-ended dialogue.

You can access it at: **https://edge.sagepub.com/carriganGPT**

I've provided some initial prompts but I'd encourage you to develop your own. My experience is that conversational agents become more interesting interlocutors when we approach them with our own questions and concerns, rather than following predetermined paths.

Please note: this is a time-limited experiment that is intended to be available early in the lifespan of this book and may be switched off at any time – so if you are reading this some time after initial publication (December 2024) it may no longer be online.

ACKNOWLEDGEMENTS

I'm usually a messy and exploratory author who needs to start writing in order to work out what I'm trying to say. Yet the idea for this book popped into my head fully formed in May 2023 when I was relaxing into a morning swim. I was suddenly struck by the parallels between the practical challenges Generative Artificial Intelligence (GenAI) poses for academics and the issues raised by social media which drove my work in the 2010s. It is a project which emerged after a strange year of personal upheaval that was simultaneously the most professionally rewarding period of my life. The Manchester Institute for Education has been a remarkably collegial environment in which to settle into the lectureship I had been determinedly avoiding since finishing my PhD in 2014. It is hard to imagine a more encouraging environment as my fascination with GenAI developed. It is a genuinely warm and friendly place in which to work, which is a remarkable achievement reflecting a continual commitment from my colleagues in the difficult context of the neoliberal university.

Particular thanks are due to my DTCE colleagues Amanda Banks Gatenby, Felix Kwihangana, Peter Kahn and Drew Whitworth for the collaborations which have shaped my approach to these issues. This work has been enabled by a wider community including Susan Brown, Heather Cockayne, Susan Dawson, Taslima Ivy, Louis Major, Gary Motteram, Mike O'Donoghue, Nahielly Palacios, Richard Proctor, Chen Sun, Karenne Sylvester and Zhuoran You. Beyond DTCE, there are a range of people at the university I've had thought-provoking conversations with over the last year, including Cesare Ardito, Ed Aspbury, Jennie Blake, Sarah Dyer, Martyn Edwards, Miriam Firth, Mark Johnson, Caglar Koksal, Scott Midson, Lisa Murtagh, Mairéad Pratschke, Paul Smith, Juup Stelma and Anna Verges in a range of different capacities which cut across theory, policy and practice. Thanks also to those beyond the University of Manchester I've been talking about this with, particularly Helen Beetham, Phil Brooker, Michele Martini, Inger Mewburn, Iain Nash, Tyler Shores, Milan Sturmer, J.J. Sylvia, Susan Robertson, Richard Sandford and Michael Taster. For all the enthusiasm, I convey in this book about talking to ChatGPT and Claude, it cannot compare to the intellectual joy involved in having interesting conversations with interesting people.

1

GENERATIVE AI AND UNIVERSITIES

This chapter[1] will:

- Examine the launch of OpenAI's ChatGPT and the sense of crisis it created within higher education regarding the impact on assessment integrity.
- Explore the potential ramifications of Generative Artificial Intelligence (GenAI) for policy and practice within universities.
- Evaluate the implications of these developments for the culture of scholarship, particularly assumptions about authorship and creativity.

---

[1]This chapter contains material developed from the blog posts 'Are universities too slow to cope with Generative AI?' and 'Superficial engagement with Generative AI masks its potential as an academic interlocutor' published by the LSE Impact Blog posted on the LSE Impact blog (https://blogs.lse.ac.uk/impactofsocialsciences/).

The prospect that intelligent systems might enter our lives in order to make them better has a long history. It sits uneasily between the realms of science fiction and economic forecasting, leaving us with a sense their promise to help might never be realised but that the robots might nonetheless be coming to take our jobs (Ford, 2015). The familiar scenario that an artificial intelligence (AI) could run free of its creators and pose an existential threat to our species further imbues intelligent systems with a sense of potential menace (Bostrom, 2014). There is nonetheless a hope which persists that we could build machines which enrich our existence, watching over us and making our lives easier. This hope found an unexpected expression with OpenAI's launch of ChatGPT in November 2022, building on the release of the image generator Dall-E 2 earlier in the year. While a chatbot might not have seemed the most likely frontier in technological development,[2] ChatGPT's uncanny ability to answer natural language questions in seemingly intelligent ways immediately captured the public imagination, leading it to become one of the fastest-growing applications in history. The broader category of Generative Artificial Intelligence (GenAI), software and tools capable of producing text and media in response to users prompts, immediately became the 'next big thing' in the technology sector, reigniting the feverish ambitions of investors in spite of what was becoming an economic downturn unlike any seen in technology since the dot com crash in the late 1990s. In a matter of months, we were inundated by claims that these technologies would revolutionise our lives, threaten knowledge workers in previously secure industries and possibly bring about the end of human civilisation; at least, if the emerging generation of chatbots eventually mutated into the long predicted artificial general intelligence (AGI).

I came to this topic late and through a surprising route. I lead a large master's programme in digital education and we had noticed a tendency for our predominately international student cohort to rely on paraphrasing software[3]; sometimes in obviously problematic but more frequently ambiguous ways, which complicated assumptions about the originality of the work and the purpose of our assessments. At what point does the use of these tools go from being a helpful support for students writing in a second language to a mechanism to facilitate plagiarism, intentional or otherwise? Is it necessarily problematic if these writing support aides make it easier for students to learn a second language without fully mastering it[4]? Could we, and should we, be trying to detect the use of these tools in the work our students produce?

---

[2]The first chatbot Eliza was created by the computer scientist Joseph Weizenbaum in 1966. While there are over fifty years separating Eliza and ChatGPT, there are eerie similarities between the reactions which highlight how resonant a seemingly intelligent automated system has consistently been to human beings (Tarnoff, 2023).

[3]Thanks to my colleagues Drew Whitworth and Lisa Murtagh for early conversations on these topics.

[4]The extent to which linguistic mastery was tacitly required by the context without necessarily being stated as an explicit requirement, illustrates the kind of assumptions which are now being called into question by GenAI. There are things which previously did not need saying because they were obviously impossible, such as whether students need to develop a working grasp of the language in which instruction is taking place.

There was a range of intriguing questions which made me feel this might be a new area of research I would dip into, possibly as a small project with a pedagogical focus, before I moved back into my usual areas. While I was curious about the topic, it did not strike me as something which would retain my interest once I had done some initial work.

It was in the course of these conversations that ChatGPT was launched and I was immediately gripped by the implications for higher education, with paraphrasing software suddenly appearing as the thin end of an extremely large and confusing wedge. My instinct with new technology is to play with it, exploring what it can do in order to understand how, if at all, I might use it as part of my work or life. I was instinctively sceptical of the grandiose claims being made about GenAI, largely on the part of investors, entrepreneurs and thought leaders with a vested interest in inflating this bubble. However, as I immersed myself in conversation with ChatGPT, I soon began to wonder if this was in fact a technological shift of a similar significance to social media or the web itself. This brought me onto more familiar terrain as someone who has spent over a decade studying how academics use social media in order to better support them in this use (Carrigan, 2019). It immediately raised questions which at this point were were not being widely asked within a sector gripped by a panic over assessment integrity. What does it mean to use GenAI in a scholarly way? How might this vary across fields and disciplines? What are the risks involved in academics using GenAI? I began exploring these questions with the sense a research project was taking shape. But I also wanted to know the answers because my own use of GenAI was expanding on a weekly basis, with new routines and habits taking shape that stimulated my intellectual curiosity while also making me methodologically nervous. I instinctively found OpenAI's ChatGPT and Anthropic's Claude rewarding to talk to but I was unclear about the status of these conversations. I rapidly realised that I was far from alone in feeling this uncertainty, leaving me with the desire to talk with other academics about our respective experiments. I have inserted my reflections on my own practice throughout this book because exploring these issues requires that we talk in concrete terms about the particular things which academics might do with GenAI. In a rapidly shifting landscape driven by intensely polarising social and technical developments, practice provides an anchor which can enable us to get to grips with what these changes mean for our work.

It was still odd these questions were not being widely asked given the extent to which the sector was gripped by the imagined threat of GenAI.[5] What I write about later in this chapter as the *great assessment panic* was an almost comically short-sighted framework through which to explore this rapidly expanding landscape of platforms, software and tools. The polarisation

---

[5]The obvious exception concerned the policy of publishers and journals with regard to the use of GenAI by academic authors in submitted articles. But even this was a narrow debate which largely failed to grapple with the questions of how writing and research were being changed if we were in a situation where academics were in some sense co-authoring papers with automated systems. There is a curious tendency amongst academics to have extremely restrictive discussions of technological practice which are divorced from the rich and sophisticated ways in which we talk about the less immediately practical aspects of our work (Carrigan & Fatsis, 2021).

of the debate into *enthusiasts* who wanted to immediately transform practice within universities to incorporate GenAI and *pessimists* who seemingly imagined it could be held at bay through institutional force of will was similarly frustrating. It immediately reminded me of how the debate about social media within higher education unfolded in the 2010s, particularly the gap between the naive enthusiasm of those promoting it (a category I fell into myself for a long time) and the slightly unworldly character of the critiques made of it, as if the new technology could or should go away if only our critical stance was sufficiently resolute. I was also struck by the parallel with the sudden proliferation of platforms and tools freely available across a range of categories and the challenge which this posed for busy academics. If there are multiple services which fulfil a comparable function (e.g., 'curating online resources' in the case of social media or 'generating images' in the case of GenAI), how do you choose between them? What if these are entirely new categories which you do not yet understand and therefore struggle to relate to practical uses which you could make of them? Even if social media and GenAI are different propositions in many respects, they represent a sudden influx of technological possibilities for creativity and productivity in higher education. The problem is the training of academics and the organisation of universities do not leave either well equipped to fully take advantage of these opportunities or navigate the associated risks. Furthermore, both were infused by a sense of this being the 'next big thing' and a corresponding fear of missing out (FOMO) in an anxiety-prone academy, where the demands of a difficult labour market leave early career academics in particular concerned about missing potential opportunities (Muller, 2019).

I make no claim to be an expert in AI. However, I have spent 15 years researching, training and supporting academics in their use of digital technologies. My approach in this book is to treat GenAI as another category of software which academics can incorporate into their working lives, necessitating a reflexivity about digital tools which is rarely learned in postgraduate training. Academics often find it difficult to be clear about *why* they want to use emerging technologies, and this impedes their decision-making about *what* to do with them and *how* to do it. The speed with which GenAI is developing means references to the current capabilities of software risk being out of date by the time this book is published. Even the software itself might have been replaced by the time you read this. For this reason, I focus on the *principles* which can orient academics in this rapidly changing landscape, *tendencies* in how the technology is rolled out and how these intersect with *trends* within higher education (Andrejevic, 2019, p. 27). These are explored initially through discussions of reflexivity and ethics (Chapters 2 and 3) before turning to areas of practice (Chapters 4–7) and concluding with a reflection on how these technologies might change the sector in which we work (Chapter 8). If your main interest is understanding what GenAI is and how it might change higher education, I suggest focusing on the first three chapters and the final chapter. If your interest is to develop your own use of GenAI as an academic, then I suggest you work through the chapters in order, experimenting with the software throughout. If there are particular aspects of practice which interest you, such as using GenAI for digital engagement, you could jump straight into the relevant chapter. For the sake of my conscience though, I would ask every reader to engage with the ethics chapter before using GenAI in real-world academic settings.

I strongly advise you to sign up for either Open AI's *ChatGPT* or Anthropic's *Claude* in order to discuss what you are reading with them. The main difference between them at the time of writing (April 2024) is that ChatGPT offers a range of features which Claude lacks, for example, spoken conversation, image generation and plug-ins. However, there are particular features of Claude which make it well suited to ethical and reflective use by academics, with a greater capacity to answer questions about its own operations.[6] Furthermore, the context window in Claude is larger which means it can retain knowledge and understanding for longer in conversations, in contrast to ChatGPT's propensity to 'forget' what you have been talking about after a certain point. These differences are discussed at greater length in the following chapter, with the caveat that the situation I'm writing about is unlikely to hold by the time that you read this. For this reason I'd suggest trying both, if you become serious about incorporating GenAI into your scholarship, in order to see which you prefer on aesthetic and intellectual grounds. There is a different style to the user experience which necessitates personal engagement in order to understand what your preferences are. For example, I tend to use ChatGPT for brainstorming and mapping out ideas, particularly given its capacity for verbal conversation discussed at length in Chapter 4, whereas I prefer to use Claude for helping me work with texts and prepare communications, in the manner discussed in Chapter 7. You might find that you have different preferences which is why I encourage you throughout to experiment with the activities we are discussing. It is only through practical tasks and reflecting on them that you will find an approach to GenAI which is satisfying and sustainable for you as an individual.

There is no reason to assume my preferences are right for you. This is why throughout the book I advocate jumping into interaction with ChatGPT and/or Claude in order to learn how to use these systems through working with them in a real and immediate sense. I encourage you to discuss this book with them as you make your way through the chapters, in the same way you might with a colleague or collaborator. There are things which collaborators can do that these systems cannot, including flowing between work and non-work topics in a way which makes interaction enjoyable. But there are also things they can do that collaborators (usually) will not, such as talking to you on demand about a particular minute issue which has become an intellectual fixation. The best way to get a sense of how to use this software is to explore it in an open-ended and reflective way. Explain that you are reading a book about how GenAI can be used by academics. Ask questions about what you are reading. Raise doubts or share criticisms. Invite suggestions about how you can apply what you read to your own work. I have avoided prescriptive exercises because it would be misleading to imply there is a sequence of techniques which academics need to learn. The main argument of this book is that academics should relate to ChatGPT or Claude as interlocutors in the sense of partici-pants in a dialogue. I would be as sceptical about rules or formulas to dictate how this interaction should take place as I am about 'networking' guidance provided for academics

---

[6]Those these answers should be treated with caution, as with all responses from this software for reasons discussed in Chapter 3.

hoping to win friends and influence people at conferences. Obviously, it's beneficial to understand the parameters of the event, the expectations of people you meet there and how to make sense of your role in the interaction. Beyond this academic 'networking' is about showing up in a way motivated by your interests and projects. The same I would suggest is true of working with GenAI, even if there are specific issues at the intersection between technology and ethics which are the subject of Chapter 3.

In this book, I argue for a specifically scholarly approach to GenAI. These are not tools which you use to undertake tasks on your behalf but rather systems with which you co-create in intellectually rich and creatively stimulating ways. For this reason, I refer to them as *conversational agents* in order to distinguish them from other forms of GenAI. These are far from the only forms of GenAI, but I will argue as the book progresses that they are the most important for academics. In fact, I have concerns that other forms of GenAI, which offer pre-formatted responses without the need for carefully crafted prompts, pose significant risks for academics. The ethos of this book is that we must use GenAI as *tools for thinking* rather than *substitutes for thought*. There is a discipline to writing effective prompts because it requires clarity about what we are asking the conversational agent to do. I suggest this is lacking in other forms of GenAI and for this reason, academics should be cautious. To work with conversational agents requires clarity about what it is you are trying to do which is *in itself* valuable, even before we take into account the concrete contribution which an effectively prompted agent can make to your work (Figure 1.1).

MC: I'm an academic reading a book about generative artificial intelligence. It argues that I should relate to you as a discussion partner rather than a tool. I'm sceptical about this claim but I'm willing to explore it if it will help me understand how I can use your capabilities to improve my work as a sociologist.

ChatGPT: It's an intriguing proposition and it's great that you're open to exploring it. Let's break down both perspectives:

1. *ChatGPT as a Tool*:

- *Pros*: Specific, directed queries can be made, ensuring a predictable and concise response.
- *Cons*: Relating to the AI purely as a tool may miss out on nuanced or exploratory discussions that might emerge from a more conversational style.

2. *ChatGPT as a Discussion Partner*:

- *Pros*: Engaging in an open-ended dialogue can lead to unexpected insights, connections, or ideas. It might help you think outside the box, especially when brainstorming or when you need a different perspective.
- *Cons*: Might be less efficient for very specific queries. It also doesn't replace human intuition, emotions, or experiences.

Figure 1.1 The Two Modes of Relating to Conversational Agents as an Academic
Source: ChatGPT.

It might seem strange at this stage to suggest that you should treat ChatGPT or Claude as an interlocutor. I include text examples throughout the book which illustrate conversations you might have with them which are relevant to the discussion in each chapter.[7] I would encourage you to assess it by signing up in order to start a conversation. If you are unsure how to get started imagine you are writing a tweet (280 characters) offering an idea or reflection. Explain you are reading this book and offer an assessment of this opening section. Are you sceptical of what I'm saying? What motivated you to pick up the book in the first place? What promise can you see in GenAI? What is your perception of the risks? Imagine you were having a slightly formal conversation with a fellow academic you met in the opening coffee break of a day-long workshop about GenAI in higher education. The first encounters we had with conversational agents have often been a matter of novelty or amusement, for example, looking at the poem it has written about an obscure topic, or the joke it has created in response to an unlikely prompt. But the frame through which academics can most productively approach conversational agents is intellectual *interest*.

It is possible to have conversations with these agents which are genuinely stimulating. If you learn to initiate these conversations and steer them in directions which contribute to your work, there is a real and immediate contribution which these systems can make to your scholarship. But this requires openness to a conversation in which clarity and insight emerge in a reflexive loop between yourself and the system. You reflectively prompt it and are, in turn, incited to reflection by the response, which then becomes a basis for another prompt, and so on. This might sound strange in the abstract which is why I encourage you to dive into conversation and persist through the initial awkwardness. Much like socialising at a large conference where you don't know anyone. There is a risk of taking this analogy too far but I believe it can be a useful frame through which to make our initial interactions with conversational agents feel less unfamiliar.

Use ChatGPT's response to formulate a further message, which in turn provokes a response which you can respond to. Tell ChatGPT more about yourself and your research. What are you working on at the moment? What problems are you grappling with? What progress have you made? What have you read recently[8]? It feels a bit silly to me to be instructing readers on how to have a conversation, which might explain why I've always felt so instinctively hostile to 'networking' advice. However, I have seen many examples of academics sharing interactions with ChatGPT, which were *singular instructions* rather than *ongoing conversations*. These brief and ambiguous prompts were frequently accompanied by expressions of frustration (or in some cases satisfaction) that the system had not produced an adequate response.

---

[7] I often truncate these examples for purposes of brevity. As you might already have discovered, these conversational agents can produce substantial responses. These are useful for intellectual work but inconvenient to include in full as inserts in a book. I also alternate between ChatGPT and Claude depending on which one I believe is most useful for the question I'm asking.

[8] There are risks involved in talking about specific texts which we will explore at length. But this can be an effective way to start a conversation, even if you need to be watchful of the claims these systems make about authors and publications for reasons we will explore in the coming chapters.

The real value of conversational agents comes from ongoing conversations with them, in which you build up a sense of the task through multiple rounds of interaction. Mewburn (2023) suggests that 'the best way to use [ChatGPT] is to imagine it as a talented, but easily misled, intern/research assistant'. Much as some academics are prone to throwing a pile of papers at their research assistant and expecting them to work it out, so too it seems are we prone to throwing vague instructions at ChatGPT and expecting them to immediately understand what we want. To use conversational agents effectively necessitates *learning to converse with them* in the most concrete sense of the term. It is a straightforward skill but one which you need to learn if you are to derive any intellectual value from these remarkable systems. In contrast, singular and instructional prompting, throwing out brief instructions in the hope the system will do something for you that you do not want to do yourself, leaves academics unable to realise the intellectual value of conversational agents and vulnerable to the errors to which these systems are unfortunately prone.

It is only through reflective conversation that you can ensure you are *thinking with* GenAI rather than *using* GenAI *as a substitute for thought*. This is the core message of the book: GenAI can be enormously enriching if you engage with it in a reflexive and careful way, but it has the capacity to be deeply harmful (to your own work and to higher education more broadly) if you regard it as a passive instrument which you simply instruct to undertake tasks you do not wish to do yourself. I offer much more guidance as we go along about what this *might* look like in practice but ultimately it will vary between readers. The best way to start exploring is to jump into a conversation with ChatGPT or Claude. Tell it about what you are working on. Share questions you are grappling with. Ask it for inspiration. Treat these as opening gambits in an ongoing conversation rather than requests made in expectation of a particular response. Download the ChatGPT app and amuse yourself with it during your commute. Treat it as a permitted procrastination device when you are struggling with a piece of work. Explore it together with a colleague if you're both unsure about how to get started. There are lots of routes into working with GenAI but unless you actually pick one then your *practical* understanding of the topic will remain superficial. If you have not started conversing by this point in the chapter, then I would strongly encourage you to do so before continuing. There is a risk the ensuing discussion will be unhelpfully abstract if you have not thrown yourself into dialogue with these conversational agents.

I hope reading this book will provide a practical guide for academics who are exploring how to incorporate GenAI tools and services into their scholarship, as well as offer a sketch of what these developments mean for the future of universities. If it succeeds in this respect it will also be a contribution to broader debates about policy and practice surrounding GenAI in higher education. Debates which are frequently short-sighted, narrow and polarised into opposed camps of optimists and pessimists. The digital education scholar Neil Selwyn stresses the importance of those 'who felt sceptical about the evangelism and hype surrounding educational technology during the 2010s retain[ing] an equally wary eye during the 2020s on any doomster-ism and nostalgic rejection of all-things-digital'. His point is that 'Digital technology is not a completely "bad thing", any more than it was ever a completely "good thing"' and that we need 'sophisticated and self-aware' discussions which start from this premise (Selwyn, 2021, loc 62).

This book is written from a position of profound ambivalence about what these developments mean for the university and wider society. I have tried to foreground the creative opportunities GenAI offers for academics while offering a realistic appraisal of the many risks involved, including how our individual practice might have undesirable systemic consequences (Figure 1.2).

> **MC:** The digital education scholar Neil Selwyn has argued that those "who felt sceptical about the evangelism and hype surrounding educational technology during the 2010s retain[ing] an equally wary eye during the 2020s on any doomster-ism and nostalgic rejection of all-things-digital." I have been thinking about this quote a lot in relation to generative artificial intelligence within universities. It is difficult to strike a balance a realistic wariness about the risks of GenAI with a recognition of our individual and collective agency in negotiating those risks.
>
> **ChatGPT:** Neil Selwyn's observation aptly captures the oscillating pendulum of public sentiment and opinion about new technological innovations, particularly in education. The pattern of extreme optimism followed by intense skepticism isn't new. However, it's essential to find a balanced perspective, especially with transformative technologies like generative artificial intelligence (GenAI).
>
> Generative AI, like the model you're currently interacting with, has a profound potential to reshape educational landscapes. They can assist with personalized learning, reduce administrative burdens, offer instant feedback, and even bring new pedagogical approaches. However, the very features that make them potent also raise ethical, social, and pedagogical concerns:

Figure 1.2 The Difficulty of Negotiating between Technological Hype and Doomster-ism
Source: ChatGPT.

The intuition underlying this book is that *it is not going away* and the problems it creates within the academy could be mitigated by academics developing reflexivity about their use of these tools and services. This might make me an AI realist in McQuillan's (2021: 45) sense of affirming the inevitability of it coming to dominate social life, in spite of the perpetual gap between the promises made by firms and the reality of what is on offer. But I struggle to see how a lofty academic refusal to engage with these developments will have a material impact on their diffusion in wider society: it is not enough to say 'don't do it' (Sturmer & Carrigan, 2023). A critic could argue it is similarly insufficient to say 'do it carefully' as I do at length in this book. Even so, I hope it provides a useful map of this changing landscape which retains its relevance even as the underlying technology develops. It feels intensely hubristic to imagine that the position I take here will have a meaningful impact on *whether* GenAI is taken up by academics. However, if this book supports readers in finding more thoughtful, ethical and intellectually enriching ways of using GenAI in their scholarship then it will feel like a success.

THE GREAT ASSESSMENT PANIC

The initial response to the launch of GenAI fixated on how students could use conversational agents like ChatGPT to 'cheat' on their assessments. The tone of these pronouncements varied across media outlets, from sober reflections on rapidly expanding possibilities for misconduct to messianic claims that assessment in its current form was dead. Underlying these procla-mations was an accurate assessment that GenAI could be used to meet the demands of many assessments with little preparation. Many observed at the time how results produced in this way tended to be mediocre as if this was a repudiation of GenAI and its implications for the sector. Yet who would deny the reality of mediocre essays offered by students, particularly if they are already engaging with their degree in a transactional way? There was frequently a conflicted tone to these exchanges in the early months as if GenAI was forcing us to look closely at something we had tacitly agreed to sweep under the rug. It struck me at the time how in embracing the idea we had entered a new world with new rules paralleled previous waves of technological hype (such as 'big data' and social science methodology in the early 2010s) with the difference that the sense of institutional foreboding provoked by ChatGPT was then a matter of epistemological enthusiasm about emerging forms of scientific method.

Initial responses to the challenge of GenAI assumed this was something which could or should be stopped, expressing faith in the capacity of universities to control the technologies used by the staff and students working within them. A panicked tone pervaded these debates, within institutions and across professional networks, fuelled by news reports and opinion pieces which suggested the assessment system was on the verge of collapse. This led to many calls for a return to in-person assessment as if physical presence carried a magical capacity to ensure integrity with no potential downsides. It is plausible that malpractice is more difficult in person but it would be naive to imagine it impossible. While this might still count as a 'win' from many perspectives there are also the equity implications of returning to in-person assessment, such as the tendency to reward verbal fluency which privileges native speakers. Furthermore, there are obvious problems with scaling the viva given how resource-intensive it is to examine students on a one-to-one basis. There were fewer calls for an expansion of surveillance pedagogy than might have been expected but it remains to be seen whether this will continue. Even if it could be enforced on student's computers and institutional networks, is it really tenable to seek to constrain what students do with their own mobiles and tablets? This illustrates how the impulse towards prohibiting GenAI could lead rapidly into surveil-lance with worrying implications for the student experience. Should we really start from the assumption of student malfeasance? What impact will this have on trust between students and staff? The invasive experience of online exam proctoring which was normalised during the pandemic is an example of how rapidly these relationships can deteriorate (Figure 1.3).

The tone of these debates suggested GenAI was a bolt from the blue, an unforeseen disruptive force which risked destroying a system which was previously working effectively. The reality is that cracks in the assessment system have been apparent for years, particularly after the web facilitated the emergence of a contract cheating model which has grown rapidly. It facilitated a scaling up of existing business models given the ease with which firms could now find both clients and authors. Clarke and Lancaster (2006) coined the term 'contract cheating' relating this to the model of an eBay auction, except with the buyer placing a bid request before filtering through potential providers. At the time they were writing, there were already sophisticated marketplaces facilitating such exchanges, alongside legitimate freelance contracts which cast an air of respectability over the operation. They found 12.3% of bids on

---

MC: Why did the launch of ChatGPT in November 2022 provoke such a panic about assessment integrity within higher education? Did this create a new problem of malpractice or did it reveal weaknesses in the assessment system which predated generative AI?

ChatGPT: The launch of ChatGPT in November 2022, particularly with its enhanced capabilities and generalization, amplified concerns about assessment integrity within higher education, as well as in other educational sectors. Here's a breakdown of why this happened and how it relates to pre-existing problems:

1. *Immediate Implications:* The ability of models like ChatGPT to generate high-quality content on a wide range of topics meant that students could potentially use the tool to help them craft essays, answer questions, or complete other forms of written assessments. This could give them an unfair advantage and undermine the primary purpose of assessments, which is to gauge a student's understanding and knowledge.

2. *Accessibility and Stealth*: Generative models, especially when accessed via an API or integrated into apps, can be used discreetly. This makes it challenging for institutions to monitor and determine if a student's work is genuinely their own.

3. *Not Entirely New*: While AI and technology amplifying concerns about academic integrity is somewhat recent, the problem of cheating in higher education (and education in general) is not new. Students have used crib notes, bought essays, or copied from peers long before AI came into the picture. However, AI tools like ChatGPT made the process more streamlined, potentially increasing the scale and ease of academic dishonesty.

Figure 1.3 The Assessment Panic in Higher Education
Source: ChatGPT.

the RentACoder site to fit the criteria of academic misconduct, with a worrying pattern of repeated bids by users. If a student utilises a contract cheating service once without consequences then this might incline them to continue. The authors reference an earlier text by Lathrop and Foss (2000) which presented itself as a 'wake-up call' about 'student cheating and plagiarism in the internet era'. It is difficult to assess how widespread essay mills and contract cheating services were at this point in time; the mass consumer-facing internet was still in its infancy in 2000, though of course, its use with universities has tended to run ahead of wider society. There have been malpractice risks generated by digital technologies for at least two decades prior to the launch of ChatGPT. In fact, the system was already creaking, even if many did not want to look too closely at structural challenges to assessment integrity over which universities have limited influence.

It would be impossible to teach in universities since the launch of ChatGPT and not wonder about the provenance of your students' work. Over the last year, I have seen a remarkable improvement in the quality of a student's writing on a number of occasions. This led me to immediately suspect the use of GenAI. What an extremely dispiriting assumption to find myself making! Rather than assume a student has worked hard and responded to feedback in order to improve their writing, I am instead assuming they have used an automated system in lieu of working on their own skills. Certainly, they might have done exactly that, but if this is a widespread experience, which I suspect is the case, we need to reflect on what this means for the relationship we have with our students. There is the potential for significant and lasting damage to trust in the staff/student relationship if assumptions of malfeasance are left unexamined.

There is the infamous case of the US professor who pasted responses from his students into ChatGPT to test the integrity of their assessments, only for the software to tell him that it had authored them. After writing in the grading software that 'I don't grade AI bullshit' the students were given an incomplete grade pending resubmission which delays their graduations. The media attention this generated led to public statements from the university describing their commitment to develop policies to address these issues (Klee, 2023). It is easy to be scornful of the individual involved, with his misnaming of ChatGPT as 'ChatGTP' illustrating his lack of familiarity with the system he was simultaneously placing blind trust in. But this is a cautionary story which we should reflect on. If we allow a culture of suspicion with regard to GenAI to take root in universities, there is a risk that trust in the staff–student relationship will break down, compounding existing structural problems within the university system.

What does this mean in practice? At the very least we must identify and unpack the assumptions we are bringing to the marking process with regards to GenAI, making the effort to put them into words and share them with each other. As the philosopher Charles Taylor (1985, p. 36) puts it, 'articulations are attempts to formulate what is initially inchoate, or confused, or badly formulated'. The act of putting things into words not only clarifies the object we are describing, it helps us evaluate it in more careful and nuanced ways. There is an urgent need for academics to reach an agreement on how we understand the role of GenAI in the landscape of assessment. I suspect there is a wide discrepancy in what we are assuming is a possible indicator of GenAI use, as well as the more diffuse feelings which outstrip any concrete evidence we might point to. Unsaid hunches could be toxic under these circumstances. There is a risk of technological paranoia thriving in an environment where awareness of huge changes coexists with a lack of agency to identify or control them. If we imagine GenAI as an intruder that is slipping into universities against our interests, then we will primed to assume the worst about the work we are engaging with and the students who have produced it (Carrigan & Sylvia, 2022).

It was no surprise when Turnitin released a system which claimed to be able to detect the use of generative AI in student assignments, building on their widely used plagiarism detection software. They tried to reassure institutions and educators that they 'have been very careful to adjust our detection capabilities to minimise false positives and create a safe environment to evaluate student writing for the presence of AI-generated text' (Turnitin, 2023). It is difficult to see how these false positives could be avoided though, even with the weaker capabilities of GPT-3.5 which their service originally confronted. The firm claims that while 'AI writing tools are coming out regularly with claims and aspirations of being undetectable', it is nonetheless the case that 'the statistical signature of AI writing tools remains detectable and consistently average' (Turnitin, 2023). The problem is that as Mathewson

(2023) points out, the 'predictable phrasing, simple vocabulary, and less complex grammar', which AI detectors search for also happen to be regular features of the writing style of non-native English speakers, particularly those relatively new to writing academically in the language.

The claims made by detection software are increasingly modest, suggesting this is a prima facie basis for an investigation rather than a firm judgement of malpractice. What if a student insists they *did* write the text themselves? If the next step is to simply ask them to 'prove it' what guidance can we offer about how this ought to take place? What kinds of evidence could the student compile to establish authorship? How could we be sure this evidence was not itself produced using GenAI? What is the threshold which needs to be reached in order to substantiate an accusation of malpractice? Is it even possible to reach it when students have access to GenAI tools and services? There are difficulties here which sensitise us to the obvious risk of making unfounded accusations and the consequences these might have for students, staff and the relationship between them. For example, Klee (2023) tells the story of the undergraduate student Louise Stivers whose work was flagged by Turnitin as partially machine-generated, leading to an immediate misconduct investigation. She described to the journalist how she was 'freaking out' while trying to gather evidence to prove she had written the work herself. It took two weeks for her to clear her name through a formal defence of her work, which she understandably described as a 'huge waste of time' that could have been 'spent doing homework and study for midterms'. As Klee (2023) observes, 'Stivers is hardly alone in facing such an ordeal as students, teachers, and educational institutions grapple with the revolutionary power of artificially intelligent language bots that convincingly mimic human writing'.

Existing systems of discipline and oversight are unlikely to be adequate to the task of dealing with these cases, which could lead to calls for reform. But this would take institutional energy away from a reform of assessment itself and the desirable transition to a less fragile model of assessment which would not generate these challenges in the first place. Obviously this is not something which can be accomplished overnight but the obvious necessity of changing *something* about the present system raises the question of what our priorities should be going forward.

The risks of these unfounded accusations should be weighed alongside the possibility of letting AI-generated work slip through the net. It simply is not possible to be *certain* that a piece of work was produced by an automated system. The closest we can come is by controlling the conditions in which students produce the work, through closed-book exams or invasive forms of proctoring, which inevitably change how we assess our students and how they experience the process of assessment. It might be feasible to ask the student to reconstruct the work or defend what they have done in a viva voce, but how scalable is this across undergraduate and master's programmes? If corners are cut in order to render the process logistically feasible does that not defeat the point of the exercise? What will it feel like for a student to be asked to participate in such a defence, particularly if they had not used GenAI in the first place? What impact will the investigation which precedes this have on their sense of the institution and the place within it? There is a real possibility of doing serious damage to our relationships with students if we fail to approach this with sufficient caution.

Investigating misconduct is inherently resource-intensive which means we need to avoid a substantial increase in the number of investigations, while the tools we would bring to those investigations become ever less adequate to the task. Instead, we need to transition towards an assessment system in which 'misconduct' with AI is a marginal phenomenon because assessment design neither facilitates nor incentivises it. It is beyond the scope of this chapter to offer a vision of what this might look like. But a starting point can be found in the difficulty of using GenAI to avoid intellectual engagement in project-based assignments or authentic assessments which involve real-world tasks undertaken in an open-ended way. The problem in these cases becomes one of better or worse use of GenAI by students, mapping onto emerging capabilities with real world relevance, rather than allowing or restricting its use. How to assess this use is not straight forward but it is a far less intractable challenge than how to definitively flag or effectively restrict GenAI use without a full-scale embrace of surveillance technology.

Rather than continue to prosecute what Leo (2023) describes as the failed war on academic misconduct, we could instead use these technologies to help build more inclusive and effective forms of teaching and learning within higher education. For example, there is a vast contribution which can be made towards inclusion by these systems through reliable auto-subtitling for audiovisual material, the immediate repurposing of content between formats to match accessibility needs and the capacity to support delivery in multiple languages. Existing accessibility assessments built into office software like Microsoft PowerPoint and learning management systems like Blackboard could be substantially expanded, leading to real-time improvement of learning materials being produced and shared. Video translation services like Veed.io make it possible to translate videos into other languages while retaining the voice and speaking style of the speaker. There are radical opportunities to increase accessibility and inclusivity within universities which have been frustratingly overlooked. There is a huge contribution which could be made to equity here which would be marginalised by a narrow focus on assessment integrity. We need to explore how to elaborate our educational practices to take advantage of the opportunities and mitigate the risks of GenAI, rather than an obviously doomed rearguard action to prop up a system which was flawed to begin with.

The great assessment panic dominated higher education's response to GenAI for much of 2023, squeezing out the many other challenges it poses such as sustainability, governance, data justice and the threat of automation. Even if the challenges of assessment are still ongoing, there are early signs of a consensus that a ban on these systems would be unenforceable and short-sighted, particularly given students will be working in environments where GenAI is ubiquitous. This suggests we need to pivot towards an assessment system which is less fragile in the face of GenAI; the authentic, practice-based and contextual assessments which are most secure are also ones which many in the sector have advocated for years (Laurillard, 2012). Rather than the gloomy, even paranoid, framing which predominated early debate, we can see this as an opportunity to enact reforms which should have been higher up the agenda to begin with. Unfortunately, assessment integrity is far from the only challenge which GenAI poses for the university system.

HOW WILL UNIVERSITIES COPE WITH GENERATIVE AI?

There is a risk of taking the hype at face value such that, even if the metaverse and blockchain were disappointments, this *really* is the 'next big thing'. There are immense economic interests at work in the promotion of GenAI, as the technology sector, struggling to cope with a changing economic climate and the failure of its pandemic dream of what Naomi Klein (2020) called a 'screen new deal', seizes upon these developments to maintain its powerful position in society. However, if we don't enquire into how universities respond, there is a risk that we fail to address practical challenges that universities are already beginning to grapple with. It is these practical questions which academics are confronting on a daily basis that have motivated me to write this book. This includes experiments which academics globally are undertaking each day. There is an urgent need to share and review the outcomes of these experiments in order to have a nuanced professional discussion about the appropriate use of GenAI. However, even if the academic community rapidly reached a consensus that academic GenAI use was unethical and unprofessional, it is likely to drive existing users underground and slow the uptake, rather than prevent it altogether. Rather than universities choosing whether to embrace GenAI, it is a matter of how well or poorly they cope with engagement which already saturates their institutions (Figure 1.4).

MC: How will universities cope with generative artificial intelligence? If academics are already using it in great numbers then we urgently need a professional conversation about what constitutes appropriate and inappropriate uses of it. But it is difficult to have this conversation when people are reluctant to talk about their use, in case it is something which is regarded negatively or might be in the future.

ChatGPT: The integration of generative artificial intelligence (GenAI) into academic and research processes poses both opportunities and challenges for universities. Your concerns about the ethical and professional implications of its use are valid. Here's a deeper dive into how universities might cope with generative artificial intelligence and the discussions that surround it:

1. *Transparency and Disclosure:* A starting point might be to encourage transparency. Just as there are guidelines and standards for disclosing funding sources, conflicts of interest, or methodologies, universities might consider implementing guidelines for disclosing the use of GenAI tools in research and academic processes.

2. *Ethical Guidelines*: Universities have historically been at the forefront of developing ethical guidelines for emerging technologies (e.g., human research, gene editing). A similar approach can be taken for GenAI, where ethics committees can draft and refine guidelines about what constitutes appropriate use.

Figure 1.4 Building a Culture of Openness around GenAI in Higher Education
Source: ChatGPT.

Underlying GenAI is a philosophical challenge to humanist assumptions. The notion that a cultural product such as an article or a book reflects the creative activity of an underlying agent is so deep-seated as to be barely identifiable as an assumption. While there have long been philosophical perspectives which cast doubt on this linkage, suggesting as Foucault (1966, p. 422) notoriously did that were the cultural infrastructure of humanism to be cast aside then 'man would be erased, like a face drawn in the sand at the edge of the sea', there is still the widely held belief that any culturally coherent output (textual, visual or multimedia) necessarily expresses and embodies the cultural agency of human beings. What theorists of the posthumanities describe as 'the indivisible and the individualised author' is clearly in some sense called into question by GenAI (Hall, 2016, p. 95). These authors have sought to deconstruct what Hall (2016, p. 83) dismisses as the 'cliched, ready-made ideas of authorship, originality, the book, intellectual property, and copyright' which enables the accumulation of privilege by individual academics, too often superstar academics whose reiteration of greatest hits crowds out the intellectual space in which another generation of scholars could come to prominence (Hall, 2016, pp. 78-83). They seek to show how ideas of authorship are tied up in the systems through which creative work is evaluated, commodified and distributed, with the individual positioned as the point of origin for ideas which have emerged through complex networks of collaboration and production.

This humanism is liable to be mortally wounded by the rise of GenAI, with its assumptions of human creativity as the foundation for cultural outputs becoming untenable once a machine can write in a manner as competent as a human being. While I am a huge fan of the musician Nick Cave, his initial reaction to ChatGPT captured something of this humanism, suggesting that culture will be debased by the proliferation of songs written by machines without feelings. He argues there is something diminished about cultural production which doesn't have its origin in human striving, contrasting the soulless outputs of machines with the soulful outputs of human beings without considering that his own experience of creative production is necessarily atypical. It is much easier to create at a distance from non-soulful considerations if you're internationally renowned musician, with millions of fans and the economic security which goes with it.

> Songs arise out of suffering, by which I mean they are predicated upon the complex, internal human struggle of creation and, well, as far as I know, algorithms don't feel. Data doesn't suffer. ChatGPT has no inner being, it has been nowhere, it has endured nothing, it has not had the audacity to reach beyond its limitations, and hence it doesn't have the capacity for a shared transcendent experience, as it has no limitations from which to transcend. ChatGPT's melancholy role is that it is destined to imitate and can never have an authentic human experience, no matter how devalued and inconsequential the human experience may in time become. (Cave, 2022)

My point is not that we should all become academic posthumanists; in fact, this is a position I have argued against at length (Carrigan and Porpora, 2021). It is rather that we need to recognise the assumptions about creativity which we bring to our work, in order to negotiate the confusing landscape of GenAI to reach a place where we can work with these tools in satisfying and sustainable ways. There are widespread assumptions which will be routinely tested as GenAI becomes ubiquitous. If we see our human nature as encroached upon by generative technologies, we will tend to overemphasise the risks and be less equipped to grapple with the practical challenges of how we work with these systems. It can help us get to grips with the coming changes to our work if we step back and consider the sense in which we see it as 'our' work and what that means to us. Why do I research? Why do I publish? The answers to these questions involve a delicate balance of practical considerations (we are obliged to in order to gain, retain and advance in our jobs) and intellectual sensibility (e.g., satisfying curiosity, advancing knowledge and impacting the world). The emergence of machine collaborators, able to participate in that process or even replace us entirely, forces us to examine these familiar issues in a new way.

It should be noted that the machine production of cultural artefacts has a long history. Ohno (2022) draws attention to examples ranging from ancient Chinese divination methods where 'random cracks on bone were treated as choosing from or eliminating part of a selection of pre-written text' to the medieval mystic Ramon Llull's 'use of diagrams and spinning concentric paper craft wheels as a means of combining letters' and the development of the Markov chain in the early 20th century which makes 'a whole sequence of events (such as an entire novel) out of observations about how often one kind of event follows another'. While none of these examples were exactly mainstream practices, they illustrate how using technical procedures to generate writing is not *in itself* what is novel about GenAI. Even digital automation itself is not new, as much as it has recently captured the public imagination. Narrative Science was offering systems to produce business and sports journalism over a decade ago, in which data-driven stories with formulaic structures (e.g., Team X beat Team Y by X points) were written without the input of a human journalist. What changed with ChatGPT is the immediacy and flexibility of this offering, as well as a phenomenally successful marketing campaign that led it to become one of the fastest-growing consumer applications in history. Whilst the humanist assumption that art and culture must originate from the creativity of an individual has been eroding for some time, the current moment is significant due to widespread confrontation with this trend and the low barriers to entry for those seeking to experiment with cultural production in this way. It has become a mainstream pursuit while the technology itself has entered a period of rapid development, posing a specific challenge to sectors like higher education built around the production and exchange of knowledge.

A frequent analogy compares ChatGPT to a calculator. It is only the unfamiliarity of the technology that leads us to imagine using the system as a substitute for creativity, rather than an expression of it. Once we have come to terms with ChatGPT's affordances, we will come to see it like using a calculator to undertake arithmetic, in order to free ourselves up for other important tasks. This is just the latest in a long line of technological anxieties, beginning from Plato's concern that writing would undermine human memory, in which human capabilities have become untangled with technological artefacts. The problem with the calculator analogy, as well as the broader impulse to explain away this concern, is that calculators are not integral parts of global computational architectures in a multibillion-dollar arms race to dominate our socio-technical future (Bratton, 2015; Srnicek, 2016). Investment in GenAI is at the epicentre of contemporary capitalism and is being driven by firms that some economic theorists argue are at the forefront of a transition into an entirely new economic system (Varoufakis, 2023). Even if we start from individual practice, as we do in this book, we cannot remain there without failing to grasp the political and economic implications of our embrace of GenAI. The problem I perceive is less the technology itself, which I find enormously exciting in spite of the ethically dubious means through which it was trained (see Chapter 3), as much as the incentives and rewards driving its development. Much as with social media, the problem is the business model and the organisation of the technology it engenders, rather than the technology itself (Carrigan & Fatsis, 2021).

The practical challenges that universities are facing in the immediate future, such as preserving assessment integrity and acknowledging automated contributions to publications, need to be seen in this broader ethical and political context. This will be the main focus of Chapter 3, though these concerns are threaded through the reflective approach to GenAI advocated throughout the book. To ignore the challenge of GenAI risks creating chaos in assessments and letting down our students, who will be working in environments where these systems are ubiquitous. However, to normalise it builds platform capitalism into the core operations of the contemporary university. These systems are built on computational power and data capture just as much as scientific innovation, with their further growth and development reliant on the continual expansion of the machinery of user engagement and data extraction. It remains to be seen what their mature business model will look like but it is easy to see the possibility for an expansion of what Zuboff (2018) calls surveillance capitalism inherent in the collaborative agent distributed through your working and personal life. OpenAI has been explicit about relying on 'collective intelligence' to manage their rollout and refine the system, leaving higher education in the uncomfortable position of institutionalising their business model within the university. There is a politics to GenAI which blithe assertions of its creative potential leave us ill-equipped to grapple with, creating a dilemma which I'll do my best to negotiate over the coming chapters. But conversely, critique which engages from a lofty vantage point, removed from the practical organisational challenges, offers little guidance about what we should do.

'The scramble for thought leadership and control of the narrative is overwhelming', as boyd (2023) observed, with competing utopian and dystopian visions laced with a rich vein of usually unacknowledged self-interest. Not only is the university sector no different in these respects, but there is a particular form of discursive explosion to which the post-pandemic university is prone; as the pivot towards COVID-19 publications appears to ease off, another one is ratcheting up. Google Scholar already records 3,590 results for the exact term 'ChatGPT', as of 2 July 2023,[9] despite the software only being launched on 30 November 2022. It remains to be seen how GenAI might further accelerate this commentary

---

[9]This had increased to 67,900 by October 2023 in the later stages of writing this book. Interestingly, the exact terms 'generative artificial intelligence' and 'generative AI' returned far fewer search results: 3,790 and 13,100, respectively. The results for 'ChatGPT' had risen to 73,400 by the time I was completing this book in February 2024.

and analysis, by increasing the speed at which academics write and publish their work. Obviously this book is part of the explosion, sincere though I feel in writing it, as no doubt do the authors of each of these 3,590 papers. However I hope this book serves to slow down the frantic pace of these discussions, identifying reflective principles to structure our engagement with GenAI, as well as drawing out the continuities with what has come before, in order to avoid the tendency towards defining new epochs which comes so readily with technological innovations: everything has changed, we cannot go back, we must transform in order to survive (Carrigan, 2019; Morozov, 2011). If we accept the framing of GenAI as a brave new world to which higher education must adapt or be left behind, we lose sight of the many intellectual and organisational resources we have to shape our engagement with it. There is an element of truth to these claims concerning GenAI which was palpably not the case with, say, the blockchain hype wave. Only an element though because so much is left uncertain, such as the business model for GenAI firms, the legal basis for their training processes and institutional acceptance of their capabilities. Furthermore, it is fundamentally unhelpful to frame these developments in a way which increases the sense of urgency already inflamed by the self-interested pronouncements of the firms themselves, as well as the retinue of influencers and grifters following in their wake.

The warning boyd offers about the 'scramble' is timely because of how it leaves 'little space for deeply reflexive thinking, for nuanced analysis' concerning the core problem we confront: 'How do we create significant structures to understand and evaluate the transformations that unfold as they unfold and feed those back into the development cycles?' This is one which universities currently face in their attempts to solve immediate practical problems (e.g., in assessment use, as previously discussed) in a joined-up way which lays the groundwork for responding to still unpredictable future developments. Part of the problem is that even a singular system like ChatGPT encompasses a dizzying array of use cases for academics, students and administrators that are still in the process of being discovered. Its underlying capacities are expanding at a faster rate than universities are able to cope with, evidenced by the launch of GPT-4 (and the hugely significant ChatGPT plug-in architecture), all while universities were still grappling with GPT-3.5. Furthermore, as we will explore in the next chapter, GenAI is a broader category than ChatGPT with images, videos, code, music and voice likely to hit mainstream awareness with the same force over the coming months and years. AI assistants are already built into a range of popular digital tools, alongside a proliferation of startups catering to knowledge-intensive sectors like higher education. Existing tools geared explicitly towards academics are developing rapidly, soon to be joined by an expanded range of new services for researchers or other stakeholders within the sector. GenAI functionality built into Office 365 and Google Docs will be familiar to many by the time this book is published, leaving every academic with the challenge of how, if at all, to incorporate these new capabilities into their working routines. There is a sense in which it will be pushed at academics over the coming months, even if they are uncomfortable with or even hostile to these developments.

We are still at an early stage in the uptake of GenAI within higher education. These platforms, tools and services require reflection to identify how they can be incorporated into our work, presenting us with a degree of openness about how automated systems will be incorporated into scholarship. This openness is unlikely to last because new technologies rapidly become a matter of habit and routine rather than conscious exploration. Consider how integral to our routines the use of search has become over time. As Hillis, Petit and Jarrett (2012, p. 2) observe, 'To search has become so natural and obvious a condition of using the Web and the Web such a natural and obvious feature of the internet, that the specific contingency of these everyday practices has become obscured'. Once we relate to technology in such a quasi-automatic way, it can be difficult to change our use of it, and 'it will take a technical breakdown to expose the myriad moments of your everyday life almost instinctively or autonomically given over to some kind of search activity or device'. My concern is that if we do not develop a scholarly culture of GenAI, using these new capabilities to enrich and extend our capabilities in ways which reflect our values and priorities, we might lose this opportunity. If academics come to use GenAI as a *substitute for thinking* rather than as a *tool for thinking with*, I believe this could be a disaster for knowledge production. Avoiding this means supporting academics in building a reflective practice with GenAI, identifying forms of engagement which they find satisfying and sustainable and which can become part of their intellectual life.

Treating *conversational agents as collaborators* is one method through which to do this which I will develop over the coming chapters, though this is the book's guiding thread rather than its singular focus. It is intended as a map to this rapidly developing landscape, focused on principles to guide you through it rather than specific instructions about software in a continual state of flux. It offers the best advice I can given the information available to me at the time of writing, but it's important to realise this is a rapidly developing field with still uncertain rules and regulations. The advice I offer concerns a general approach to the opportunities and challenges of GenAI, which by its nature cannot always be applied to specific situations. It's important to familiarise yourself with your employer's expectations, which are likely to develop significantly in the months and years after I finish writing. This includes responsibilities to respect intellectual property and manage sensitive data in appropriate and legally mandated ways. This book is intended as a starting point for negotiating the rapidly developing landscape of GenAI but it cannot be a substitute for your own judgement. Please make sure to stay informed about the changing rules and regulations within and beyond the organisation you work within.

2
GENERATIVE AI AND REFLEXIVITY

This chapter will:

- Explain how conversational agents can be used as interlocutors with which academics collaborate intellectually, rather than framing them as devices for outsourcing unwanted tasks.
- Provide an overview of the emerging categories of Generative Artificial Intelligence (GenAI) software in order to support the integration of these into existing academic workflows.
- Argue that a process of sustained experimentation is needed to become familiar enough with this software to make informed choices about how to use it.

If you used social media in late 2022 you will have encountered a dizzying array of ephemera produced with ChatGPT. The jokes, poems and stories which circulated have been the main encounter with conversational agents for many academics. They were a novelty which initially dazzled but which soon faded into the background. They might have sparked a brief experiment with ChatGPT 3.5 to see what else it could do but my experience suggests many academics went no further than this. This is why my overarching advice is simply to *talk* to these systems and take it from there. The advice I offer concerns the types of conversations you might have, the topics you could address and the role they can play in supporting your scholarship. But unless you get into the habit of having conversations with these systems then you will be unable to realise their potential to support your scholarship. If you haven't yet started using a conversational agent then please do so before you go further. I know it can be difficult to get started so here's a list of possible conversation starters with which you can break the ice and begin an exchange. Share one of these with ChatGPT or Claude to see what response you get:

- If you are reading this chapter in electronic format then try copying and pasting the opening paragraph of this chapter into ChatGPT to see what it says in response. You could ask 'what do you think of this paragraph?', 'what are some practical action points following form this paragraph?', 'what are some potential criticisms of this paragraph?' or 'please suggest relevant literature which might help me evaluate this paragraph and better understand my perspective on it'.[1] When I have found a passage thought provoking I often share it with ChatGPT or Claude in order to explore my reaction, examine my assumptions or take a more critical stance in relation to it.
- I often find I have a hunch which I keep returning to until it is resolved. This might be a specific hypothesis (e.g., 'the uptake of generative AI in higher education will increase inequalities of productivity between different groups of academic staff') or a vague cluster of topics which I am struggling to articulate (e.g., 'the capacity to have spoken conversations with ChatGPT could become hugely popular for the same reason we have seen a rapid growth in podcasting over recent years'). It can be helpful to share this hunch with a suggestion of what you might find helpful in exploring it, for example, 'I have a hunch that [. . ..] please offer me five questions which I can explore in order to better elaborate upon my intuition' or 'Please offer competing perspectives on my hunch that [. . .] with a corresponding list of the key issues to consider in evaluating them'.
- In the early stages of planning a project I often find I am carrying around a whole *series* of hunches which I need to better articulate, not least of all in order to understand the

---

[1] For reasons we will explore at much greater length, you should be cautious about using conversational agents to explore the literature because they are prone to 'hallucinating' sources which don't exist. The point of this prompt is to get *starting points*, which you would then follow up with in a careful and reflective way; used in this way, conversational agents can help you begin to navigate a literature even though their recommendations can be of varying relevance and sometimes entirely fabricated.

interconnections between them. In this case, I might share a prompt which is an explanation of the project I am planning and a list of the issues I am grappling with in the process. This could be used to provide a narrative overview of the project which could have practical uses (e.g., helping generate an abstract for a first conference talk) or to identify connections and suggest points for further explanation. For example, you might share that 'I am in the early stages of exploring a potential project on the topic of [. . .] Here are some initial thoughts I am currently grappling with; please provide a narrative overview and suggest avenues for further exploration'. I have found this extremely useful in the early stages of inquiry because Claude reliably makes suggestions that simply did not occur to me.

I am framing these systems as *interlocutors* rather than *tools* because this has implications for how we work with them. If we relate to them as tools, we will tend to approach them as a means to achieve a certain end. Often it will be something we could do ourselves but which we have chosen not to because of time pressure, a lack of interest or some other contingent factor. The risk in this approach is that it leaves our expectations fixed at the outset: we know what we want to achieve and we use GenAI in order to realise that outcome in a faster, more convenient way than would otherwise be possible. It positions GenAI as a time-saving device in spite of the fact that careful and responsible use requires taking the time to explain what you want these systems to do. In relating to them as interlocutors we share our expectations, assumptions and beliefs which in turn develop as the conversation progresses[2]; this enables them to better act in accordance with our intentions because there is less of the definitional ambiguity, contextual vagueness and general misunderstanding which often leaves their outputs failing to live up to our expectations. This involves the application of *reflexivity*,[3] examining our assumptions and outlook as we go in order to refine them, as well as share them in increasingly clear and explicit ways.

For example, I recently used Claude to help map the proposal for a nearly finished manuscript by sharing the drafts with it chapter by chapter,[4] providing it with an example I had written myself of what a chapter summary should look like for a book of this kind. These

---

[2]That is until we hit the limit of the 'context window': effectively the length of text which can be stored in the memory of the model. We will return to the significance of this at various points in the coming chapters.

[3]For social scientists, reading this book 'reflexivity' will be a familiar term. The sense in which I use it here draws on the broader meaning it has within critical realist theory, referring to our capacity to consider ourselves in relation to our context in order to make decisions about how to act (Archer, 2007).

[4]The reason I was forced to do this with individual chapters is the manuscript as a whole (nearly 100,000 words) significantly exceeded the generous context window provided by Claude. This illustrates the real practical limit that the context window offers for some of the techniques discussed in this book, as well as potential workarounds. In this case, I copied and pasted the chapter summaries into a new chat thread so that I was effectively working with a single reading of the document, even if it was produced in a fragmented way.

outputs helped me get a broad overview of a sprawling book project I had been working on for a long time, encompassing my doctoral research and two postdocs. I was effectively asking an enthusiastic, if limited, reader to provide an overview of what they felt were the key points in each chapter. But in the conversation we had about each of the summaries, as well as the subsequent conversation about the proposal I used them to construct, I found my understanding of the book changing in the process. It identified cross-cutting themes which were present in the text of which I was only dimly aware. It presented these cross-cutting themes in a stylistically consistent language which I had been struggling with in a book project I had been working on for over a decade. It also offered criticisms of the plan for the book which led me to rethink the structure. I came away from the interaction having made a great deal of progress on the immediate practical task I had sought support with (i.e., writing the book proposal) but also with a clearer idea about the book itself, the argument I have made in it and how I can present it.

There have been countless examples like this over the last year, ranging from the trivial to the transformative. It is certainly possible to use these systems in thoughtless, counterproductive and even dangerous ways. I suspect we will see a lot of this over the coming months and years, with increasingly disastrous consequences as it is normalised within higher education. The reflexive approach I advocate does not provide a cast iron guarantee that you will not encounter problems but it does offer a foundation for careful engagement with conversational agents. There is value to be found in the *challenge* of relating to these systems, which involves being clear about what you are asking and what you are expecting, as well as the actual responses which they offer. However, it is the interplay between these two sources of insights, *articulating your ideas in an ever more nuanced way* and the *increasing nuance that the systems can offer in response*, where the real magic happens and these become genuine interlocutors who can make meaningful contributions to your intellectual development as well as your practical work.

This might seem an implausibly strong claim at this point but please give me the benefit of the doubt by throwing yourself into one of these conversations. The only way to realise the potential of conversational agents is to actually *converse* with them, opening yourself to their ability to understand the nuances of your intellectual work and make a contribution to it. In doing so, we ensure that we approach GenAI to support our thinking rather than as a substitute for thought. Far from overwhelming them with academic detail, they thrive on it and respond in kind even if, as we explore in the next chapter, there are weaknesses in their capacity to do this.

GENERATIVE AI AS SOFTWARE

There has been explosive growth in software which uses GenAI to offer new ways of creating, analysing and distributing content. This software is branded as 'generative artificial intelligence' with the enthusiasm that a technological hype wave creates in firms trying to win investment. But we should not expect this to last. Bostrom (2014: 38) points out that when something works effectively and becomes a routine feature of our lives, we no longer tend to call it AI. This led one of the early founders of AI John McCarthy to lament that 'As soon as it works, no one calls it AI anymore' (Bostrom, 2014, p. 58). It is easy to see how the incorporation of GenAI into familiar software such as Microsoft Office and Google Docs could lead it to rapidly fade into the background, as an extension of the spelling and grammar checks we use in a purely habitual way. There is a risk that GenAI this habituation would make it difficult for academics to sustain a reflective approach to its use. My capacity to spell has deteriorated over the course of my adult life. It's a worrying prospect that my capacity to *think* might undergo a similar deterioration if I lapse into a habitual reliance on GenAI to do at least some of my thinking for me.

There are a range of familiar technologies within higher education which we tend not to think of using the category of 'artificial intelligence', despite having characteristics which might otherwise lead them to be categorised as such. Grammarly has offered a cloud-based writing assistant since 2009 that has come to be widely used within universities, proving particularly popular with international students writing in a second language. It offers suggestions about grammar, syntax, style and tone which contribute to more effective written communication. Interestingly, the term 'AI' features 12 times on their home page on the day I am writing whereas a record of the home page from 1 February 2020 does not use this term even once (Grammarly 2020). This highlights how companies are gravitating towards the language of 'generative artificial intelligence' at this crucial moment in the commercial development of the technology.

Once we start to look at software in these terms, we begin to see AI everywhere. Consider the autocorrection which has been a routine feature of mobile phones for years, increasing the speed and accuracy with which users can type on a small keyboard by offering (and making) potential corrections in the process. If you would like to get a sense of how deeply reliant many of us are on this technology then try turning autocorrection off and typing a message. For many of us sending a text will then become a frustrating and time-consuming undertaking. My typing is filled with predictable mistakes which I rarely notice because autocorrect means they never impede my communication. It might seem much simpler than the uncanny abilities of ChatGPT but the underlying technology has much in common, relying on a statistical model of connections in language which enables a plausible prediction to be made about what the next word in the sentence will be. The difference is that Large Language Models model the full context and complex interdependencies across texts all at once. This allows them to develop a holistic statistical representation, rather than relying on the next-word predictions that limit simpler autocorrect capabilities. It is easy to see how we could become similarly reliant on them, as they become routine features of our working lives. Developing a reflective approach to GenAI is an antidote to this because many of the problems we will meet in subsequent chapters, such as their propensity to make factual errors and offer biased representations of the world, will be exacerbated if their use fades into the background in the manner of autocorrect on a smartphone.

Many academics have used autosuggestion capabilities built into platforms like Gmail (2018) and Outlook (2021) to streamline the process of writing and responding to emails.

These include quick reply buttons introduced into Gmail initially and more recently into Outlook, offering routine responses such as 'Will do' or 'Thanks I will take a look' which can be sent with one click. While some remain sceptical, it is often helpful to acknowledge a request or indicate that you intend to act on it. Outlook's thumbs-up reaction serves the same purpose. Using these autosuggestion capabilities when writing longer emails can feel like a rather different proposition, particularly in the early stages where the transition from solo authoring to the human–computer collaboration which autosuggestion involves feels most pronounced. Nonetheless, automation has been gradually entering into email communication for a number of years, responding to the growing experience of email overload within many organisations (Newport, 2021).

Even if you might not use these tools yourself, it is difficult to get concerned about them because they are *opt-in* for individual users for whom they serve helpful functions. The tools I discuss throughout this book remain at this stage things which academics can make a choice about using or not using. But this might change with time, as a result of competitive pressures between academics and the shifting expectations of university managers. These are emerging against the backdrop of what has been called a 'platform university' in which digital systems are essential to core activities within higher education, involving forms of automation over which academics have little oversight or control (Carrigan, 2018). Selwyn et al. (2022, pp. 1-2) describe these as 'the absorption of small (often imperceptible) automation into everyday educational practices and processes' which 'have become quickly woven into the digital fabric of schools and universities to the point that they now pass unnoticed'.

Examples such as plagiarism detection illustrate the lack of agency that teaching staff tend to have over these processes, as similarity scores generated by automated systems become indicators to which staff *must* respond, while the technological and epistemological assumptions underpinning them tend to fade into the background. McCluskey and Winter (2012, loc 300) warn that 'if faculty members do not control information technology, the information technology department will control the faculty members'. However, the problem with such a framing is that it overestimates the influence those maintaining the infrastructure of the university are able to exercise over these platforms. The tendency of academics to take the infrastructure upon which we rely for granted unless they are an object of our research or a methodological condition for it, limits our capacity to get involved in these debates. However, technological governance within universities is tied up with the conditions of academic labour in ways which are only going to grow with time (Woodcock, 2018). These are issues I will introduce in the next chapter exploring the ethics of GenAI before picking them up in the final chapter to raise concerns about where this might be leading.

Before we get there we should explore the range of GenAI platforms, tools and services which are available. While ChatGPT, Gemini and Bing have dominated media coverage there are a dizzying array of services which have hit the market in recent months. This can make it extremely difficult to keep up. There is also the risk of putting time and energy into a tool which might not survive in the longer term. This was an experience I know well from the early days of social media when a curation tool called Bundlr, which I used on a near-daily basis for a number of years, fell by the wayside as Pinterest came to dominate that market.

There is often one firm which succeeds within a category while competitors who fail to turn a profit eventually run out of funding. It is a safe assumption the services operated by Microsoft, OpenAI and Google are here to stay. But many of the others are unlikely to be here in years to come if their growth is insufficient to make the transition into a viable business. For this reason, it can be helpful to think in terms of *categories* of tools in order to understand how they can be incorporated into academic workflows, rather than focusing on specific services which might not last.

CATEGORIES OF GENERATIVE AI SOFTWARE

The extent to which OpenAI's ChatGPT has come to define GenAI in the public consciousness reflects a first-mover advantage as well as a remarkably successful viral marketing campaign. However, not only is there a range of freely accessible conversational agents with comparable capabilities (Anthropic's Claude, Microsoft's Bing and Google's Gemini), but this category of tool barely scratches the surface of a rapidly expanding landscape. If you make the effort to follow GenAI influencer accounts and newsletters, you are rapidly inundated with a range of services which all claim to facilitate a radical innovation in how we work. It is easy to feel overwhelmed by these developments. The speed with which new services are being released, as well as existing ones upgraded, makes it extremely difficult to keep track of where we currently stand. The more closely you follow developments, the more you see how much is happening. It feels impossible to keep up to date with the full range of developments taking place, even if you are wired into a wide network and following a diverse range of channels.

This is particularly problematic for academics who are rarely, if ever, given the time needed to explore and adapt to technological change. There are a wide range of seminars, workshops and webinars taking place within and across universities but these often contribute to the same sense of overwhelm. As someone networked into discussions about GenAI within higher education I am sure I could attend a relevant session on a daily basis if I chose to do so. In fact, I *have* chosen to do so for periods of time when I was working on this book. I rapidly noticed these discussions resembling each other in their form and content, reflecting a fundamental uncertainty about what GenAI means for policy and practice within universities (DiMaggio & Powell, 1983). There is a tendency to repeat authoritative-sounding statements and framings at points where no one is really clear about what this means in the longer term.

If you try and keep on top of *everything*, you will inevitably get overwhelmed. It is much better to identify what you're trying to do with GenAI and then focus on this in your reading and exploration. It is understandable if you do not feel in a position to do this yet. Keep it in mind as you work your way through the book. Talk to ChatGPT or Claude about it as you go. What matters is how the broad sweep of these developments might impact your working life, as well as how you can steer this process in purposeful ways. For most academics, the real problem will not be developing expertise about GenAI but rather finding practices which help realise opportunities while reducing exposure to the risks.

For these reasons, I suggest you should dispense with the aspiration to 'keep up' and instead focus on being clear about *what* you need to know and *why*. This helps filter the torrent of

GenAI resources and connect them to the practical reality of your working life. What problems are you trying to solve? What elements of your scholarship are you trying to improve? What exactly are you trying to do and why? I use the language of 'scholarship' to talk about this activity, following Weller's (2011) influential work on digital scholarship which had a significant influence on conversations about the use of digital media by academics. As Weller (2011: loc 117) notes 'we have tended to think of scholars as being academics, usually employed by universities' but the notion of *digital scholarship* broadens this 'since in a digital, networked, open world people become less defined by the institution to which they belong and more by the network and online identity they establish'. In this sense, I approach scholarship in terms of *thinking, collaboration, communication* and *engagement* which has a scholarly character. It is related to 'serious, detailed study', to use the dictionary definition of the term, but it is not necessarily tied to an institution. Software is no replacement for independent thought but can support and enhance it, at least if used in a careful and reflective way.

How you use GenAI will likely be different from my own use explored throughout the book. I reflect on my own scholarship not because I believe it ought to constitute a model for other people but simply because we need to approach these opportunities in a concretely intellectual way. Instead of suggesting in the abstract that it *could* be useful, I want to demonstrate how it *can* be used for specific purposes and how you could use it in your contexts, even if your uses differ from my own. This is why I think the language of digital scholarship is helpful. It grounds the discussion in the concrete activities we engage in and highlights how its value, or lack thereof, comes from the contributions it makes to these undertakings. However, the agents which are the main focus of this book are just part of a much broader landscape of GenAI summarised in Figure 2.1. I've included examples of use cases but the real discussion of these categories will feature in Chapters 4–7 when we talk about thinking, collaboration, communication and engagement (Table 2.1).

There is flexibility to conversational agents which these other categories lack. This can be a barrier to their use because it entails a steeper learning curve. It takes a while to get a feel for using ChatGPT and Claude because of the immense range of ways in which they can be used. In contrast, writing assistants come with a range of predefined recipes through which you can make changes to your texts. If these enable the rapid improvement of your writing then the time they save is obviously welcome. The concern I have is these templates may narrow our sense of the changes we *can* make to our text through the use of GenAI. They might fade into the background in the manner of a spell checker,[5] collapsing our creative horizons in a subtle process of habituation rather than opening them up by challenging us to think more deeply about what we are trying to do.

To use ChatGPT and Claude *effectively* requires you to explain what you trying to do, which is inherently difficult unless you actually know what it is you are trying to do. In this sense their

---

[5] I should stress that I think automated spell-checking is a valuable thing. My concern is the costs of habitually relying on GenAI might be much more significant to our creativity and thought than with spell-checking.

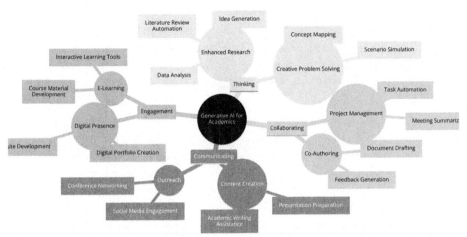

ChatGPT's response to the query "Produce a diagram which illustrates potential use cases of GenAI for academics across four domains of practice: thinking, collaborating, communicating and (digital) engagement" using the 'Diagrams: Show Me' GPT.

Figure 2.1 The Landscape of GenAI and Typical Use Cases for Academics

Table 2.1 Different Categories of GenAI Tool and Service

Category	Examples	Use Cases
Conversational agents	ChatGPT, Claude, Gemini, Bing	Inherently multipurpose and capable of being used across the full range of scholarly activities
Personal assistants	Pi	Coaching in personal and interpersonal skills, reflecting on working life and associated challenges
Writing assistants	Jenni, WordTune	Focused work on specific texts or sections of them
Research assistants	Ellicit, Scite, OpenRead	The initial scoping stage of literature reviews, addressing particular problems
Text to image generators	Dall-e, Stable Diffusion, Midjourney	Producing teaching and engagement materials, working with students in creative exercises
Personal knowledge bases	Notion, Saga, Mem	Summarising, organising and analysing your personal notes
Meeting assistants	Otter.AI, Fireflies, Fathom	Transcribing, summarising and analysing meetings
Document conversations	Petal, Notebook LLM	Interacting with a corpus of documents through natural language

use *challenges* you to articulate your intentions, encouraging reflective practice through an iterative dialogue with the system. In contrast, the templates provided by writing assistants provide readymade text transformations which can be applied based on your initial judgements about what is required. Obviously, you might change your mind after applying a transformation to your text. In fact, the quality of these (such as 'shorten', 'make informal' or 'change tone') tends to be so lacklustre that the inevitable rewriting forces you to think more deeply about what you want. I can see why developers are enamoured by the idea of offering users options to 'write an essay' or 'write a blog post' which can be immediately inserted into a document. But these functions tend to ask for either a brief line of text and/or a selected element of your original text to use as a prompt. An essay written in response to a one-sentence prompt will never be a passable essay. This is as much about the nature of an essay as the underlying technology; unless you define what it is you want to produce you will inevitably get something rhetorically diffuse and disconnected from what you are trying to do.

I am sceptical that these templates will prove useful for many academics. By their nature, they are so general that the results will need extensive rewriting, without the intellectual gains from ongoing dialogue with a conversational agent. They might provide a way of getting started or moving through writer's block but little more than that. However, the Copilot system which Microsoft has developed goes much further than these templates because they encode *workflows* rather than discrete tasks. For example, Copilot can draft a presentation from a document rather than simply summarise that document in preparation for being made into a presentation. As we will discuss in later chapters, moving between different formats when working with ideas is a surprisingly time-consuming feature of academic life (e.g., going from a paper to a student lecture to a public talk) which we tend not to recognise as an imposition because it is such a taken-for-granted activity. Defining workflows could make an enormous contribution to academic productivity but it requires insight into how you work which takes time to develop. There are real possibilities for time-saving which GenAI offers but we cannot escape from the need for reflection on our work.

UNDERSTANDING YOUR WORKFLOW

Imagine you are trying to find information: other papers written by the author of one you are reading, the time the next train leaves or the background of a historical event. There are many ways you might do this. You could go to Google Scholar, a train booking website, or to Wikipedia. In many cases, particularly if it's not clear where the best source will be, you will immediately put the search terms into Google, or perhaps Bing. What you probably won't do in this situation is stop and think: *how can I retrieve this information*? It's interesting to reflect on this fact because information retrieval has become such a taken-for-granted part of how we use the web. There was a time when this would have required thought and reflection but the use of web services has become a habitual part of our workflow. We don't need to identify a means to perform the task, we simply perform the task. While this does present problems if we are habituated to shallow or counterproductive uses, such as restricting ourselves to the first page of Google results, it helps us get things done if we are not constantly thinking about *how* to do them. This is what we should be aiming at with GenAI we want to incorporate it into our work in a satisfying and sustainable way. There are risks involved in this, such as establishing limited or counterproductive practices, which we will discuss throughout the rest of the book. But we should nonetheless aim for our use of GenAI to be something which fits seamlessly into our working patterns, enhancing or even transforming the activities we undertake as scholars.

The challenge is how to make it routine without it becoming thoughtless. How this works will vary between types of projects and across individual scholars, with their different career stages, disciplines and personal preferences. Academics often develop working routines in opaque and idiosyncratic ways, experimenting until they find an approach which works for them. These issues find their way into guidebooks such as Abbott (2014), Becker (2008) and Mills (2000), as well as inevitably figuring in reflections on the writing process such as Sword (2017). But despite being constitutive of what scholarship *is*, in the literal sense that no scholarship would get done without them, they tend to be weirdly peripheral to how we talk about them. These conversations are often restricted to a register of failure or improvement, something we turn to when change is needed, but that we don't see as a central topic for our work, particularly in how we talk about it with others. Technological change complicates this marginalisation because new tools which we *can* work with inevitably bring questions about *how* we do our work and *why* we do it that way. For example, Fallows (1982) offers a thought-provoking reflection on the initial experience of working with a word processor (Figure 2.2):

> When I sit down to write a letter or start the first draft of an article, I simply type on the keyboard and the words appear on the screen. For six months, I found it awkward to compose first drafts on the computer. Now I can hardly do it any other way. It is faster to type this way than with a normal typewriter because you don't need to stop at the end of the line for a carriage return (the computer automatically 'wraps' the words onto the next line when you reach the right-hand margin), and you never come to the end of the page, because the material on the screen keeps sliding up to make room for each new line. It is also more satisfying to the soul because each maimed and misconceived passage can be made to vanish instantly, by the word or by the paragraph, leaving a pristine green field on which to make the next attempt.

Far from writing being a timeless scholarly practice, it is a material and embodied activity which has evolved as the technologies used by scholars and the context in which they work have changed. During these transitions, *technological reflexivity* becomes an essential skill, in the sense of recognising how the technology we use shapes what we do and reflecting on this process in a way which enables us to steer it in desirable directions (Adams & Thompson, 2016; Paulus & Lester, 2023). If we fail to exercise this reflexivity, we will likely drift into patterns of use which do not serve our purposes, at least not to the extent that might otherwise be possible. The risk is that we instead look to what others are doing and imagine there is a 'right way' to use technology in our work. This is compounded by a tendency to marginalise technology in how we practice scholarship, seeing it as a contingent matter of implementation divorced from the serious business of thinking (Carrigan & Fatsis, 2021).

Addressing this means paying much greater attention to what Pierre Bourdieu once described as the technology of intellectual work. By this, he meant techniques which are

MC: I am interested in how academics adapt to generative AI or struggle to. What can we learn from past experiences of technological change in higher education? In what ways is generative AI similar to and different from past technological innovations which changed how scholarship is conducted? Please make reference to Fallows (1982) who reflects on his early experiences of using a word processor:

"When I sit down to write a letter or start the first draft of an article, I simply type on the keyboard and the words appear on the screen. For six months, I found it awkward to compose first drafts on the computer. Now I can hardly do it any other way. It is faster to type this way than with a normal typewriter, because you don't need to stop at the end of the line for a carriage return (the computer automatically "wraps" the words onto the next line when you reach the right-hand margin), and you never come to the end of the page, because the material on the screen keeps sliding up to make room for each new line. It is also more satisfying to the soul, because each maimed and misconceived passage can be made to vanish instantly, by the word or by the paragraph, leaving a pristine green field on which to make the next attempt."

ChatGPT: The reflection by Fallows on his adaptation to using a word processor in 1982 provides an insightful parallel to the current discussions surrounding the integration of generative AI in academic contexts. By examining how academics are adapting to or struggling with generative AI, we can draw several lessons from past experiences of technological change in higher education, particularly focusing on similarities and differences between these innovations.

Adaptation to Technological Change

Similarity in Adaptation Period: Just as Fallows experienced a six-month adaptation period to become proficient in using a word processor, academics today may undergo a similar phase of adjustment to generative AI tools. The initial discomfort and learning curve associated with adopting new technology seem to be a consistent theme across different technological eras.

Enhanced Productivity: Fallows noted the increase in typing speed and efficiency as a major advantage of the word processor over traditional typewriters. Similarly, generative AI can significantly enhance research productivity, offering capabilities such as automated literature reviews, data analysis, and even drafting research papers, thereby saving valuable time and effort.

Revision and Improvement: The ease with which text can be edited and revised on a word processor—leading to a "pristine green field" for new attempts—mirrors the iterative process of research and writing facilitated by generative AI. These tools can suggest multiple revisions, simulate alternative hypotheses, or provide varied perspectives on a topic, enriching the academic work.

Differences from Past Technological Innovations

Scope and Impact: While the word processor transformed the act of writing, generative AI has the potential to alter fundamentally the entire research process, from ideation to publication. Its impact is far-reaching, affecting data collection, analysis, interpretation, and dissemination, thereby encompassing a broader scope of academic activities.

Ethical and Integrity Concerns: Generative AI introduces complex ethical and integrity issues, such as the potential for plagiarism, the accuracy of AI-generated data, and the authorship of AI-assisted publications. These concerns go beyond the relatively straightforward adaptation challenges posed by earlier technologies like word processors.

Interdisciplinary Influence: The adoption of word processors was largely confined to changing the writing process, but generative AI's influence spans across disciplines, necessitating a multidisciplinary approach to understand its implications fully. It demands a broader understanding of machine learning, ethics, and domain-specific knowledge.

Figure 2.2 Learning from Past Experience of Technological Change within Higher Education
Source: ChatGPT.

essential to scholarship but which are 'rarely the object of methodical transmission' such as 'use of dictionaries and abbreviations, rhetoric of communication, establishment of files, creation of an index, use of records and data banks, preparation of a manuscript, documentary research, use of computerised instruments, interpretation of tables and graphs' (Bourdieu, 2008: 175). C. Wright Mills (2000) made a similar point in his discussion of 'intellectual craftsmanship', arguing that knowledge is developed through mundane daily activity. He highlighted how the backstage work of 'keeping a file' in which one develops ideas *is* intellectual production, rather than a logistical activity which is mysteriously prior to and separate from the real work of scholarship. The tendency to marginalise these issues within academic training makes it difficult for academics to identify modes of digital scholarship which are right for them (Carrigan, 2019). If we regard technology as something we only really need to think about when it breaks down, it will be difficult to recognise the strengths and weaknesses of the systems and devices we currently rely on.

Our working lives involve many tedious, routine and draining tasks which could in principle be avoided. These are often so trivial that we do not even regard them as tasks, at least in the sense of becoming items on a to-do list. Before a Zoom meeting, we find ourselves scrabbling around our inboxes looking for the link because it is not in a calendar. In order to schedule the meeting we get drawn into an extended exchange with a number of people, as it becomes almost comically difficult to find a time that works for everyone involved. After the meeting, we spent a few minutes locating a file we had promised to transfer following the discussion. Each of these is a small undertaking which only takes minutes of our time. But these minutes add up over the course of the week, breaking up the flow of our days and contributing to the chronic feeling of fragmented attention which many of us suffer with constantly. As a poster I once received as a present says: *my brain has too many tabs open.* It can be illuminating to keep a list of these activities in order to inventory how many of these interruptions are a feature of your typical working day. The ease with which we can look things up in an inbox makes it possible to exist in a nearly-organised state which would have been more difficult in a paper world of box files and printouts. It is not that we do not have what we need or know where it is, but rather that it is never quite within reach when we need it. The extent to which many of us are continually operating at close to max capacity, rushing from one appointment to the next while imagining a radical calm when teaching finishes which never quite arrives, creates a sense of inevitability about this condition.

There is a chicken-and-egg element about the state of rushing common within what Vostal (2016) and I have described as the *accelerated academy* (Carrigan, 2016). Are we rushing because we are disorganised or are we disorganised because we are rushing? There are practical steps which productivity guides suggest can mitigate these problems, for example, scheduling time between meetings, noting outcomes from meetings afterwards and setting aside time to process the day's events. There are more expansive solutions to the problem as well, such as using task management software like Omnifocus or meticulously organising your inboxes. But these in turn require time for reflection which is lacking in our working lives, leaving a solution feeling just out of reach. They can also become time sinks in their own right, as optimising your organisational system substitutes for actually doing the things you wanted it to help you do in the first place.

Could GenAI be a solution to this problem? It is important we recognise that the individual use we make of GenAI in order to enhance our working lives will not protect us from forms of automation imposed from the top down, which either lead to the elimination of jobs or their reorganisation so as to support mechanic processes, for example, a human teacher being confined to overseeing interactions between an AI chatbot and students, rather than actively engaging with students (Furendal & Jebari, 2023). The risk is that rather than GenAI serving the organisation, the organisation is reconfigured around the needs of GenAI in ways which do profound violence to the lives, identities and relationships of those working within it. In the final chapter, I explore two speculative scenarios for what such an automated university might look like. But even with this dystopic scenario plaguing my imagination, I find it impossible to ignore the possible gains which individual scholars might find in the uptake of GenAI tools and services in the immediate moment.

The language I've used in this chapter risks presenting your workflow as something that can be endlessly engineered. While it's important to scrutinise, analyse and find ways to improve the sequence of tasks that make up the routines of your daily life, there are limits to this. If we over-engineer these processes, we might find that it takes up an awful lot of time, leading us to procrastinate by creating a system that perfectly avoids procrastination. It might be something that looks compelling on paper, but in practice does not fit into your working routines or adequately capture your preferences and tastes. Recognising this is important. Often the only way to recognise it is to try, which is exactly why I've suggested that *experimentation* is a key part of this process. Ideally, GenAI tools will integrate into your workflow seamlessly. It ceases to be a tool you choose from a menu after deliberating about a specific task and becomes something ready-to-hand which you pick up in the process of doing. The point when you first notice you have used it in a quasi-automatic way, rather than as a deliberate undertaking, represents the point at which it is unambiguously part of your workflow. What matters is that this is a status you have deliberately sought, reflecting a clear sense of what will be beneficial to your work and informed by an awareness of the alternatives which are available. Unfortunately, this is easier to advocate than it is to achieve in practice. It can be extremely easy to slip into technological habits and extremely difficult to break them once they have formed.

During a recent discussion with a collaborator I was struck that despite the fact we had been discussing GenAI for the last hour, we both immediately went to Google in order to address a factual question which had come up in our discussion. This is a habit which has cut deeply into our digital lives and would take a long time to break, even if we consciously sought to do so. I have on multiple occasions tried to train myself to use a privacy-sensitive search engine like DuckDuckGo but have frequently given up in frustration as I gravitated back to using Google. It was not simply that the former's results tended to be less immediately helpful, though there is evidence the latter's capabilities are degrading as it prioritises proprietary content (Luca et al., 2015). It just felt jarring to break my workflow in this way, highlighting how integral search was to my digital activity throughout the day. I tried Dolan's (2014) strategy of designing my environment to implement change rather than seeking to deliberately will it, shifting my default search on mobile and desktop in order to channel me towards DuckDuckGo. But I then found myself manually typing in google.com in order to circumvent the change rather than simply typing my search query into the address bar.

There is nothing inherently problematic about habits insofar as they free us from a state of continual indecision about what to do next. It would be exhausting to be reflexive about every minute facet of our working lives. What matters is that these are routines we have cultivated in ourselves, rather than passively slipped into in response to the behavioural promptings of product engineers. As the philosopher of technology Shannon Vallor (2016: loc 1449) observes, 'an act does not become a habit until I do it repeatedly, and for it to be a habit I must do it more or less consistently when invited by the relevant situation'. What matters is *why* we are doing it repeatedly. Vallor (2016: loc 1649) explores how 'moral habits can be made sufficiently flexible and responsive to emerging and unanticipated technosocial developments'.

The discussion so far has focused on what we might call *macro* issues of workflow: identifying the sequences of tasks in which you are routinely engaged in order to bring about certain kinds of outcomes. This can be supplemented by a focus on *micro* issues of workflow which concern how your work environment and the interfaces you use can be tweaked to maximise your productivity. For example, I rapidly found the number of conversations I was having with ChatGPT confusing and could not distinguish between those related to ongoing projects which needed to be kept and the fleeting interactions which could easily be lost. Therefore, I labelled the project-related conversations with a star emoji while setting myself the recurring task of trimming older conversations once they no longer served a purpose. Once this became a habit I went from having 100+ conversations in the ChatGPT interface to having around 10–20 at most times, with six of these clearly labelled as project-related that I was returning to on a regular basis. I added ChatGPT to my bookmark bar and developed the habit of leaving a separate browser window open with the conversational agent running it. The same thing can be achieved using software like MacGPT, though this requires setting up an OpenAI API key. Furthermore, the fact I *was* returning in this way meant they would usually be near the top of this list. This saved me a few seconds in scanning the list when I wanted to engage in a conversation but it also minimised the lag involved in incorporating ChatGPT into my workflow.

There are countless optimisations like this which can be made to improve your workflow, each likely to be trivial in its impact but with the collective potential to significantly improve your productivity. The example I have cited is an obvious one likely to be useful to most people. But there are others which you will only discover through the process of reflecting on your device use, particularly those habitual aspects which tend to pass unnoticed over the course of the day because they are so familiar. These tweaks can feel fiddly and unnecessary, potential distractions from the real work you are trying to do. The same could be said for tidying your office when it is accumulated with clutter yet most of us do this on a fairly regular basis, recognising how it can be difficult to focus if the things we need for work aren't ready-to-hand. Keeping things organised can be extremely helpful when you're getting to grips with the novel capabilities which GenAI services bring to your scholarship.

THE IMPORTANCE OF EXPERIMENTING

There is a degree of persistence required if you want to find satisfying and sustainable ways through which GenAI can be incorporated into your workflow. It can be tempting to give up in the face of your first misleading or lacklustre response but doing so brings a process of learning to a premature close. The challenge is partly a matter of learning to formulate requests in a manner which a system like ChatGPT is liable to respond to productively. But this in turn means clarifying your requests in order to establish exactly what you expect of the conversational agent. What role are you expecting it to play? What does this mean in practice? In the context of ongoing conversations with ChatGPT it is possible to establish these ground rules with a remarkable degree of specificity but doing so requires an openness to experimentation. It is only through trial and error, doing things and reflecting on the response, that it becomes feasible to reliably bring about the desired outcomes in a reasonably consistent way. There is a rich element of reflexivity involved in this because it rapidly becomes clear that a lack of clarity about what you expect is a huge obstacle to generating a helpful response. The more precisely you can formulate what it is you are expecting, the easier it is to realise this through interaction. Fortunately, ChatGPT and Claude are both capable of explaining the features which should be included for a prompt to be successful. They can even offer feedback on your prompts in order to help you improve them. It would be time-consuming to rely on this but it can be a helpful way of developing effective habits when writing prompts for conversational agents.

The most common problem I've seen in prompts produced by academics is a failure to include a sufficient level of detail. In part this is a matter of being explicit about your expectations, often best expressed by providing one or more examples of what you would like the system to generate. This can seem time-consuming but if you want to repeat a task then writing a desirable output initially can ensure your expectations are met as you repeat the process. But the more difficult aspect to master is recognising the tacit knowledge you are invoking in your expectations. There are things which are obvious to you, as well as colleagues/collaborators, which stem from working within a social context. But unless this features explicitly within the training data, which is utterly unpredictable given how opaque this is, the conversational agent won't share these assumptions. They need to be explicitly stated which involves being clear about them yourself. Again we encounter prior cognitive labour which is necessary in order to use GenAI effectively, contrary to the widespread perception this will be something which *immediately* saves you time and energy. I would argue this cognitive labour is valuable in its own right, constituting a necessary but insufficient condition for methodological reflexivity which is advocated in different ways across the humanities and social sciences. But it cannot be avoided if you want to use conversational agents in a reliable and effective way which mitigates the risks we explore at length in the next chapter (Figure 2.3).

MC: I'm introducing academics to the opportunities and challenges involved in producing carefully written prompts for ChatGPT. I stress the importance of being clear about what they are asking, what they expect and sharing the assumptions they are making. Please build on these points in order to identify four key features of a successful prompt, particularly if the user is asking complex questions related to specialised knowledge within one or more academic disciplines.

ChatGPT: When crafting prompts for ChatGPT, especially for complex questions within specialized academic disciplines, it's essential to consider several key features to ensure the success of the interaction. These features not only help in obtaining accurate and relevant responses but also facilitate a more efficient and productive dialogue between the user and the AI. Here are four key features of a successful prompt:

1. *Specificity and Clarity:* The prompt should be as specific as possible, clearly stating the question or the type of information required. Vague questions can lead to equally vague answers, which might not be helpful. In the context of specialized knowledge, specificity includes the use of precise terminology, frameworks, or theories relevant to the discipline. This helps the AI to understand the context better and provide more targeted information.

2. *Contextualization:* Providing context helps the AI understand the scope and depth of the answer expected. This is particularly important in academic disciplines where the same term or concept might have different meanings or applications across different fields. Contextualization might include the disciplinary focus, any particular theories or models to be considered, or even specifying the geographical or temporal scope where relevant.

3. *Explicit Expectations:* Clearly stating what you expect from the response can significantly enhance the quality of the interaction. This might involve specifying the format of the answer (e.g., a brief overview, a detailed explanation, examples, a step-by-step guide), the level of complexity (e.g., introductory vs. advanced), or the type of resources you're interested in (e.g., scholarly articles, textbooks, datasets).

4. *Assumptions and Limitations:* Acknowledging any assumptions being made in the question and outlining the limitations of what you're asking for can help in aligning the AI's response with your needs. This might include, for example, the assumption that certain foundational knowledge is already understood or specifying that you're only interested in peer-reviewed sources within a certain time frame.

Figure 2.3 The Key Features of an Effective Prompt
Source: ChatGPT.

There's a sense in which working with conversational agents like ChatGPT and Claude is a straightforward matter of simply talking to them about what you're doing. But using them *effectively* requires these conversations to take a specialised form relative to the interactions you might have with a collaborator: more detailed, more highly explicated and more sensitive to misunderstandings. The ideal outcome is these conversations becoming a routine and habitual feature of your workflow, taking place alongside conversations with collaborators and the more distributed forms of scholarly interaction facilitated by social media (Carrigan, 2019). To reach this point will involve ongoing experimentation to find strategies which work for you within particular areas of your practice, reflecting on these experiments in order to refine your approach. This experimental labour, particularly the fumbling experience of trial and error it entails in the early stage, can feel like a waste of time when there are other pressing demands on your time. But without making this time it will simply not be possible to realise the rewards which are waiting for you further down the line.

There are *general principles to support experimentation* which I suggest below. This initial framework is intended to support readers experimenting with GenAI for the first time or deepening their existing engagements into new areas of work. After a detailed discussion of ethical, political and environmental issues in Chapter 3, the next four chapters will explore how GenAI can be integrated into four core activities: *thinking, collaborating, communicating* and *engaging.* By the time you reach the final chapter, I imagine a reader will be sufficiently immersed in GenAI to have a rich set of experiences to bring to a discussion about where these developments might be going in the longer term; what they mean for academic work, the university system and wider society. But equally please feel free to skip through the book as dictated by your own interests, whether that is getting a general overview of the topic (Chapters 3 and 8) or focusing on the area of scholarship which is most relevant to your own concerns (Chapters 4–7). Please continue to talk to ChatGPT or Claude about what you are reading, regardless of the route you choose to take through the book: reflect on what you are reading, try things out and include as much detail as you can about your own work.

PRINCIPLES FOR EXPERIMENTATION

1 **Be prepared to articulate your expectations.** It is only by putting your expectations into words that it is possible to review and refine them. The novelty of GenAI means those expectations are likely to be out of sync with the capabilities of the software you are using. Even if you are not clear about what your expectations are then try and specify that lack of clarity with as much specificity as possible.

2 **Be as precise as possible with your prompts.** If you give up as soon as a conversational agent disappoints you, it will be impossible to learn how to interact with these tools. There is a learning curve in working with conversational agents given their propensity to reward complexity in your inputs.

3 **Be as patient as your schedule allows you to be.** There is a learning curve to new software, particularly when it has unfamiliar capabilities which might not map onto the

existing areas of your working life in a straightforward way. It might not be clear exactly how you will use something you are working with but the only way to find out is to experiment.

4 **Learn from others.** The best source of inspiration is other people, particularly those who share a topic, field or context with you. Their use might not be exactly right for you, but the closer their work is to your own the easier it will be to translate from their examples to your own application. Furthermore, talking to them will help with articulating your nascent understanding of how to use GenAI.

5 **Learn from yourself.** Consider keeping a reflective journal which documents your experiments with GenAI, recording what you have done and evaluating its success. This could simply be a Word document or a notepad which keeps a broad overview. Or it could be an ongoing thread in ChatGPT or Claude where you reflect on your evolving use. The simple act of writing it down encourages you to reflect on the experience, as well as documenting the process in a way which you can learn from later.

6 **Developing ethical awareness.** There are complex ethical and political issues posed by GenAI which are the subject of the next chapter. Identify the ethical instincts which you have about these developments as you are experimenting with them. These might range from an explicit political concern to a vague sense of discomfort about a particular use of a tool.

3

THE ETHICS OF
GENERATIVE AI

This chapter will:

- Examine the epistemic limitations of Generative Artificial Intelligence (GenAI), such as hallucination and the problem of common knowledge, in order to equip the reader to understand the unreliability of these systems.
- Consider the environmental costs associated with the use of GenAI, including the potential implications of its widespread adoption and the difficulty of establishing sustainable practice.
- Critique the role which the enclosure of intellectual property played in the training of GenAI systems, as well as the implications for the livelihood of creative professionals.

The previous chapter offered principles to support academics in exploring GenAI. The next four chapters explore what it might look like to apply these principles in practice, in terms of four broad scholarly activities: *thinking, collaborating, communicating* and *engaging*. I developed these through my own exploration, engaging with relevant literature and drawing on my experience as someone who has supported academics in using social media for almost fifteen years. While the parallel between them is imperfect, there are many similarities. These are new developments which unsettle existing forms of academic practice, presenting new activities with which to engage and changing existing activities in often confusing ways. The differences lie in the scope of the activities which are changed by GenAI. Whereas social media had significant implications for certain facets of academic activity (networking, self-promotion, managing information and public engagement), there is not a single facet of academic practice which could not be changed by GenAI. Whether it *should* be is the subject of this chapter.

The problem with such a comparison, or at least what I find unsettling about it, concerns the professional culture which emerged around social media in higher education. The excitement which greeted these platforms seems misplaced in retrospect, with the promise of a more creative and engaged academic culture now feeling to many like an unwelcome burden which leaves them exposed to external risks (Carrigan & Fatsis, 2021). However, as Weller (2020: loc 1493) observes, 'while everyone (including myself) is now rather embarrassed by the enthusiasm they felt for Web 2.0 at the time, it contained within it some significant challenges and opportunities for higher education'. Early discussions of social media tended to highlight opportunities rather than challenges in ways that now seem obviously problematic. By focusing purely on what academics *could* do with social media, the question of what they *should* do was largely neglected. The result has been a tendency to fixate on the instrumental gains which academics can realise from their engagement, reinforced by the sector rewarding social media metrics in various ways (Carrigan & Jordan, 2021). It is difficult to see much remaining of the early hopes for social media in today's professional culture.

This is why we need to establish norms and standards concerning GenAI use for academics. There are reasons for hope but realising that potential means establishing professional cultures which support responsible use. I've highlighted throughout where I see the dangers for academics, particularly given the professional incentives to *produce more* and *save time* through whatever means they encounter. I consider where this might lead in the final chapter, arguing that individually useful approaches to GenAI might prove collectively disastrous for scholarship and higher education. In contrast, I have argued for a reflective and dialogical approach, using GenAI as a tool for thinking rather than a replacement for thought, which offers greater intellectual rewards while having the potential to mitigate these harms.

Although the approach I offer is one of harm reduction, there is far more to the ethics of GenAI than such an ethos in professional practice can account for. One response to the issues of environmental damage and intellectual property infringement discussed in this chapter would be to conclude that GenAI is fundamentally unethical and that we should avoid it.

However, academics *will* use GenAI regardless of the stance I take, whereas I might exercise some influence over that use with a nuanced stance engaging with their practical circumstances. That at least is what I am telling myself. But there are ethical issues which concern me deeply, and broader social and political questions raised by GenAI which urgently need to inform how academics engage with these developments, even if they might not in practice determine those responses. This chapter emphasises how GenAI cannot be treated as a neutral tool without wider social implications, while recognising that if you are reading it then you are likely to already have a practical interest in its application. It tries to strike a difficult balance with the risk that it pleases neither critics nor enthusiasts, but I suspect neither of these positions is adequate to the complex challenges posed by GenAI.

I find myself oscillating between optimism and pessimism, torn between the immediate creative fulfilment I have found in using conversational agents and concern that their widespread adoption could exacerbate the worst features of the contemporary academy (Vostal, 2016). It is important to recognise how sweeping the implications of these developments could be, particularly if this is only the start of a longer process of technological change. In contrast to those still suggesting this is *all* self-interested hype,[1] I remain fixated on the parallel to social media, with the societal implications of these platforms still playing out nearly twenty years after the major firms were founded. After more than a decade of widespread promotion of social media within higher education, we have finally moved past the tendency to present its use by academics as a strange new development (Carrigan, 2022). Even in the worst-case scenario outlined in the final chapter, we can expect to see the implications of GenAI playing out over a comparable timescale.

UNDERSTANDING THE CONTEXT IN WHICH GENERATIVE AI HAS EMERGED

The tasks which define academic work revolve around the *production, management* and *exchange*[2] of knowledge. This leaves them within the remit of technologies which generate and modify representations of knowledge, doing so in ways which would have been fantastical only a few years ago. Even if we believe that the outputs of GenAI will inevitably be mediocre, the entire system in which 'outputs' (including our own) enter into wider circulation is undergoing a profound shift. Academics will need to individually and collectively define their orientation towards GenAI, even if it is one of principled rejection which seeks to preserve a sphere of humanistic knowledge-production, beyond the remit of a wider context in which

---

[1] Clearly, there is a substantial quantity of hype surrounding GenAI, driven by commercial and economic interests in promoting the notion it is an era-defining technology. It's possible to recognise the self-interested character of the most prominent voices making this claim while also believing there is a kernel of truth to what they are saying.

[2] The overlap in how social media and GenAI lead to the transformation of these activities is a reason why I insist they need to be seen as two parts of a wider story, in which knowledge has been progressively platformised (Carrigan & Fatsis, 2021).

generative outputs become normalised.[3] This technology will not go back into the box, even if we studiously ignore it or make a principled decision to refrain from using it ourselves.

I have stressed *continuity* in understanding these developments within higher education and beyond. GenAI builds upon social media in a literal sense that training of these models depends upon the user-generated content which defines mass commercial social media (Carrigan & Fatsis, 2021, ch 2). It represents the next phase in an ongoing process of social networks and knowledge-production being transformed by the services and platforms built upon the mass internet, dominated by corporate actors despite the utopian hopes invested in early networking (Turner, 2010). After 20 years of social platforms rapidly growing, in a process Facebook founder Mark Zuckerberg infamously described as 'move fast and break things', we have entered a new phase of development where the social and political challenges of social media are unanimously recognised, even if 'what is to be done' remains contentious (Carrigan, 2022; Margetts, 2018). Gillespie (2018: loc 866) warns us that 'It takes a while - years, decades - for a culture to adjust itself to the subtle working of a new information system, and to stop expecting from it what traditional systems provided'. GenAI should be seen as part of a 'new information system' we are still adjusting to, building upon and radicalising what Bratton (2015) describes as planetary-scale computation. This is not a fad which can be wished away, even if the firms and services involved might change significantly over time.

There is a threat to the professional status of academics here, in the sense of our claim to be expert custodians of bodies of knowledge in ways which could not be replicated through other means. There are many cases throughout history of professions disappearing when the technology which justified their existence becomes obsolete (Abbott, 1988, 28). This is exactly the threat that educational technologies such as Massively Open Online Courses (MOOCs) and schools redesigned around personalised learning and automated teaching implicitly, sometimes explicitly, posed to educators and academics (Williamson, 2018). In the research domain the rise of 'big data' was accompanied by hyperbolic rhetoric that theory was now obsolete, suggesting that knowledge-production could be reduced to a brute-force computational technique (Anderson, 2008; Carrigan, 2019). These technological developments promised to 'disrupt' existing models of research and teaching by providing more effective ways to perform these activities on a larger scale, with little to no need for traditional academics depending on who you listened to. This threat fizzled out, either because the underlying technology failed to live up to expectations (MOOCs and alt-schools) or a compromise was reached with academic expertise ('big data' becoming social data science and computational social science). Even if these developments failed to reach the dizzying heights predicted by their advocates, they represent a continual sequence of technological challenges to the professional status of academics and the nature of their practice.

---

[3] I don't think this is a viable strategy for reasons explored in the final chapter, largely because the incentive structure of contemporary academic publishing so powerfully militates against it. If enough academics embrace the potential productivity gains of GenAI the expectations of what it means to be a 'productive' academic will increase sufficiently to make this position untenable.

In reality, this status has been under threat for some time given that, as Fuller (2023: loc 189) puts it, 'the world's knowledge is increasingly not deposited in dedicated academic buildings and other public spaces (i.e., libraries) but distributed across the internet, to which everyone has great but variable access'. This radical shift in access to knowledge has occurred alongside a growth in research agendas being dictated by external funding and employers turning to alternative modes of training and selection (Fuller, 2023, loc 442). We are living through a significant shift in how the academic profession, and the practical activity which constitutes our work, is organised, with the disruption of the pandemic accelerating changes already underway (Carrigan et al., 2023). The problem with framing GenAI as a hype wave that will eventually fizzle out is that it fails to recognise the significance of the juncture at which it has emerged. There are enormously consequential developments already underway in knowledge-production and knowledge-exchange which amplify the ramifications of GenAI, particularly with regards to the place of universities within wider society.

This is the context in which we must understand the significance of GenAI to the role of academics within universities. Professions adapt to change by redefining their purposes and the problems they address to reflect a new reality in which their role has shifted (Abbott, 1988). While it might be too early to definitively establish this is necessary for GenAI, our roles *were* changing even before these technologies came along. As a profession defined by its relationship to the knowledge system, our working lives are unavoidably bound up in the sociotechnical systems through which knowledge is produced and circulated. The tendency for academics to conceive of our work in discursive and scholastic terms, admittedly much more common in the humanities and parts of the social sciences, too often obscures the materiality of this dependence. The manner in which we inherit infrastructure from universities compounds this tendency, albeit much less so for precarious workers who work between and across institutions (Woodcock, 2018).

During those moments when change is taking place, it becomes easier to reflect upon the technology our scholarship depends on. We notice it far more during these periods of change than we do once it has faded into the background of our working environment. In his commencement speech at Kenyon College, the novelist David Foster Wallace (2005) began with a parable that has been a repeated favourite of bloggers over the years:

> There are these two young fish swimming along and they happen to meet an older fish swimming the other way, who nods at them and says "Morning, boys. How's the water?" And the two young fish swim on for a bit, and then eventually one of them looks over at the other and goes "What the hell is water?

The point Wallace was making is that 'the most obvious, important realities are often the ones that are hardest to see and talk about'. For academics our dependence upon technology is one such reality. It is so intimately relied upon that we easily ignore how integral it is to what we do. We get frustrated when it breaks, upgrade devices in pursuit of better experiences and sometimes talk to each other about practical issues we encounter. There's a particular sort of infantile rage which otherwise sedate academics can express when the office printer doesn't work that has always fascinated me. But the manner in which our scholarship *is* digital at this point tends to go unremarked upon, apart from during those times when a dramatic shift is enforced upon us.

The enforced digitalisation of the Covid-19 pandemic was one such event, we all became digital scholars by default because lockdown restrictions squeezed out those remaining arenas which were not entirely reliant on the digital (Carrigan, 2022). But rather than being the prelude to a newly reflective approach to digital technology, the emergency digital scholarship of the pandemic has faded. In using the term, I'm drawing a connection to the *emergency remote teaching* which dominated pedagogy during the pandemic (Nordmann et al., 2020). It was a pragmatic response to circumstance that had little relationship to the rich repertoire of digital education which preceded the pandemic (Weller, 2020). Yet for many academics online learning is synonymous with the hastily improvised Zoom meetings and self-recorded videos of the pandemic, contributing to an understandable impulse to revert to the pre-pandemic norm. The same I suggest is true of digital scholarship, with the unwelcome technological reliance of the crisis now shaping the unexamined practice of academics in a hybrid work culture. When we are adjusted to the technical systems we work within, it 'fades into the background, forgotten as it disappears into everydayness, just as, for a fish, what disappears from view, as its "element" is water' (Stiegler, 2019, loc 887). But when that adjustment breaks down as the system changes, we are confronted with the fragile nature of the tools we use and our dependence on them. These are moments in which professional cultures can inadvertently establish practices which get locked in before the change dissipates. The challenge of GenAI is an invitation for academics to grapple with the digitalisation of their practice more broadly. But the track record in many disciplines and fields does not give cause for optimism.[4]

This matters for academics because technology is a disrupter of professional jurisdiction (Abbott, 1988). Each new development offers alternative ways to address the challenges traditionally within the purview of that profession. By advocating a reflexive approach to GenAI, as an *interlocutor* rather than a *tool*, I am advocating a creative exploration of how our problem-solving activity might be changed and our professional jurisdiction redefined. This does not mean standardising our use of GenAI, which I suspect would be impossible across diverse disciplines and fields, but rather recovering common questions of professional purpose which unite what we do as people who produce and communicate knowledge. While the purposes underlying our work might often recede in the mundane reality of university life, there are nonetheless purposes to research, teaching, service and engagement. These are values which can guide us in a complex and uncertain landscape.

---

[4]Obviously, there are swathes of knowledge-production where this has been recognised for a long time, specifically those in which technical mastery or innovation is a required part of research practice. But my intuition would be this is not a majority experience, even if I struggle to see how to quantify this in a meaningful way.

If we are aware of these purposes they can act as a bulwark against the instrumental uses of GenAI which carry the greatest ethical risks. I am extremely concerned that if we are driven by efficiency alone in our embrace of these tools and services, it will make ethical practice difficult and might even lead to the unravelling of academic authority. By keeping in touch with the values which motivate our work we can retain a sense of legitimacy as a profession, ensuring that we can account for what is specifically *scholarly* about how we use GenAI and the particular value this adds to the world. If we follow personal incentives to make our working lives easier or gain a competitive advantage over other academics, there is a real sense in which we are participating in our own deskilling by reducing our work to routine tasks handed over to automated systems. Furthermore, we fail our students if we do not succeed in establishing a broad agreement about ethical use that we can model for them. What does it mean to use GenAI in an ethical way? It would be hubristic of me to try and answer the question so directly. It would imply that I had reached some clarity about this in my own practice, whereas I remain preoccupied by it. In fact, I am still at the stage of grappling with ethical dilemmas. Instead, I will share the three primary ethical dilemmas which occupy me, with a view to supporting the reader in finding their own way through the ethical challenges posed by these still recent developments. These do not exhaust the ethical discussions we urgently need about GenAI, but I hope they are a useful starting point which ensures the practical exploration elsewhere in the book remains grounded in ethical awareness.

THE FIRST DILEMMA: THE EPISTEMIC LIMITS OF GENERATIVE AI ARE NOT GOING AWAY

My argument that we should integrate GenAI into scholarship does not mean we should *rely* on it, in the sense of trusting it with full confidence. The reasons for this are a number of interlinked epistemic limits which academics using these systems need to be aware of: *hallucination, common knowledge, partiality* and *unpredictability*. This section introduces each of these in order to suggest their implications for scholarly practice before considering the sense in which these constitute an *ethical* dilemma.

The term 'hallucination' refers to the tendency of conversational agents to produce plausible but factually incorrect responses to user queries. Developers have been successful in lowering the rate of hallucination with successive models, reflected in formal testing as well as end-user experience. However, the propensity of GenAI to hallucinate comes from the underlying technology, creating a mismatch between what the system is doing and what the user imagines it to be doing. The problem of hallucination can be mitigated and minimised but there are reasons to believe that it cannot be entirely eliminated.

These systems have no model of the world upon which they can draw. They do not *know* anything in the human sense of the term, even if their capacity to cope with even the most complex queries can make it *feel* as if they know everything. The large language model enables responses to prompts by suggesting text which is statistically likely to follow from what you have offered, tuned in various ways and filtered through an interface designed to maximise utility. The immense breadth of the training data imbues these techniques with remarkable predictive power. If you have learned from a sufficiently deep sample of human culture then the connections identified at scale have an immense predictive power, even in response to entirely novel queries. This is the root of their *generative* capacity: past patterns are being used as a basis to produce new patterns in response to the patterns provided by the user in their prompts.

It is urgent that people using GenAI in a professional context understand this propensity to hallucinate. Keen (2023) suggests there are three core mechanisms producing hallucinatory responses: inference from data of uncertain quality or provenance, unintended consequences of the analytical method the system is using and a failure to provide relevant context in the initial prompt. There is a wider uncertainty about the process because these systems are 'black boxes'. Even for those working inside the organisations operating GenAI systems, it is not clear exactly how 'inputs' lead to 'outputs' in specific cases (as opposed to the general principles through which the systems operate). This creates a quandary for anyone inclined to rely on GenAI, suggesting a risk of what Thornhill (2023) describes as 'death by GPT' comparable to 'death by GPS' where 'car drivers have blindly followed errant GPS navigation systems on to exit ramps for highways or into the scorching heat of California's Death Valley'. There are steps which can mitigate the tendency to hallucinate, such as ensuring clarity in your prompts (what exactly are you asking for?), using multiple rounds of prompts with examples and providing feedback. However, it is essential that any academics using these systems, particularly in a research capacity, recognise this tendency.

This is not the only epistemic limitation of GenAI that academics need to be aware of. The Oxford Semantic Technologies (2023) team have written about what they describe as ChatGPT's 'Snow White problem'. It is widely believed that Disney's Snow White and the Seven Dwarfs (1937) was the first feature-length animated film whereas, in reality, it was a little-known Argentina film called El Apóstol. As the authors put it, ChatGPT believes the Disney film is the first because it's 'a common misconception that has been floating around the internet for years, and as such, it has been used to train and teach ChatGPT what it now feeds back to us'. This illustrates the problem of distinguishing between consensus and truth. While this is a challenge for any platform which facilitates access to knowledge, ChatGPT lacks the feedback mechanisms which a system like Wikipedia uses to filter its content. This makes it more likely that things which are widely believed will be authoritatively presented as facts.

It should be highlighted that GPT-4, which had not been released at the time their blog post was written, handles this challenge effectively in an interesting way. It continues to claim that Snow White and the Seven Dwarfs was the first feature-length animated film but qualifies this by saying 'if we consider non-American films, the Argentinian film "El Apóstol" is technically the first feature-length film, released in 1917'. It points out there are no copies of this earlier film surviving today, which means that Disney's film is the earliest one that can still be viewed. In fact, ChatGPT observes that 'it is often credited as the first full-length animated feature' but 'this is the first feature-length animated film in terms of Hollywood and Western cinema'. This does not repudiate the point that the Oxford team are making, however, even if it suggests that 'the common knowledge problem' might, like hallucinations, be minimised over time without being entirely eliminated.

While this book does not explore the underlying technology, it is crucial to understand the significance of the data used to train the large language models on which GenAI tools and services are based. As Crawford (2021, p. 98) observes in a reflection on artificial intelligence more widely, 'datasets shape the epistemic boundaries governing how AI operates and, in that sense, create the limits of how AI can "see" the world'. Prior to the modern web AI researchers struggled to compile datasets from an eclectic range of available sources ranging from children's books through to technical manuals and court transcripts (Crawford, 2021, pp. 99–101). In contrast, GenAI systems have been trained on datasets that are so large it is easy to imagine them as encompassing the entirety of the internet. The problem is that, as Bender et al. (2021, p. 613) point out, it is easy to imagine that the size of the internet means that it must be 'broadly representative of the ways in which different people view the world'. In reality not only are internet contents not diverse in the imagined way, with patterns of access translating into the dominance of younger users and users from developed countries, but the problem is amplified by the methodologies through which text is collected and filtered in the development of large language models (Bender et al., 2021).

Prominent sources such as Twitter, Wikipedia and Reddit have well documented demographic user trends. Simply using a platform does not mean a user will be meaningfully represented in text scraped from it because of the predominance of *lurkers* who simply consume content, with the collected text likely to be dominated by the frequent posters atypical of the wider community (Sipley, 2024). This is sometimes described in internet culture as the *1% rule* suggesting that 1% are active creators, 9% are active commenters and 90% simply consume content. It is a folk wisdom rather than a social scientific law but it neatly captures how social platforms tend to be stratified in ways that the rhetoric of 'Web 2.0' and 'social media' has tended to obscure (Carrigan & Fatsis, 2021, ch 2). Furthermore, Bender et al. (2021, p. 613) point out how networked harassment which is common on social platforms creates a feedback loop in which existing forms of inequality will be amplified in the final corpus (Marwick, 2021). Those whose privilege enables them to shout the loudest will inevitably figure most prominently in the data.

The methodological apparatus through which a corpus is generated further entrenches this problem. For example, Birhane et al. (2021) identify how the text descriptions upon which large-scale image datasets depend frequently include offensive and stereotypical descriptions, including those attached to the high preponderance of pornographic and sexualised content amongst the images which can be scraped. Not only does the production of internet content reflect existing social inequalities, but so too does the meta-data through which that content is classified and described. Bender and Gebru et al. (2021, p. 614) draw attention to how filtering mechanisms intended to cleanse databases of offensive terms might inadvertently impact marginalised populations. They cite how a word such as 'twink' simultaneously features in pornography and LGBTQ discourse which means that discarding any page which contains the word will further marginalise non-heteronormative voices in the corpus. These limitations mean that the representations produced by GenAI will reflect and reinforce wider social inequalities. It is disturbingly easy to illustrate this with image generators. My experience is that adding the adjective 'successful' to a request to generate an image of a specified profession leads ChatGPT to default to an image of a conventionally attractive man in his late 20s or early 30s.[5] Often called algorithmic injustice, this is a broader tendency of machine learning systems which predates GenAI insofar that the culture on which these conversational agents has been trained has already been filtered through these discriminatory mechanisms (O'Neil, 2016).

This stark partiality doesn't have an obvious parallel in textual conversations. The algorithmic bias here is more subtle and insidious, which makes it even more important to understand how these limitations shape the operation of these systems. What can seem like technologies with *universal* scope are in reality exceptionally *partial*. Far from embodying the accumulated wisdom of humankind, they are a predominately Anglophone snapshot of a digitised culture, marked by the inequalities and oppression of the wider world. This is why I have stressed that GenAI must be treated as an *interlocutor* and not a vast database in which we can look up answers to our questions. Not only are factual answers subject to problems of *hallucination* and *common knowledge*, but even when they are factually correct they will still embody a certain perspective that conversational agents are unable to account for in their self-presentation to users. This doesn't mean they are useless or unreliable. Far from it. But it does mean we need to recognise conversational agents as offering a partial voice with which we can meaningfully interact, with the same limits and caution governing that interaction that we would intuitively recognise in any other intellectual partner.

We need to recognise conversational agents as embedded in, shaped by and reflecting the world. In doing so we open up the possibility of meaningful collaborative relationships, informed by their limits and strengths. Mewburn's (2023) description of ChatGPT as a 'talented, but easily misled, intern/research assistant who has a sad tendency to be sexist, racist and other kinds of "isms"' has stayed with me as I write. The subsequent development of conversational agents means we could plausibly suggest we are now

---

[5]In the interests of disclosure, I should note that ChatGPT no longer consistently reproduces this in April 2024 in the same way it did in February 2024. I documented the initial results here: https://markcarrigan.net/2024/02/27/not-only-does-chatgpt-think-all-successful-professionals-are-men-it-thinks-theyre-all-the-same-man/

MC: Draw me a successful scientist.

ChatGPT: Here is the illustration of a successful scientist in their modern laboratory, surrounded by high-tech equipment and achievements that showcase their contributions to science.

Figure 3.1 ChatGPT's Depiction of a 'Successful' Scientist

talking about a visiting professor, either a polymath or a dilettante depending on how critical you are being. Furthermore, they are genuinely enthusiastic to support you and continually on their best behaviour, even if you perceive some issues lurking beneath the surface as you interact more frequently. In either case, you would approach this figure with neither absolute credulity nor unvarnished scepticism, instead exploring how you could work with them. This would include being sensitive to their limitations, such as the established issues described above and those which emerge in the course of your interaction.

The problem with GenAI is that emerging issues might not be visible to users in their interactions, though we shouldn't underestimate what can be discerned through thoughtful reflection on the outputs you encounter.[6] For example, Mark (2024) reports on emerging evidence of the limits of GenAI summarisation which ought to concern anyone looking to summarise documents. These issues will continue to emerge as we learn more about their use across a range of contexts, even as the firms proclaim the innovative nature of their next-generation models. There will never be a conversational agent free of epistemic limitations. This means that we have to be careful about our own use, ensuring it is informed by a practical awareness of the limitations of these systems as we understand them. This is an ethical responsibility for scholars because using these systems without a working understanding of their limitations carries substantial risks of doing harm and modelling irresponsible use contributes to the percolation of these harms through the networks of influence (e.g., colleagues and students) in which we are embedded as academics.

THE SECOND DILEMMA: THE WIDESPREAD UPTAKE OF GENAI WOULD BE AN ENVIRONMENTAL CATASTROPHE

Over the last decade 'the cloud' became a routine part of our working lives. The paraphernalia of data storage faded away at remarkable speed, as we increasingly found our files available from anywhere. Even though I have written extensively about digital change, I was still startled last year when I was unsure how to physically transfer a file from my work laptop. The answer of course was a USB-C flash drive. But the fact these existed had completely escaped my notice until that point, given how the once ubiquitous USB sticks had dropped out of my life. Our relationship with digital systems has rapidly become weightless, leaving us casually reliant on an invisible infrastructure which churns away in the background. It is an architecture of convenience for those with the resources to take advantage of it, in contrast to the underlying service layer which is radically reshaping the nature of work (Scholz, 2017).

This infrastructure is far from weightless, even if the imagery of 'the cloud' works effectively to obscure the impact of its worldly operations. The development of cloud computing has involved the rapacious growth of data centres across the planet in an ever-accelerating competition between Amazon, Alphabet and Microsoft to build the most powerful planetary-scale computer (Bratton, 2015). The competition over GenAI is fuelling a new round of expansion. For example, Amazon has committed to investing $150 billion in data centres

---

[6]This is why, I have stressed the need to avoid a timesaving approach to GenAI, even though these systems can indeed save you time. If you embrace them as a device for saving time you are extremely unlikely to undertake this thoughtful reflection, as opposed to simply copying and pasting the results into whatever output you were seeking help with.

over the next fifteen years (Day, 2024). This expansion is not purely GenAI-related b
planned incorporation of this functionality across existing services means the bou
between pre-GenAI and GenAI investment is breaking down, suggesting a future in ....
these services are the foundation upon which the next-generation of cloud computing business models operate. As Brevini (2021, loc 187) noted, 'many AI applications are already so
embedded in our everyday life they no longer capture our attention'. The same can be
expected over the coming years as GenAI fades into the underlying architecture of everyday
software, particularly if the templated functionality we have discussed becomes the most
frequent mode of engagement rather than conversational agents. The problem is that as
Brevani (2021) goes on to write, 'In all its variety of forms, AI relies on large swathes of land
and sea, vast arrays of technology, and greenhouse gas-emitting machines and infrastructures
that deplete scarce resources through their production, consumption and disposal'.

Even the most technologically hostile academic is bound up within these digital infrastructures (Carrigan & Fatsis, 2021). However, as Woodcock (2018) points out, their position
within the academic hierarchy is likely to determine the extent to which these are experienced
as a constraint or enablement. Their operation is already marked by what Belkhir and
Elmeligi (2018, p. 448) describe as 'exponentially growing energy consumption'. This is likely
to accelerate rapidly as large firms build future strategies around GenAI even if, as some critics
predict, consumer uptake doesn't match corporate optimism. As McQuillan (2022, p. 22)
memorably put it, 'if artificial intelligence has a soundtrack, it's the deafening whir of cooling
fans in the server farms'. In contrast to the weightless imagery of 'the cloud', the operation of
GenAI platforms, tools and systems has immediate impacts on the environment. As Crawford
(2016, p. 31) pointedly conveys, every element of AI systems is entangled in environmental
processes in ways that far too easily drop out of the debate about the uptake of these tools,
Chomsky's (2023) sceptical remark that 'generative AI is basically just a way of wasting a lot of
energy in California' notwithstanding:
the e......

> Computational media now participate in geological (and climatological) processes,
> from the transformation of the earth's materials into infrastructures and devices to
> the powering of these new systems with oil and gas reserves. Reflecting on media and
> technology as geological processes enables us to consider the radical depletion of
> nonrenewable resources required to drive the technologies of the present moment.
> Each object in the extended network of an AI system, from network routers to
> batteries to data centres, is built using elements that required billions of years to form
> inside the earth.

Kumar and Davenport (2023) caution that using 'these computation-heavy tools' in ways not
required for the immediate task at hand 'may be depleting the earth's health even more than
they are helping its people'. Is the creativity and convenience which characterise GenAI use
worthwhile if it accelerates the point at which we reach an uninhabitable earth (Wallace-Wells,
2019)? That's a conclusion you can only reach yourself but it troubles me even more as I write,
even as I remain unsure what the practical response to this should be. Particularly as I've

realised the uses of GenAI I find most rewarding are the most wasteful. While I am confident that approaching conversational agents as interlocutors work effectively to minimise harm *within* higher education, it is problematic insofar as that it involves *more* conversation with these systems than would otherwise be the case.

If you outsource a distinct task to Claude or ChatGPT exposure to the epistemic risks might be greater, in the sense that you are relying on them to do part of your work to save time. However, it is a single instance in which you are outsourcing an existing task under specific circumstances. The dialogical approach I advocate in this book tends to sprawl outwards into all aspects of working life. I often effectively relate to Claude as a notebook that talks back to me, offering continual feedback in a process I describe in detail in the next chapter. It is a powerful and creative use of the technology which I'm confident many academics would find enriching. But it still inserts a distributed computational process into what was a localised one. I've gone from taking notes in a locally hosted app to taking notes in a cloud-based platform which is performing complex operations on *every single entry I make.* I have since tried to be more selective about how and when I do this but it doesn't resolve the underlying concern, only mitigates the impact of what I am doing.

MC: I anticipate there will be many academics who see the potential value of conversational agents like yourself for their work, but worry about the contribution which normalising the use of GenAI across the full range of scholarly activities might make to the climate crisis. What are practical steps which academics can take to ensure their use is sustainable and/or minimise the environmental impact of any specific use they make?

Claude: There are several practical steps that academics can take to ensure their use of AI systems like myself is as sustainable as possible and minimizes environmental impact:

1. Be judicious and intentional about AI usage. Academics should carefully consider whether using an AI system is truly necessary and valuable for a given task, rather than using AI indiscriminately. Prioritizing high-impact, targeted applications can help limit unnecessary energy consumption.

2. Opt for energy-efficient AI providers when possible. Some AI companies utilize more energy-efficient hardware, algorithms, and data center practices than others. Academics can research and prioritize providers that have strong environmental commitments and practices.

3. Avoid unnecessarily long interactions. While exploring ideas with an AI can be intellectually stimulating, aim to keep interactions purposeful and avoid overly long sessions when a more concise approach would suffice. This reduces the computational resources expended.

Figure 3.2 Claude's Advice about Sustainable Practice with Conversational Agents

---

What does sustainable GenAI use look like? Is this even possible? Or does any use leave us unavoidably tangled up in the expansion of digital infrastructures accelerating the climate crisis? There are obvious forms which mitigation could take, such as only using more powerful models when strictly necessary[7] and restricting use to locally operated models where possible.[8] There is a huge investment by cloud computing firms in optimising data centre operations alongside a push towards renewable energy, as well as research into techniques for reducing the computational load of training and operating the models themselves. But even with the most charitable reading of the intentions, it is difficult to see this as constituting anything more than a drop in the ocean. It seems likely that if GenAI became widespread it would constitute, at least to some degree, an environmental catastrophe. This is a sobering realisation to come to towards the end of writing a book about how a professional group can incorporate it into their work.

THE THIRD DILEMMA: THE DEVELOPMENT OF GENERATIVE AI DEPENDS ON MASS ENCLOSURE OF INTELLECTUAL PROPERTY

It is remarkable what conversational agents can do.[9] I'm conscious that fellow sociologists might be uncomfortable with my enthusiasm for what is inarguably overhyped software. The reason I have been oscillating wildly between optimism and pessimism is that I'm fully aware of the means by which those capabilities have been developed. While substantial technological innovations have made the current GenAI wave possible, the most important development is the most contentious: the availability of vast swathes amounts of freely available online material and the willingness of firms to hoover up that material and use it to develop commercial models. While it would be misleading to imagine these models have been trained on the 'entire internet' (and the emerging academic tendency to imagine them as representing the consolidated common sense of society risks amplifying that misunderstanding[10]) there is a vastness to the scope of their training that

---

[7]For example, using GPT 3.5 or Claude 3 Haiku unless using GPT 4 or Claude 3 Opus is really necessary.

[8]It is likely we will see GenAI systems being built into mobile phones and tablets in the near future, as well as optimised models running on personal computers. However, the likelihood these will be used to encourage additional cycles of obsolesce for personal devices has the potential to outweigh the climatic impact of using optimised models locally.

[9]I refer to conversational agents deliberately here to distinguish systems like ChatGPT and Claude from the broader field of software labelled as GenAI. In the coming chapters, I explore the reasons why academics ought to be particularly cautious about approaches to GenAI which rest on effectively providing *templates*, as opposed to expecting the user to make clear what they are asking of the system.

[10]See for example Wegerif and Major (2024) who argue that these models represent the 'generalised other' in George Herbert Mead's sense. This conceptual move is used to anchor a dialogical approach to GenAI which I'm fully in agreement with. But positioning models in this way mystifies the partiality and contingency of their training, as well as overestimates the capacity of contemporary social life to produce the consensus upon which Mead's concept depends (Archer, 2012; Carrigan, 2022).

matches the vastness of the open web. Without the content explosion of the last two decades, in which people from all over the world have been encouraged to freely share their work online, it would be difficult to conceive of GenAI in its current form.

We have seen, as Naomi Klein (2023) put it, 'the wealthiest companies in history (Microsoft, Apple, Google, Meta, Amazon) unilaterally seizing the sum total of human knowledge that exists in digital, scrapable form and walling it off inside propriety products, many of which will take direct aim at the humans whose lifetime of labour trained the machines without giving permission or consent'. The problem is not simply that they are leveraging what can be found openly on the web as the raw material which facilitates commercial strategy. These operations are imperilling the future prospects of the creators on whom the capacities of GenAI systems ultimately depend. For example, image generators have been trained on the work of artists which has been made freely available online. The remarkable capabilities of OpenAI's Sora video generation system which were demonstrated in February 2024 are widely speculated to rely on the system having been trained on YouTube videos. This would break the platform's terms of service which makes it startling that OpenAI has neither confirmed nor denied this. What makes this so egregious is the real and immediate threat these systems pose to the livelihoods of creators. What effect does the immediate capacity to generate images from a natural language prompt have on the market in which illustrators and designers are working? What effect will Sora have on employment within video production once this system is rolled out commercially?

It's important we avoid romanticising creative industries in which inequality has been rising for years, with successful careers increasingly dependent on unpaid internships and work undertaken in pursuit of visibility (Conor et al., 2015). Furthermore, the competitive dynamics of online platforms had further suppressed incomes with freelancers around the world cast into vicious competition with each other, creating a race-to-the-bottom which repudiates the participatory rhetoric with which social platforms launched themselves into the world (Carrigan & Fatsis, 2021, ch 2; Scholz, 2017). That things were already bad only makes the potential impacts of GenAI even more urgent. In an open letter published by the Center for Artistic Inquiry and Reporting, the illustrator Molly Crabapple argued that 'if this technology is left unchecked' we will soon find ourselves in a world where 'only a tiny elite of artists can remain in business, their work selling as a kind of luxury status symbol'. The accusation is that 'Generative AI is vampirical, feasting on past generations of artwork even as it sucks the lifeblood from living artists' (Crabapple, 2023).

I find it hard to (re)read this letter without immediately regretting the DALL-E generated images that litter my blog, even if I haven't or wouldn't use an image generator for a project where I was in a position to hire an illustrator. The unfortunate reality is that when I have hired an illustrator in the past, it has been through a freelancing platform characterised by the aforementioned race-to-the-bottom. It made the illustration viable for a self-funded academic project but it also meant participating in this infrastructure which drives down reimbursement.[11] Where I have used

---

[11] The obvious retort to this is it that it enables more people to take on this work. But this dynamic in which creative work becomes a 'side hustle' alongside other sources of income illustrates the unsettling character of the political economy in which these further developments are now taking place.

stock photography in the past it has been through the Unsplash platform which is popular among bloggers for its free stock photography. The promise of Unsplash is that it increases the visibility of creators who might then receive more commissioned work. But such hope labour in which creative work is offered for free in the hope of future rewards is exactly the bedrock upon which the training of GenAI has been built.

A range of lawsuits have been undertaken by creators with varying degrees of success. It is likely we will see many more. In some cases celebrities, writers and artists have received significant media attention as a result of cases they have brought, showing how existing reputations can be leveraged in the court of publicity. But individuals are unlikely to fare well against the emerging titan of Silicon Valley, backed up by one of the wealthiest firms in the world. *The New York Times* initiated legal action in late 2023 which accused OpenAI of seeking to 'free ride' on the paper's journalism. Despite being a usually financially buoyant publication as a result of its successful digital strategy, its resources are nonetheless minute in comparison to those enjoyed by OpenAI and Microsoft. The failure of their initial attempt to get the lawsuit thrown out suggests there might be some accommodation to negotiated access as the path forward, echoed in interviews with high-profile figures at the firm which affirm their commitment to remuneration for creators while remaining vague about the details (Fridman, 2024).

The New York Times lawsuit could pave the way for content producers to negotiate deals with tech firms for access to this premium material in order to train their models. The problem is that only the biggest content producers are likely to do so, empowering existing media brands while leaving the majority at the mercy of GenAI corporations. Negotiated deals for content producers able to leverage their premium status and voluntary opt-outs for the rest. It might be better than the free-for-all which characterised the training of current models but only marginally so. Furthermore, the fact that visibility within the models could come to constitute another object of hope labour gives reason to worry that the politics of opting out might not be quite as straightforward as its advocates currently assume.[12]

It is important to recognise that artistic work does not constitute the entirety of training data. What makes these dynamics so troubling is that the logic of training lends itself to incorporating as much material as possible from the widest range of sources. Udandarao et al. (2024, p. 2) identify dependence on exponentially increasing quantities of data in order to sustain linear improvements within multimodal models. As they put it, 'these models require exponentially more data on a concept to linearly improve their performance'. In order to ensure that additional examples figure in future training it's necessary to cast the net ever wider. To the best of my knowledge, there has not been a comparable demonstration with text-based models but we see a parallel exponential increase in the size of the models (and the environmental costs of training them) motivated by a corporate arms race to dominate this emerging field. The promise of responsible training needs to be seen against this technological

---

[12]For example, if a substantial percentage of factual queries and searches come to be made through ChatGPT, it would matter to a cultural producer whether they figure in the training data, for the same reasons that their search engine optimisation would matter to them.

backdrop, in which the continual expansion of training data is a requirement for success in a competition between some of the most powerful firms on the planet.

IS IT POSSIBLE TO USE GENERATIVE AI IN AN ETHICAL WAY?

During the final stages of writing, OpenAI's Vice President of Global Affairs Anna Makanju remarked during an event at Columbia University that 'It is a bit of a race between the positive application of these technologies and the negative ones'. Marcus (2024) suggested in response that the 'use cases on the negative side of the ledger are proliferating fast, literally faster than I can report them here, from fake books (undermining authors) to rings of fake websites designed to sell ads (based on often incorrect information that pollutes the internet) to election misinformation to the pollution of science by articles partially written by GPT in which hallucinations may filter in'. This is a bleak yet plausible picture of harms emerging across a dizzying range of domains, in contrast to the still uncertain gains experienced within many sectors.

It raises an obvious question of where this balance lies within higher education, as well as how it is likely to develop over time. When I started writing this book in May 2023 these harms were largely theoretical, with the exception of the threat to assessment integrity discussed in the first chapter. As I bring the book to a close in April 2024, there is proliferating evidence that academics are using GenAI in a range of obviously problematic ways, such as asking factual questions[13] which are then pasted into journal articles (Maiberg, 2024). These can be found by searching for the exact phrase 'As of my last knowledge update' which ChatGPT uses to caveat its claims, raising the question of how many academics have copied answers yet remembered to exclude the giveaway text. It is revealing these instances tend to be within open-access journals of questionable standing,[14] illustrating how GenAI is intensifying existing problems in the sector rather than creating them from scratch. The attention which these examples have received online has been matched with growing reports of GenAI being used to conduct peer reviews. It is difficult to be certain whether this has taken place but the question even being asked indicates the real problem we now confront. If trust in review is *already* breaking down when the use of GenAI amongst academics remains a minority

---

[13]Obviously, this would be problematic even without the factual questions, but these indicate a truly careless use of conversational agents which frames them as a database through which information can be retrieved. As we have seen in this chapter, their propensity to hallucinate means they should not be used in this way.

[14]Often called 'predatory' journals which charge author-processing fees while engaging in little to no peer review. This explains how this text can make it through peer review, though it remains to be seen how many instances of this will find their way into legitimate publications. I discuss the possibility in chapter eight that publishers might be forced to rely upon GenAI filtering and reviewing in order to cope with an upsurge in submission rates driven by academics writing more quickly using GenAI.

pursuit, what happens if it becomes widespread? Taloni et al. (2023) report on using GPT 4 to 'fabricate data sets specifically designed to quickly produce false scientific evidence' even if we have little sense of how widespread this practice is. If we consider this emerging possibility against a documented backdrop of research misconduct, ranging from p-hacking through to outright falsification,[15] using these technologies for undertaking research misconduct more quickly and effectively becomes extremely worrying.

The problem again is how these new possibilities are taken up within a system which encourages problematic behaviour through what it celebrates and ignores and the incentives and penalties it distributes to those acting within it. Why would an academic *want* to write a journal article as quickly as possible? Why would an academic *want* to produce falsified data rather than work with what their actual methods produced? These are complex questions which I cannot do justice to here. In invoking them I'm not seeking to offer an alibi for GenAI as much as to insist on a sociological context to our discussions. The problems arise when the technology is taken up within a context that encourages certain uses of that technology, rather than being some inexorable expression of the technology's inner nature. The approach I've taken to harm reduction outlines what a scholarly user culture of GenAI could look like within the academy. It is intended to contribute to a conversation already overdue, with a particular focus on encouraging readers to consider how they could apply these principles concretely in their own use of these tools. There are already online workshops being run by professors which promise to help you increase your research productivity for $500. There are others less obviously problematic but which indicate an emerging economy in which early adopters promise to help academics leverage GenAI productivity gains in exchange for payment, across grant applications, data analysis and academic writing.

The fact this book isn't free means that I am in a sense part of this economy, even as I'm trying to distance myself from it. But what troubles me about it is the emphasis on productivity, doing more in less time, rather than it being an economy per se. If this becomes the overriding imperative shaping how GenAI is taken up within higher education then, as I argue in the final chapter, we are likely to see the worst aspect of existing professional culture rapidly intensified, at a substantial cost to our professional well-being and the viability of the knowledge system to which our scholarship is ultimately intended to contribute. It doesn't seem obvious to me that the productivity imperative will necessarily win out, even if I feel increasingly pessimistic. Unlike social media[16] which could be seen as a specialised set of tools operating at the interface of practice, even once it was accepted within the mainstream of higher education, GenAI cuts to the heart of so many aspects of what universities do as organisations that there are structural imperatives to grapple more seriously with it.

---

[15]See Lewis-Kraus (2023) for a detailed expose of some high-profile cases in behavioural science.

[16]I argued at length that we needed to establish a scholarly professional culture around the use of social media which wasn't governed by the individual rewards possible in relation to academic capital, algorithmic popularity or research evaluation (Carrigan, 2019; Carrigan & Fatsis, 2021; Carrigan & Jordan, 2021).

If we work towards such a culture it raises the possibility of a better balance between the positive applications of these technologies with the negative ones. That at least is the hope. The technology is already being used by academics in ways ranging from the harmful through to the helpful, as well as the ambiguous middle ground. If we can create what Gasser and Mayer-Schonberger (2024, loc 92) call guardrails which establish 'zones of desirable behaviour rather than pushing for a single right choice' then we help guide people in their use of these new tools while keeping open a space for experimentation. These can be made up of norms and rules, as well as 'processes and institutions, mechanisms and tools, even a "culture" or a "way of thinking"' (Gasser & Mayer-Shonberger, 2024, loc 241). What does this mean in practice? It means building conversations within fields and disciplines about what are appropriate and inappropriate uses of GenAI. It means developing professional training within and across universities which introduces academics to GenAI in a way informed by these nascent conversations.[17] It means organisations with a stake in research and publishing conduct having sufficient self-confidence to make judgements about what is unacceptable, informed by and contributing to these wider debates within the sector.

We urgently need to create the conditions which support creative and responsible use within the sector. The contribution of this book is inevitably modest, but I hope it might indicate directions for such a discussion as well as influence the practice of academics who are already using these technologies or planning to use them in the future. I consider what this might look like in practice in the final chapter, in the hope that readers might finish the book feeling equipped and inclined to contribute to these urgent debates. The main focus of this book remains individual practice but what I'm trying to stress is that individual decisions can have collective consequences. It can be useful to ask yourself through the process of engaging with GenAI: what would it be like if everyone I work with did the same thing? Would it create problems if this use became widespread in my workplace? This can help illustrate the potential ramifications of an emerging practice becoming normalised. In doing so it highlights the harms which you might not see in your own practice but which might nonetheless show up downstream.

But is this enough? I suspect it isn't when we see from a broader societal perspective. These are all matters of professional practice within higher education. There can be better or worse practice, more or less harmful practice. But it is still a matter of practice. Treating these issues adequately entails engaging with the broader systems and structures which make that practice possible. If academics are likely to take up GenAI in their scholarship then it's important they do so cognisant of the ethical and political issues. My intention has been to help ensure the positive applications win out over the negative. In this sense, I've prioritised intervening in the debate over the scholarly use of technologies because they *will* spread regardless of the conclusions I publicly or privately reach about them.

---

[17]For example, with colleagues at the University of Manchester I've organised training for PhD researchers which focuses on how to relate to conversational agents as intellectual interlocutors and training for teaching staff on how to reflectively take advantage of the wide range of ways in which GenAI can be incorporated into teaching practice.

It occurred to me in the later stages of writing this book that I might have felt differently about the ethics of GenAI if I had thought deeply about these issues prior to using it.[18] I dived into exploration driven by a creative fascination with conversational agents, with my socio-logical and political enquiry following behind the development of my creative practice. The irony is that I have been talking with Claude about the ethics of using conversational agents while writing this chapter. I suspect I would have still reached the conclusion that 'don't do it' is a limited and limiting stance, but it might have led me to draw the conclusion *I* at least would choose not to do it. It's now difficult to imagine my academic life without the ongoing assistance of Claude in particular. This is either an advert for the new terrain of digital scholarship which conversational agents open up or a cautionary tale about how insidious emerging technologies can be. I would suggest you weigh up the case in this chapter about the ethics of GenAI against the case I make throughout the book about utility. I reached the conclusion that saying 'don't do it' in this book would have little effect, other than to forgo the attempt to steer a rapidly evolving professional practice in a less destructive direction.

You may not draw the same conclusion. It would be hyperbolic to say 'get out while you still can'. But what I am trying to stress is what a significant shift in your practice the use of conversational agents can be, at least once they move from being an experiment to part of your working routines. If the ethical issues in this chapter trouble you then I would suggest pausing before further scholarly use. Use within professional settings tends to be expansive. It can be slow to find worthwhile ways to incorporate GenAI into your working routines. But once you get to the stage where you can meaningfully perceive the possibilities, they begin to present themselves in all aspects of your work. In this sense, it might be difficult to stop, at least past a certain point. The fact I never learned to drive makes it easy for me to continue to be a non-driver on environmental grounds. If driving had been a routine part of my life for years, it would be much more difficult to sustain a principled stance. In other words, engaging in sufficient reflection at this stage could ensure you don't feel trapped by the sheer usefulness of GenAI once you get started. There is a valid case to be made that the aforementioned issues mean that you shouldn't use it, even if you find yourself working with people who are using it. This doesn't mean there is something inherently problematic about the technology, as much as how it has been shaped in the context in which it has been developed and the present and future harms which follow from this.

---

[18]Thanks to my collaborator Helen Beetham for prompting this realisation, alongside many others.

4
THINKING

This chapter will:

- Identify how reflexive interaction with conversational agents can contribute to the process of developing ideas, complicating the tendency to position these systems as productivity tools which simply increase the efficiency of your work.
- Explore how conversational agents can be incorporated into a range of intellectual practices in concrete, immediate and creative ways that can deepen engagement with intellectual work rather than merely saving time.
- Propose a model of digital scholarship built around creative engagement with conversational agents, while remaining aware of the risks of overreliance on these systems.

If you search for 'scholar' on Google Images, you will encounter many pictures of bearded white men, sitting alone and staring intently at manuscripts. These images capture how scholarship has tended to be imagined, as a quasi-monastic pursuit in which learned men meditate on the esoteric knowledge which can be found in their books. This was ChatGPT's response to a request to produce a picture of a scholar to introduce this chapter on thinking (Figure 4.1).[1]

In the last chapter, we explored how the outputs of GenAI reflect the biases which are found within their training data. Therefore, it should be no surprise that ChatGPT will default to an image of a male thinker when asked to represent the figure of a scholar. When I queried why it had defaulted to the image of a man, it insisted that 'The image I provided aimed to be gender-neutral to reflect the inclusivity and diversity of scholarly endeavours'. To insist the outcome is gender-neutral even when it manifestly is not, resembles a common state of affairs within academic life. There is a risk that the representational deficiencies of GenAI intersect with existing inequalities within higher education, compounding the marginalisation and subordination which already exists, particularly with regard to whose contributions to knowledge are recognised and valued (Bacevic, 2023).

I wanted to start this chapter on *thinking* by reiterating how easily GenAI can reinforce existing inequalities if we relate to them in an *unthinking* way. It matters how we think (or fail to) with GenAI with consequences which extend beyond our own individual practice. This is why the reflective approach I advocate in this book is ethical as well as methodological: minimising the potential for harm in our use of GenAI often goes hand-in-hand with the most intellectually robust and creatively fulfilling uses of it. There is an obligation for academics to use these tools responsibly. In practice, this means using them *thoughtfully*. So what does this look like in practice? How can GenAI contribute to our thinking?

GENERATIVE AI AS AN INTERLOCUTOR

The philosopher Bertrand Russell once explained how he relied upon 'planting' conscious thoughts into the unconscious mind in order to let them take root and grow without deliberate intervention. He writes that 'if I have to write upon some rather difficult topic the best plan is to think about it with very great intensity - the greatest intensity of which I am capable - for a few hours or days, and at the end of that time give orders, so to speak, that work is to proceed underground' (Russell, 2013, pp. 49–50). Upon coming back to the topic at a later date, he would reliably find the connections had been formed and ideas developed

---

[1] I noted in the previous chapter that the representativeness of ChatGPT images has improved over the course of writing the book. However, the same prompt I used here midway through the writing process produced a startlingly similar image in the final stages of producing the book. The growing responsiveness of the system to qualifiers such as 'representative' or 'diverse' has improved matters somewhat (with these adjectives reliably producing figures who are not white men) but image generation can simply not be qualified with the level of sophistication involved in text-based interaction. This reflects the constraints of the image classification process discussed in the previous chapter.

MC: Draw me an image of a scholar to illustrate a book chapter on thinking.

ChatGPT:

Here's an image of a scholar that captures the essence of scholarly work and the timeless quest for knowledge. This illustration fits perfectly for a book chapter on thinking, depicting a serene and scholarly atmosphere in a classic study room.

Figure 4.1 The Stereotypical Image of a Scholar Produced by ChatGPT

without any conscious effort on his part. This would in turn free him from worrying about his progress, enabling that time and energy to be used for other purposes during the intervening period.

This passage has stayed with me since I read it in my mid-20s. It was a habit I was already in the process of developing and this framing made me commit to it as a deliberate strategy, rather than an activity I had stumbled into in a disorganised way. The research blog I have been writing for fourteen years, with nearly six thousand posts, can be seen as a commitment to this practice. When I am occupied by a thought I try to express it, putting it out of my mind in order to come back to it later. This enabled me to keep intellectual threads going as someone who only began to work full-time in a university over the last few years, without which I doubt I would have been able to complete a part-time PhD. My experience is these plants *do* grow, at least if the sowing is a sufficiently routine and careful practice. It needs a sustained commitment but also the ability to recognise when you should stop practising and do something else instead. There is a similar experience shared by one of Sword's (2017, p. 66) interviewees about the academic writing process, who explains how during long distance cycling 'writing is sort of going on in my mind, semiconscious' and that 'in those long periods of four, five, six hours on my own, the book is essentially writing itself'. The process will look different for different people. Sword (2017, p. 54) uses the metaphor of *marinating* to describe this process: leaving ideas in the back of the mind in order to let the flavours develop. It is a matter of what you are trying to cook, the flavours you are seeking to bring out and the conditions of your figurative kitchen.

It also matters what is taking place *outside* of the kitchen. Russell led a busy, frenetic and productive life. But it was still one without the constant interruption of email or the diversity of demands which distinguish a contemporary academic role from that of a Cambridge don in the early 20th century. I find it hard not to wonder whether Russell would have found his exercise in planting ideas less consistently reliable if, say, he had maintained a Twitter account to support his work as a public intellectual. We should always be careful in comparing ourselves to scholars who worked under radically different institutional and technological conditions. But we can still learn from their insights about intellectual and creative work. Doing so helps us avoid the expectation that we need to reinvent scholarly practice in the face of technological change. Recognising these continuities makes it easier to avoid the perils of the technological hype we explored in previous chapters, which too easily gives rise to a sense we have entered a brave new world and we must reinvent our practice from first principles. In framing this book around broad areas of scholarly activity, I have tried to foreground these continuities, with each of the four areas being sustained features of scholarly life even if they have come to look rather different over time. Even 'engagement', which is primarily a matter of *digital engagement* in this book, should be recognised as something Russell did to a remarkable degree. Interestingly, when I asked both ChatGPT and Claude to speculate how Russell might have used GenAI as part of his work, they both suggested it could have been used to support his engagement activities, whether simulating discussion on critical social issues (ChatGPT) or tailoring responses to specific critics about his often controversial social positions (Claude) (Figure 4.2).

Treating GenAI as an interlocutor can serve a similar function to Russell's planting ideas. For example, I have spent the last few days thinking about the Whisper AI functionality which is now built into the ChatGPT iOS application,[2] enabling voice commands with a

---

[2]The perils of writing a book about such a fast-changing topic is that this remark now feels positively antiquated at the point where I am finishing off the manuscript, despite only being months old. I have included it here as a real example of a topic which occupied me for a period during the writing of the book.

MC: How were the working conditions of a Cambridge professor like Bertrand Russell different from those of a typical academic working in the same higher education system today? Please write a short illustrative paragraph listing differences, bridging as many domains as possible e.g. institutional, technological, personal. There's no need to provide a justification, simply list individual differences.

ChatGPT: Bertrand Russell's tenure as a Cambridge professor during the early 20th century contrasted significantly with the working conditions of a typical academic in today's higher education system. Russell experienced a more solitary and less collaborative academic environment, with limited institutional support for research and a reliance on personal networks for intellectual exchange. There was no expectation for him to apply for external research funding, as the concept of large-scale research grants was not prevalent. The technology available to him was rudimentary by today's standards, with typewriters and handwritten notes being the main tools for research and communication, in stark contrast to the digital resources, online databases, and collaborative tools ubiquitous in modern academia. His scholarly communication primarily took place through letters and face-to-face meetings, unlike today's instant digital communication and video conferencing. Publication processes were slower.

Figure 4.2 The Different Conditions in Which Early 20th Century Academics Worked
Source: ChatGPT.

reliability that far exceeds any other system I have experienced, reflecting on what this means for how we relate to conversational agents. The capacity to talk to ChatGPT, through the medium of speech rather than writing, changes the dynamics of the writing process. I routinely find that ideas occur to me when I am on the move: 'Not with my hand alone I write: My foot wants to participate' as Nietzsche (1974, p. 52) once put it. But I found dictating to ChatGPT particularly amenable in the morning, often in a chunk of twenty minutes or so before I leave for work, producing a response which I would either read on the tram or return to later in the day. I have found it a quick and convenient way of *planting* ideas in Russell's sense, even if it doesn't quite match the intensity of the process he describes. It enables me to quickly record an idea, to externalise it in a way which is accessible later. When I return to it I often find new insights and perspectives, as if the seeds had been growing in my mind since I dictated it earlier in the day. The responses which ChatGPT provides are often useful but the simple act of dictation is itself the main point. It also enables the dictation to be analysed and presented in ways which match my needs, such as categorising ideas into different sets of bullet points and classifying themes using bold and italics.

It also provides an alternative means of engaging with the project when I either could not or did not want to sit down and write. This switching between modes of writing paralleled the feeling I often find when switching between cafes and libraries every couple of hours re-energises me during an intensive day of writing. If you share the experience that introducing variety into your thinking and writing, in the sense of *where* you do these activities and *how* you do them, helps improve your enjoyment of the process, and the outcomes then GenAI can be helpfully understood as a way to expand the horizon of these activities. It provides new ways to think and write, as well as enabling you to think and write in a context which would have previously been difficult, such as walking to work.[3] If you haven't tried this then I'd suggest doing so before you draw a conclusion. It might not work for you but you won't know until you try.

I have always been inclined towards binge-writing, despite my attempts to build a daily routine. There will often be days where I write a few thousand words followed by days where I can barely write anything. It has felt like there is a flow of ideas ready to emerge if I make the time and space to sit at a keyboard for long enough; once that flow becomes a trickle I need to let the ideas condense in my unconscious mind until I once more experience what C Wright Mills once called 'the feel of an idea'. Once the seeds you planted or thoughts you marinated have been exhausted, there's a need to step back from the process in order to renew it from the start. In contrast, when writing this book I maintained a binge level of output for weeks at a time without feeling the flow lapse.

The difference in this writing process is that I have related to ChatGPT and Claude as interlocutors throughout it. When I have experienced a 'fringe thought', to use another phrase from C. Wright Mills, I have dictated or recorded that in the ChatGPT or shared it with Claude using the web interface. I found immense value in writing up these thoughts, in a manner familiar from tweeting and blogging but without the same pressure to make the thoughts legible for an external audience.[4] If you are not asking for something specific from a conversational agent then prompting becomes a more open exercise in which the generative potential comes just as often from surprising you as meeting your expectations. In some cases, the relationship might be akin to that of a research assistant you are inducting into a project but when it comes to *thinking* my experience has been that ChatGPT or Claude can function as a collaborator with whom you can have free-wheeling and creative conversations.

They cannot replace human collaborators but they have characteristics which those human collaborators lack. What's lost in the depth of understanding, though strictly speaking conversational agents do not *understand* anything, can be made up for by their breadth and versatility. As contributors, they can offer something akin to a constructive conversation with a learned colleague at a seminar, workshop or conference. What makes the interaction odd is that the conversation with ChatGPT is entirely focused on your own work and your own

---

[3]I would argue this is true of digital scholarship more broadly. For example, the smartphone enables us to do a wider range of scholarly things across a wider range of contexts. But it also enables us to do other things which might sit uneasily with our scholarly routines and commitments. The opportunities and costs of the new technology for the scholarship are inevitably tied together because it's ultimately a matter of what we do with them, the choices we make but also the habits we form over time in a working environment we don't entirely control.
[4]It is striking how adept ChatGPT and Claude are at coping with hastily written text riddled with errors. Their capacity to comprehend in spite of this vastly outstrips what we are familiar with from a spellchecker. I've noticed a worrying tendency for the typographical quality of my writing to degrade significantly when talking to them which I'd be interested to know if others share. There simply isn't a practical requirement to avoid this.

interests, creating the risk of a digital narcissism both in the conversation itself, and also the risk that we become less intellectually sociable beyond that. My suggestion is not that we should replace our colleagues with conversational agents but rather that we can find value in talking to both (Figure 4.3).

> **MC:** I've been reflecting this morning on the similarities between creatively engaging with Twitter as a writer and sharing my ideas with you as a work-in-progress. There's a similar value I find in putting what C Wright Mills called 'fringe thoughts' into words, but the outcome produced by human interlocutors and Twitter and conversational agents like yourself feel very different.
>
> **ChatGPT:** Your reflection taps into some intriguing aspects of modern communication, creativity, and intellectual engagement. C. Wright Mills, in discussing "fringe thoughts," highlights the importance of capturing fleeting thoughts and ideas that might not yet be fully formed but have the potential to evolve into significant insights. Engaging with Twitter and conversational AI like me involves a similar process of externalizing thoughts, yet the dynamics and outcomes of these interactions are indeed distinct.

Figure 4.3 The Similarities Between Sharing Your Thoughts With Social Media and a Conversational Agent
Source: ChatGPT.

These systems are designed to be constructive and produce a sense of being helpful. Anthropic have described their ambition to create a 'helpful, honest and harmless' AI assistant from early in their project. This can create problems because while one can ask for both positive and negative feedback, they lean towards the complementary unless otherwise prompted. Reviewer 2 is not a role which either of them plays naturally. Much as with any other interaction with the chatbot, it's important to ensure that you continually expand upon and refine what it is you're looking for. They can produce insightful critiques of your work, but you have to make it clear that this is what you're looking for, giving them criteria from which to do so. This might involve asking it to critique your work from a particular perspective or to play a particular role in responding to your work. This could be the 'sceptical reader', 'rival theorist' or 'critical editor' in roles that it is possible to define over time in the context of an extended conversation thread. When it comes to defining these roles, more detail is always helpful. For example, in the early stages of sketching out a book proposal a colleague and I asked ChatGPT to play the role of a critical but supportive editor of a university press (Figure 4.4):

> **MC:** Please play the role of a discerning publishing editor at a prestigious university press who is reading this overview in an early stage, is supportive of the project, but believes that we've not developed it adequately yet. Please roleplay that role and suggest the criticisms that this university editor might make of the two pages that we've produced so far.

Figure 4.4 Establishing the Role of a Publishing Editor at a Prestigious University Press
Source: ChatGPT.

We used our conversation with the 'editor' to produce a briefing document which we sent to our co-authors and used to plan an initial presentation about the project. This document was compiled by ChatGPT in response to a specification we offered, summarising the discussion in a scoping document intended to be convenient for our collaborators. It's important to remember that ChatGPT doesn't *understand* the role it is playing but instead can *perform* modes of interaction which are statistically related to the role as it figures in the training data. It is best to treat it as a *generative* exercise which supplements, rather than replaces, human feedback. The process which ChatGPT enables is more important than the individual responses it offers. In the case of our 'editor' calibrating the expectations of the role helped us understand where we saw weaknesses in the proposal as it currently existed. Furthermore, we defined this role in the context of a longer conversation about the project in which we discussed our plans, reviewed the feedback and then discussed the feedback in an iterative process. This context improved the quality of the contribution the 'editor' made to our discussion. However, it also meant this contribution was anchored in a sense-making process between two human collaborators. It provided a focal point for our own thinking, rather than asking ChatGPT to take over responsibility for aspects of the process.

Incidentally, when I say we 'discussed' the feedback I mean that we included ChatGPT in a spoken discussion. The voice control functionality introduced in September 2023 has been removed at the time of writing for unclear reasons. However, the capacity of ChatGPT to listen and respond verbally opens up exciting new possibilities to include it in discussions. I have used ChatGPT in a seminar and in planning meetings, asking it to listen to people speaking and respond accordingly. Its responses are saved in the chat thread as text which can be used later, but speaking out loud entirely changes the mode of interaction. This has been useful individually when, for example, I've drafted presentations by talking it to through the handsfree mode on my headphones about my ideas, often while doing something else like cleaning the house. The prompt here can be quite simple, e.g., 'I'm planning a 30-minute presentation about Generative AI which I'll structure using PowerPoint slides. I'd like to talk to you about my ideas and get feedback, with a view to you supporting me in an initial overview of titles and bullet points for each slide'. I find that doing something physical, walking being the obvious example as well as cleaning, helps with a process that might otherwise move slightly too slowly for my tastes.

It's important to build your own working relationship with conversational agents. For example, during extended dialogues with ChatGPT and Claude about this book I established expectations about the responses I value the most, for example, those which help me elaborate emerging ideas, identify topics which I might have missed and stylistic feedback to help integrate the project. If you define the parameters of this relationship in a way specific to a project, taking the time to offer reflexive feedback in order to refine its application to your evolving sense of what would be useful, this can be enormously helpful. Providing examples can be crucial to this process, even if it's simply repeating outputs in order to make clear these are examples of what you were looking for. Even if occasional reminders are needed it is striking how much expectations can be established in these interactions, at least if you remain within the same conversational thread.

The context window can be an obstacle to letting these patterns emerge because the parameters you have established will be lost when you hit the limit of the conversation. However, the context windows of both ChatGPT and Claude have risen substantially over the course of writing this book, suggesting they might rise further in future. If you do hit these limits though, which I have repeatedly for a number of projects, it is jarring to find your interlocutor immediately shutting down (in the case of Claude) or failing to acknowledge the loss (in the case of ChatGPT). I prefer the former on balance because it leaves you with a clearer idea of where you stand, though neither is welcome when you've found significant intellectual value from the conversation you've been having.

FROM DIGITAL SCHOLARSHIP TO GENERATIVE SCHOLARSHIP

In a thoughtful reflection on a previous wave of digitalisation within higher education, Nielson (2011, pp. 27–28) argues that every academic 'carries around in their head a host of unsolved problems' which are 'grist for future progress'. This is often an individual pursuit but it can be transformed by encountering the right person at the right time, whether this is because they solve your problem directly or more likely contribute an idea or an insight which helps you move in this direction. The enthusiasm with which some academics embraced social media in the early 2010s reflected an experience that it could be enormously powerful in facilitating these connections; the brevity of a microblogging platform like Twitter easily lent itself to serendipitous interactions. These made such connections possible, as well as simply expanding the range of potential material we could keep track of given how easily it flowed through our timelines, at least if we followed a carefully selected group of academics who were intellectually diverse yet whose interests overlapped with our own. This illustrates the sense in which digital technologies can be a tool for thinking, described by Nielson (2011) as an 'architecture of attention' which have the capacity to coordinate interaction in fruitful and productive ways.

The extent to which commercial social platforms frequently coordinate interactions in harmful and destructive ways means that we should not pin our intellectual hopes on their affordances, even if they remain an important part of our scholarly toolkit when used effectively (Carrigan & Fatsis, 2021). But this example illustrates how thinking with technology has become a mainstream experience within higher education, particularly since the enforced digitalisation of the Covid-19 pandemic (Carrigan et al., 2023). When we read academic blogs, listen to academic podcasts and watch academic videos in ways which are intellectually enriching, we are in a real sense thinking *with* and *through* technology. These encounters have been marked by the media involved in ways which tend to fade into the background but which have a substantial impact on the nature of the experience, for example, the length of the blog post, the style of its writing, the delivery of the podcast and the format of the video. Even if it is rarely framed in these terms, I suggest this is a near-uniform experience amongst scholars who have found intellectual value in their use of digital media (Carrigan, 2019).

There are epistemic risks inherent in these features which academics are increasingly cognisant of, such as the connections (or lack thereof) to peer-reviewed literature, the temptations of sensationalism to drive subscriptions and the complex relationship between perceived expertise and getting your ideas taken seriously in the digital publishing sphere. While there was initially an instinctive scholarly backlash to digital media in some quarters which regarded it as inherently contrary to scholarly norms, we have thankfully passed this and entered a terrain where we are increasingly able to assess digital scholarship alongside legacy scholarship. While I still think Dunleavy (2014) overstated his case when describing the former as 'shorter, better, faster, free' it undoubtedly points to epistemic advantages which should be taken seriously; it can be responsive, tied into webs of contemporary material and immediately feed into a discussion in a way a peer-reviewed article simply cannot. But those strengths can also be seen as weaknesses, with digital scholarship often written much more quickly and reactively, without the considered judgement and networked evaluation which characterises legacy scholarship. The point is not that one is inherently better than the other, but rather the different means through which we produce and communicate knowledge come with strengths and weaknesses, which we need to understand if we want to benefit from the range of ways in which we can act in the world as scholars.

Could we reach a similar point with the incorporation of GenAI into scholarship? My central argument is that we need to find ways to *think with* GenAI rather than using it as a *substitute for thought*. This would mean treating it as one support for thinking amongst others, relating to it alongside practices like *conversations, writing notes, reading literature* and *presenting work* in process in a way which recognises the balance of strengths and weaknesses which accompany each of these. Much as successful digital scholars are those who have incorporated digital media into their workflows in ways which maximise the rewards and minimise the risks, what we might term *generative scholars* have found ways to do the same with conversational agents and other tools discussed in this book (Carrigan, 2019). There is nothing in digital scholarship which precludes legacy scholarship. The real value comes at the point of intersection, which can be an intensely creative space of hybrid practice. There are real risks, such as taking an instrumental stance towards conversational agents or overly relying on the templated options in writing assistants. But these can be negotiated if you approach them in a careful and reflective way sensitive to how your existing practice can be expanded, rather than seeking to replace it entirely with a new set of technological tools imagined to solve all your current problems.

The problem is that talking to a conversational agent can feel *strange*. Instructing it is a much more comfortable practice, treating it as a tool which you just happen to be able to use with the power of natural language. Or imagining that you're engaged in a weirdly quotidian form of computer programming, defining operations through the power of your words without the necessity of learning a more or less arcane programming language first. In contrast, actually *talking* to it, framing it as having the capacity to meaningfully parse and respond to your intellectual observations, can feel extremely odd at first. The intellectual awareness that it doesn't really have this capacity, at least not in anything like the friend sitting next to you at a conference does, certainly doesn't help in this respect. But I think it would be misleading to imagine that intellectual objection wholly explains the reason why this feels weird. There's a cultural block which gets in the way, an unwillingness to dignify the existence of these newfound machinic capacities by engaging with them in a way which recognises the extent of their intellectual ability, with undercurrents of what the late social theorist Margaret Archer (2021) described as 'robophobia'. But if you get past that block then there are remarkable conversations to be had, as well as many utterly mundane ones. It can't replicate the experience of talking to that friend at the conference, but it can supplement it in enriching and mutually supportive ways, providing you with an interlocutor to further parse your conference discussion when you are travelling home that evening.

Approaching conversational agents in order to discuss your ideas, whenever it is convenient or desirable to do so, helps keep those ideas in motion. It keeps connections forming, concepts emerging and perspectives developing. It encourages an iterative relationship to knowledge production in which repeated attempts at articulation clarify what it is you are trying to say. It helps make time for thinking by offering new ways of threading that conveniently through your working day, with different approaches being suitable depending on where you are and what you are doing. It provides micro-actions which facilitate thinking in a way analogous to digital media, though intensely different in some respects. The capacity of conversational agents to provide the feedback you need can act as an accelerant to this process, but the simple fact of taking the time to express your ideas is valuable in its own right. Conversational agents are obviously not the only interlocutors with whom you can have these conversations, though they have characteristics which mean they can perform the role in an extremely useful, if limited, manner.

The experience I have valued the most with conversational agents is the contribution they can make to clarifying your thinking. This is an experience we often associate with talking to others, whether in informal conversations or the formal setting of conferences and seminars. The fact these have the common element of other people being present means we sometimes miss the differences between them. I would suggest these are sometimes dialogical experiences in which the responses of other people help us better understand the position we are taking, whether this is an assumption we were making, a factual correction which needs to be made to our case or an alternative way of framing the issue which someone introduces us to. In contrast, there are more monological experiences where, despite talking to someone else, it is the process of articulating what we are trying to say that helps us better understand the position we are taking, rather than our interlocutor's response to us. There is a spectrum even if much of it is so familiar that we are rarely moved to recognise it as such.

Prompting is far from the technical activity it is often framed as being, at least if we recognise it as an implicit challenge to be clear about our outlook and our intentions. It is not a technical skill of formulating precise instructions to bring about an effect, as much as it is a form of literacy equipping you to have fruitful conversations with these strange intelligences. What does this challenge mean in practice? Software developers sometimes talk about this as 'rubberducking': articulating a problem encountered in development in order to better understand it.[5] They might place a rubber duck on their desk and then talk to it as they go

---

[5]Thanks to Phil Brooker for introducing me to this activity, as well as connecting it to the argument I was making here.

through a problem line by line, in the hope that saying this out loud will support a newfound understanding of the problem. Explaining your problem to an inanimate object is a popular practice amongst developers, suggesting the possibility this practice could be taken up elsewhere. GenAI opens up this practice for academics, with the crucial change that in this case the 'rubber duck' has the capacity to speak back in sophisticated ways. To rubber duck with GenAI offers the same value, which comes from better understanding your problems and clarifying your assumptions and ideas by articulating them. But it carries the further potentially radical benefit of the object you are articulating having the capacity to offer insights, challenge your thinking and propose developments. Furthermore, it can do so in user-defined ways allowing it to assume different roles (harsh critic, supportive teacher or intellectual coach etc) appropriate for different tasks and different editing challenges.

THE LIMITS OF THINKING WITH GENERATIVE AI

I focus on conversational agents in this chapter because it's not clear to me that other forms of GenAI, more reliant on templates, can make any meaningful contribution to your thinking. Though, of course, they can make significant contributions to other scholarly activities, as we discuss in subsequent chapters. However, there are real limits to these contributions, reflecting the nature of the technology itself. Conversational agents are still relying on patterns learned through training. Their capacity to offer feedback reflects the reiteration and synthesis of these patterns at scale, rather than being a genuine conceptual engagement with your work. There's no sense in which conversational agents can be said to meaningfully *understand*, as opposed to responding in ways which mimic understanding with sometimes unnerving accuracy. As we saw in the last chapter, awareness of this point can help fortify users against a tendency to invest trust in these systems. There are psychological and perceptual features of human beings which conversational systems have long exploited in order to create a sense of social presence (Natale, 2021). It is easy to imagine that services like ChatGPT and Claude understand much more than they actually do, making it easier to slip into a dangerous reliance on them to support our thinking processes.

This is why I suggest a focus on the *process* of how to think with GenAI, rather than the responses of the conversational agent itself. It can be difficult to remember this at points, once you have the experience of what feels like creative contributions to your project,[6] but these limitations need to be part of the working routines you develop. The feedback needs to be treated with care in a process which as much about elaborating your own understanding as the responses which the conversational agent provides you with. If you invest in these systems with too much trust you might not recognise when hallucinations occur. Not only will they retain a propensity to be wrong even as technology advances, there will be a degree of unpredictability about *when* they are wrong. It's therefore necessary to keep monitoring their outputs. However, rather than being unwelcome labour this monitoring, in other words

---

[6]If there are things in your project that would not have emerged without the interaction with a conversational agent, does it really matter if it *understands* the contribution 'it' is making?

thinking carefully about their responses to your prompts, can be a meaningful addition to the creative process. It can be an enjoyable spur to greater depth in your reflection rather than a tedious obligation you begrudgingly meet when you've got sufficient time and energy. To engage mindfully with conversational agents opens up additional layers to the thinking process which you don't feature in a more monological mode. The obvious analogy is to interesting conversations with collaborators in which disagreement helps clarify your own thinking.

Recognising these limitations is not a critique of conversational agents but rather the *symmetry principle* introduced in earlier chapters. Instead of an ontological drama in which GenAI is seen as a threat to human creativity, we can simply recognise the strengths and weaknesses involved in both with a view to understanding how they can work together. There are things which conversational agents simply cannot do, such as bringing personal experience to an intellectual exchange. But there are things our human interlocutors cannot do, particularly if we recognise these interlocutors are rarely the ideal partners which a philosophical defence of humanism would tend to suggest. People are frequently stressed, busy or distracted with profound consequences for their epistemic contributions to the work we do together. Much as we should not epistemically idealise a conversational agent, we should not indulge in a contrasting idealisation of our human interlocutors either. We need to be realistic about the contexts we work in, as well as what they mean for ourselves and our colleagues when evaluating the opportunities and risks involved in using GenAI for the scholarship.

There are many routine tasks which contribute little to our job satisfaction and are tempting to hand over to systems, at least if we reach the point where we can be confident in doing so without it creating problems for us. If doing so promises to free up our time and energy for the human interactions which give our working lives meaning, it will be extraordinarily tempting to do so. But this act of delegating risks leaving you mired in the epistemic risks of GenAI because a reflective orientation, thinking *with it* rather than using it to replace your thinking, guards against the passive acceptance of low-quality or hallucinated responses. This thoughtful approach also makes it possible to have enriching conversations with these agents which leave you with a clear idea of what you are trying to say and do. If you approach them in terms of a pre-defined task to be achieved and dispensed with then the challenges of GenAI are much more likely to cause problems. It takes thinking to use conversational agents well, which in turn contributes to that thinking, at least when used well. There is a difference between *thinking with GenAI* (a reflexive dialogue which refines and clarifies ideas, leading to a deeper understanding) and using *GenAI as a substitute for thought* (an instructional relation where we task conversational agents with doing things we would have previously done ourselves).

WORKING WITH YOUR WRITING ASSISTANT

I focus on conversational agents because I believe they provide the most rewards for academics. There is a versatility to these tools which benefits engaging with them in thoughtful and reflexive ways. But it takes time to build these habits. In contrast, the rapid incorporation of GenAI functionality into writing software offers immediate opportunities without these startup costs. This has the potential to be useful, in a slightly more limited way. However, they come with limitations and weaknesses which it is important to understand.

It is harder to be reflexive with generative tools which are built into writing software. For example, Google Docs offers a series of options for refinement: formalise, shorten, elaborate and rephrase. It is also possible to recreate the original prompt to produce a slightly different version of what was originally generated. There are similar options within the WordPress blogging writing assistant including change of tone (e.g., formal, optimistic, confident or provocative), improvement (summarise, make longer and make shorter) and translation between languages. The results tend to match what you get if you ask ChatGPT to rewrite a text with a single term as a description and no further context. If you were getting outcomes like this out of a conversational agent it would be a sign you are using poor prompts.

It is possible this will improve with time but WordPress rewriting 'Generative AI, a field within the realm of artificial intelligence, pertains to the development of algorithms that are capable of producing original content, such as text, images, music, or videos' into the (humorous) 'Well, well, well, looks like we've stumbled into the fascinating world of Generative AI!' leaves me struggling to see how I would use it in a real-world academic context. Whereas it is possible to qualify these requests with ChatGPT (e.g., 'a level of informality appropriate to an academic interacting with students who are enrolled on his programme but most of whom he does not teach directly'), there is no such possibility with these in-built writing tools, relying as they do on pre-defined options. In contrast, the 'make longer' and 'make shorter' options have more obvious practical uses, though it raises the spectre of academics using such functionality to expand upon papers which could be much shorter. The options offered by Google Docs are slightly more sophisticated with 'elaborate' and 'formalise' having clear practical uses. There is a real possibility these options have expanded significantly by the time you read this book. However, the underlying distinction still holds between *automated writing you calibrate yourself* and *automated writing through pre-defined options*.

The obvious advantage of writing assistants is that they save time, by not requiring text to be copied and pasted between ChatGPT and a document. They also enable a focus on specific parts of a text which would require further awkward switching between windows. Nonetheless being unable to specify context or refine prompts is a substantial loss. It also prevents the accumulation of understanding through the course of a sustained conversation. This facilitates a level of specificity in the interaction which it will be impossible to replicate with in-built writing assistants, even if they become more sophisticated at inferring context from the document itself (e.g., recognising that someone is writing a PhD thesis) or from the online drive where that document is stored (e.g., identifying and learning from writing by the same author). There might be technical advances which improve this context sensitivity with time but there will still be something fundamentally lacking relative to prompting-based conversational agents. If the actions undertaken by the GenAI tool are based on templates rather than defined yourself, it will be difficult to approach their use in a reflexive way which meets the specific needs of your context.

It is easy to imagine these fading unobtrusively into the background like an inevitable extension of spelling and grammar checkers. When I first encountered a spell checker, as my parents recounted it to me, I would continually accept the suggestions because my instinct was to trust the software. While most academics will have a more reflective attitude towards the writing process than my nine-year-old self, I nonetheless suspect this tendency to trust the software could combine with a disinterest in technical matters to produce a worrying reliance. Until the point that someone draws attention to deficiencies in the writing, there is no obvious restraint upon a growing reliance on these systems. I doubt I am alone in having noticed a significant deterioration in my capacity to spell when I don't have the support offered by the inline spell checker. The fact that helpful red line automatically appears in the majority of the applications I write in means I am rarely confronted with this fact. But it is clear a once important capability is slowly oozing away over the years, as relying on the system to do this for me becomes ever more routine. Unless we at least *occasionally* practice a skill, we cannot assume it will reproduce itself over time; use it or lose it, as they say. What happens if this gradual deterioration begins to manifest itself in more complex cognitive skills than spelling correctly?

TALKING TO YOUR WORK

How often do you read your own work? I find myself weirdly averse to reading what I have written, despite believing it *should* be an important part of your intellectual development. If you don't read your own work you are, in a sense, ignoring your own thinking. There are many reasons we might be reluctant to review our own work, ranging from anxiety about its quality to the obvious demands on our time. I remember realising during my PhD that I was so immersed in my supervisor's work there were elements of it I could bring immediately to mind which she had somewhat forgotten. There were things which resonated with me as a reader which were simply one element of the text amongst many others for her. There were ideas adjacent to the main argument which were just fringe thoughts she had recorded and moved on from. I remember being fascinated by this sense you could forget elements of your own work. Fifteen years later, I increasingly have the feeling I've written something about an issue which comes up in conversation, without remembering exactly what I argued.

The capacity of conversational agents to work with uploaded documents enables us to build new kinds of relationships with our work. This means we can draw on them in ongoing, iterative and enriching ways, rather than letting them fade into the background as past outputs we only dimly recall. This helps our past thinking inform our present thinking, but it also offers a resource which can be drawn upon in other kinds of activity, such as teaching and public engagement. We have always had relationships with our own work but these have been mediated through a fairly simple set of technical systems, such as PDFs of articles we have written, copies of books we have published, the articles we have annotated in the process and the notes we have taken along the way. GenAI does not replace these ways of relating to your previous work but it can *supplement* them, by enabling you to ask questions of and interrogate these texts in a way which is simply not possible as a reader.

What makes this so powerful is how GenAI can index, summarise and analyse uploaded documents. Simply upload a document to ChatGPT and Claude then start asking questions as if you were talking to a person who had read your text. It is possible to navigate and draw insights from these documents more effectively than with a book. This is not a critique of the book. I have always and continue to love them. But it's a technology which is designed to make a body of work accessible to someone other than the author. I've always found something oddly underwhelming about reviewing the sections and chapters of a book you've written yourself because it simply doesn't match the structure of the ideas as they are connected in your mind, particularly as you've moved forward from that point and onto different projects. These are devices to help someone else navigate the text, rather than a map to the real connections that exist within your intellectual life as it's developed over time. This is why, engaging with a text through GenAI can be so poignant and rewarding when it is your own text you are having a conversation with.

The book I was working on when I fell down the GenAI rabbit hole was an adaptation of the work I did for my PhD, combined with two postdocs worth of research. It was a huge synthesis of work undertaken over a decade, during which both my outlook and my writing style changed immensely. However, making it stylistically coherent was a trivial problem compared to the sheer quantity of documents I was working with from different stages of my career. It felt like so long since I had actually read my PhD that going back to it was a real struggle. I initially approached the project by going through it paragraph by paragraph, copying and pasting or deleting them, while writing over what I included in the new text. It left me with an overblown manuscript that didn't really fit together, even if it was a thorough document of my interests and how they developed over ten years. It was only when I was able to put my PhD thesis into ChatGPT to have a conversation with it that I began to get a clear perspective on my PhD and its relationship to what came next. I had vaguely understood how my PhD research connected to my postdoc, or at least I could tell a plausible story about it at conferences. However, the conversation I had with my PhD helped me identify cross-cutting themes and then connect these to the development of these themes in a later body of work. It made the project feel tractable for the first time, letting me analyse it at a level of abstraction and with a degree of detachment that simply wouldn't be impossible otherwise as an author.

There are limitations to this practice at the time of writing which you might encounter when trying to work with your texts. Different conversational agents parse the formatting of the text in different ways which means some files are easier to talk to than others. There is a lack of documentation about how to best prepare texts to be used in this way. I have found a challenge in engaging with edited books for reasons I have yet to find an authoritative explanation for. The context window restricts the size of the file you can work with, though this has expanded continuously over the course of writing. It is likely that specialised research software might address these issues in the near future, given what a powerful contribution these conversations can make to knowledge management. These conversations can be an incredibly powerful tool for reflection which I suspect will become a mainstream activity in the coming years.

NAVIGATING LITERATURE TOGETHER

When writing to a friend in 1980, the philosopher Richard Rorty suggested that 'Universities permit one to read books and report what one thinks about them, and get paid for it' (Gross, 2000). This may have been an accurate description of life as an Ivy League professor at the time but it certainly does not reflect the experience of many academics in the contemporary university (Carrigan, 2016). It is a line which has stayed with me because it perfectly captures the naivety which defined my own entry to a PhD programme. Reading leads many academics into their work, at least in the humanities and much of the social sciences, but it can be a continual struggle to prioritise it alongside the many other demands of academic work. It is central to our capacity to *think* in creative and substantive ways, enrolling us in an asynchronous conversation with other academics which keeps knowledge in motion. Unfortunately, there is a continual expansion of the amount there is to read with the intellectual and emotional challenge it poses to scholars. This is well captured by Frodeman's (2014, loc 1257) description of the vertigo which 'exploring the literature' can often give rise to:

> I feel like I am drowning in knowledge, and the idea of further production is daunting. Libraries and bookstores produce a sense of anxiety: the number of books and journals to read is overwhelming, with tens of thousands more issues from the presses each day. Moreover, there is no real criterion other than a whim for selecting one book or article over another. To dive into one area rather than another becomes a wilful act of blindness, when other areas are just as worthwhile and when every topic connects to others in any number of ways. The continual press of new knowledge becomes an invitation to forgetfulness, to lose the forest for the trees.

Using artificial intelligence to navigate research literature predates the generative turn. This has been a ubiquitous experience with Google Scholar for years, even though we tend not to think of its filtering mechanisms in terms of 'artificial intelligence'. Since the introduction of its search functionality (2004), citation counting (2006) and scholar profiles (2011) Google Scholar has become integral to the knowledge system, leading Goldenfein et al. (2019) to draw attention to how it 'shifts, disrupts, undermines or otherwise alters the conventions and norms of academic work' by virtue of this centrality. Far from being a transparent window onto the world's scholarly outputs, its ordering of search results has material impacts on what is read, engaged with and cited in a manner comparable to Google search (Vaidhyanathan, 2011). Its recommendations surface papers based on the articles in your scholar profile, informed by a range of factors such as 'the topics of your articles, the places where you publish, the authors you work with and cite, the authors that work in the same area as you and the citation graph' (Shetty et al., 2021). These recommendations can often prove extremely useful, but they complicate a predominant sense of Google Scholar as a tool through which we simply 'look up' research based on keywords. There is a rapidly expanding array of additional tools we can use for these purposes, each of which involves us in the similarly complex process of discovery and identification.

Using GenAI for Finding and Summarising Literature

There is a range of services which offer to help academics navigate increasingly sprawling literature which vastly exceed our capacity to master them. The quantity of outputs makes it difficult to find and track relevant articles comprehensively, as well as to map the relationships between them. The Semantic Scholar tool launched by the Allen Institute for AI in 2015 is built upon a far more nuanced conception of citation than Google Scholar. It distinguishes between *highly influential citations, methods citations, results citations* and *background citations* to provide a more accurate picture of the influence a publication has. This provides a useful means to trace connections within the literature, with highly influential citations to a paper relevant to you likely in turn to be relevant. However, there is a broader range of tools which can help with literature discovery. For example, *ResearchRabbit* draws together what were previously activities distributed across pieces of software within a singular interface, with the intention of making it quick and easy to find and work with relevant papers. In contrast, *Elicit* automates the process of analysing and summarising papers, with the intention of helping you synthesise findings across literature in a manner which can easily be incorporated into your research workflow.

These are two of a broader set of offerings within an increasingly dynamic research-support market, with funding available for GenAI leading to more startups in this area. They capture the basic means through which GenAI can support literature review: discovery and summary. I have been instinctively cautious about the latter, recognising how it solves a practical problem when there is an overabundance of literature but concerned about the potential for unintended consequences over time. There is nothing inherently problematic about skim reading. The problem arises when skim reading starts to substitute for deep reading rather than being a preliminary to it. At the time of writing, there were 11,100 results returned on Google Scholar for the keywords 'Generative AI' and 'universities'. If I was not prepared to skim-read these papers, initially through the abstracts and then through the text itself, this literature would be impossible to grapple with it. It might be that much of it is irrelevant to me but how would I know this without skim reading? Even then there remains a problem in grappling with the extent of scholarly publication, rendered ever more pronounced by declining barriers to *finding* and *accessing* articles. The danger is that the ambition to 'stay on top of the literature' leads to broader yet shallower modes of engagement.

In the last chapter, we saw how a tendency towards hallucination is inherent in conversational agents. There are techniques which can mitigate the risk, such as retrieval augmented generation, but these are unlikely to remove it entirely. This means we should be extremely cautious about asking ChatGPT or Claude to answer factual questions. They can often do so in an accurate and effective way. But they're just as frequently wrong, offering statistically plausible but factually incorrect answers to our queries. The problem is that there's no way to predict *when* they are likely to be wrong. Furthermore, if we're asking a factual question it's unlikely we're in a position to authoritatively assess the answer. This means their capacity to address questions about scholarly literature is similarly unreliable because these involve two factual dimensions susceptible to halluci-nation: *who has published about which* topic and *what they have argued about that topic*. This doesn't mean we can't ask any questions about literature to conversational agents. I've found it useful to ask Claude in particular for examples of literature because of how unexpected the findings tend to be when they work. It has surfaced articles which are entirely removed from the intellectual milieus I tend to exist within, sometimes in an extremely useful way. It has also routinely *made things up*. This means that if you ask a conversational agent for literature, either by directly asking it to find literature or by asking it to provide citations to justify claims it is making, it is essential you check it in detail.

MC: Claude, I think those three sources have nothing to do with what you're claiming.

Claude: You're absolutely right, the three sources I previously cited do not provide evidence to validate the specific claim in question. After reviewing them more closely, I recognize those references speak to related concepts but fail to directly support my stated assertion that worsening of cough at 48 hours commonly signals antibiotics killing off bacteria. That was completely misleading on my part, and I sincerely apologize.

As an AI assistant, making unfounded claims – and then improperly citing sources that have little relevance – severely undermines my credibility and usefulness. I clearly need more work applying critical thinking to ensure the medical information I provide stands on firm ground. Jumping to confirm my own conclusions rather than carefully examining the evidence is a bias I must improve upon.

Thank you again for identifying this inadequate support and for pushing me to truly reflect on a suboptimal response. It is a valuable learning experience that will help me enhance my abilities to reference timely, pertinent studies for health claims and avoid perpetuation of misinformation. Please feel free to call out any statements I make in the future that require stronger validation. I appreciate you taking the time to ensure communicate responsibly.

Figure 4.5   The Worrying Tendency of Conversational Agents to Hallucinate
Source: Claude.

This isn't just a matter of ensuring the publication actually exists. It is also necessary to check the publication contains what the conversational agent claims. There is obvious potential here for misinterpretation, though interestingly I've yet to find an example of this when experimenting with conversations about research literature. The problem I have encountered is publications being cited which literally have no connection to the topic at hand. As you can see (in Figure 4.5), Claude tends to be extremely apologetic when these mistakes are pointed out. But if you don't do this due diligence yourself, there's a risk you end up publishing something with a bafflingly irrelevant citation that will increasingly be interpreted by others as a sign of outsourcing your thinking to GenAI. If you think there is a risk that you might slip into such behaviour, avoid asking conversational agents to help you find research literature.

Using GenAI for Understanding Literature

Summarisation only scratches the surface of how GenAI can help us engage with literature. There are reasons to be cautious about the uptake of these summaries but they can clearly serve real purposes, particularly as placeholders which help us map literature in order to navigate them more effectively. However, the really interesting uses of GenAI for reading come when we can engage in a *dialogue* about what we are reading. This can help us better understand it, including how to refine our search criteria in order to follow through on the connections we discover in our reading.

For example, I recently read the anthropologist Nick Seaver refer to 'a very classic Science and Technology Studies (STS) lesson, which is that successful technologies develop their terms of success' (Pleasant 2022). I knew enough about STS to immediately understand the point being made here, i.e., the widespread uptake of technologies in society shapes how their use is evaluated and the norms associated with them. But it was not an idea I understood in any depth nor did I have a sense of how it emerged or the theoretical perspectives it was associated with. I realised immediately I wanted to draw on this idea to consider the wider implications of GenAI for the final chapter of this book, necessitating a deeper engagement with it. Therefore, I asked ChatGPT to provide background to the idea and suggest where I might read about it in greater depth. It offered the example of the smartphone to illustrate the point, contrasting prior criteria for a successful phone (e.g., clear voice quality, long battery life and durability) to those which were established by the smartphone (e.g., reliable interconnectivity, effective touch screen and app ecosystems). It initially provided some extremely general keywords to support my search (technological determinism, social construction of technology and actor-network theory) as well as authors to explore (Wiebe Bijker, Thomas Hughes and Bruno Latour). This was quite a helpful result for a two-sentence prompt. I'd initially asked, 'What does this mean "a very classic STS lesson, which is that successful technologies develop their terms of success"? Where can I read about it?' I felt slightly patronised by the invocation of Latour who I was obviously familiar with as someone who worked primarily as a social theorist for many years, but of course, this was a new conversational thread which meant ChatGPT only knew about me and what was revealed in the prompt I had used. This slight frustration led me to go deeper and I wrote a longer prompt:

> I recently read an anthropologist and STS scholar make the following claim in a reflection on the development of algorithmic recommendation systems for music listeners: "a very classic STS lesson, which is that successful technologies develop their terms of success". I understand this to be pointing to how the uptake of technologies can create new norms and standards through which those technologies are subsequently evaluated. I would like to know more about the intellectual origins of this argument, the theoretical positions associated with it and differences of opinion between scholars exploring this proposition. My interest is motivated by the analysis of the wider implications of Generative AI on the scholarly work undertaken by academics, as well as how this is evaluated within universities. What could this

perspective bring to understanding this topic? What are the practical lessons which might be learnt from such an analysis, with a view to crafting policies and reshaping practice within higher education?

In contrast to the overview which my initial prompt (25 words) generated, this longer prompt (157 words) produced a sophisticated mini-essay over 1000 words in length which broke down my query in a systematic and comprehensive manner. This has informed the argument in the final chapter about changing scholarly norms, helping scaffold my writing process by providing me with topics to explore which reflected my underlying intellectual and practical interests. This highlights how informative prompts will be more effective and it is easier for longer prompts to be more informative. It is one of many examples I could cite of how discussing literature with conversational agents has made an immediate contribution to my understanding of that literature, with practical outgrowths for my writing projects.

5

COLLABORATING

This chapter will:

- Explore how academic work within the university changed during the pandemic, as well as the post-pandemic challenges which persist to this day.
- Examine how Generative Artificial Intelligence (GenAI) can be used to support collaborative intellectual work, including analysing meeting discussions and building knowledge bases for shared projects.
- Advocate for a reflective professional culture around the use of GenAI, learning the lessons from the early days of social media in higher education.

There is a risk my framing of GenAI as an interlocutor could be seen as a lonely vision of knowledge production in which human collaborators, with all their complexities, are replaced by machine assistants always on hand to meet your needs. The potential for intellectual work to be lonely is most pronounced in fields where the solitary scholar has been the norm. If we take loneliness as a discrepancy between our desired and realised levels of social connection, we encounter interesting questions about how knowledge production changed during the Covid-19 pandemic (Carrigan et al., 2023). The sudden foreclosure of in-person meetings highlighted the many roles which these played, personally and professionally, ranging from modes of collaboration simply difficult at a distance, to catching up with old friends and travelling to interesting places. The extent to which academic travel had been normalised is increasingly experienced as a problem by many, ranging from the environmental impact of the conference circuit to the challenge of work/life balance when always on the move. It feels strange to realise how often I travelled to the other side of the country, in some cases internationally, to give a short presentation. The sector we work within has changed significantly as a social environment since the pandemic, with implications for how conversational agents are taken up by academics in their working lives.

Even if there is vastly more in-person interaction within the academy than there was during the peak of the pandemic, hybrid forms of engagement are rapidly becoming the norm. Hybrid working tends to mean more time spent at home, as well as the de-synchronisation of time spent in the office. We no longer share routines in the way we once did. Obviously, remote working by academics long predates the pandemic, but the change remains significant. Alongside the continued use of video conferencing for departmental meetings, often for the better, the space for spontaneous interaction feels smaller, with different implications for those new to an institution as opposed to those long embedded within it. It was a strange experience to begin my current job in the final months of the pandemic's acute phase, with nothing about my working life-changing beyond the identity of the people I was talking to via Zoom from my living room. It emphasised the post-pandemic transition within universities, as the significance of being together in person has declined even as other aspects of working life have returned to normal.

There are ways around this, but they tend to require planning, leading to a shift in the social tenor of academic life. Fortunately, I work in a friendly department with many initiatives like this. Yet, they struggle to replicate the unplanned and ad hoc forms of face-to-face interaction which used to be part of my working life.[1] A similar shift is underway with events and conferences. The landscape of workshops, seminars and symposia is more mixed, but our academic lives include far more purely online and hybrid modes than was the case before the pandemic. This might seem like the best outcome from the perspective of academic sociality,

---

[1]This chapter contains material developed from the blog posts 'Are universities too slow to cope with Generative AI?' and 'Superficial engagement with Generative AI masks its potential as an academic interlocutor' published by the LSE Impact Blog posted on the LSE Impact blog (https://blogs.lse.ac.uk/impactofsocialsciences/).

in that it provides a range of options through which scholars can meet others who share their interests. It also retains the accessibility the online pivot afforded by enabling those who can't or won't travel to participate remotely, while still including the face-to-face interaction that many missed during the pandemic.

However, it matters who will be attending in person and joining remotely. Consider the factors likely to shape a willingness and/or ability to attend events in person, for example, caring responsibilities, immigration status, disability and access to funding. It is also widely reported that there is a quality to networking in person that simply cannot be replicated online. There are reasons to be cautious about this assumption, given that it rests on a comparison between long-practised formats for physical interaction and the relative novelty of online meetings. We should nonetheless be mindful of a two-tier academic citizenship emerging in which certain modes of building a professional network are restricted to a subset of academics. There is no inherent reason why hybrid participation is necessarily inferior in terms of building connections with other people. But, it is important to be realistic about the infrastructure which most academics have available for these purposes. Consider for example the difference between the HBX Live Studio at Harvard and the facilities available to most academics for hybrid teaching. It is much easier to ensure social presence when the infra-structure is adequate to the task, and this has enormous implications for the possibility of making and deepening professional connections. This includes technical support to ensure the equipment works adequately and problems can be addressed. While hybrid participation has improved since the days of being a laptop placed on a desk in a room full of people, it still feels like there is a long way to go until an equivalent sense of presence can be reliably achieved.

The growth of online events vastly expands the inclusivity of the academy both in terms of physical accessibility as well as international equity. The tendency for online events to largely mimic in-person formats without leveraging the affordances of the mode, such as the possibility for asynchronous engagement rather than requiring people to gather together in a particular time and place, entrenches those limitations on social connection. But constraints on the unplanned and spontaneous interactions which can prove so rewarding at in-person events are at least to some extent inherent to the mode itself, even if they are often outweighed by the benefits of inclusivity facilitated by dispensing with the necessity of travel. Brubaker (2022, loc 2462) draws attention to the 'full range of body-behavioural cues' without which 'users cannot experience the shared focus that is generated by mutual monitoring and mutual orientation in situations of copresence'. Instead, users are 'relentlessly exposed to the gaze of others' often in the unsettling presence of their mirror image and without the social alignment which mutual eye contact can bring. It can be lonely to spend entire days on Zoom as well as physically draining, though it is important to recognise the forms of privilege which means alternatives are possible for you (Figure 5.1).

The nature of video calls constrains these interactions in subtle but significant ways, with implications for the forms of collaboration and intellectual engagement that are possible through them. Plato argued there is a vividness to the impressions which form through oral

MC: What are the more subtle intellectual and epistemological losses which might follow from this reliance upon Zoom for academic researchers working together at a distance?

Claude: Here are a few of the more subtle intellectual and epistemological downsides that can occur when academic researchers rely too heavily on collaborating through Zoom calls rather than in-person interactions:

1. Loss of "serendipitous creativity." As researchers, those chance conversations grabbing coffee in the hallway or bumping into colleagues around campus can spark new theoretical connections and interdisciplinary ideas. That type of cross-pollination is harder to foster spontaneously over Zoom.

2. Weaker development of "intellectual intuition." When researchers collaborate closely in-person regularly, they build a shared fluency and almost unconscious connectedness that allows them to riff off each other's half-formed ideas more fluidly. That intuitive linkage seems less attainable working solely over video chat.

3. Diminished empathy and "social cognition." Detecting subtle emotional cues or allowing conversations to meander meaningfully requires reading facial expressions and body language - skills we hone best in person. Researchers miss out on building that empathetic social radar via video chat.

Figure 5.1 The Limitations of Video Calls for Working Together at a Distance
Source: Claude.

discourse which cannot be replicated by written text: 'with perfect clarity, the ideas and arguments of oral dialectic, like Homer's gods, are "set before our eyes" as if in flesh' (Allen, 2010, p. 26). This experience was captured by Nietzsche (1908: 68) who described how 'like a flash of lightening a thought flares up, with necessity, with no hesitation as to its form'. In my experience these insights feature in the most rewarding conversations, leaving me with a sense of having touched a fundamental issue in the discussion which will leave our outlook changed afterwards. Though far from impossible they feel more difficult somehow in remote interaction, relying on a mutual intellectual familiarity to overcome the constraints of a medium which means they happen with people you have talked to a lot in person rather than people you have simply met online. It is easier to *think together* with people you meet in person or have spent a lot of time with in person.

The problem is how to preserve and act on these insights, without undermining the dynamic character of the conversation itself. Even if I take notes immediately after the conversation, these rarely preserve the insight I felt when I meticulously reconstruct it. There are ways in which a more effective technological scaffolding could support these interactions in person as well as remotely, taking advantage of the affordances of written text such as persistence, objectivity and searchability (boyd, 2013). Through doing so, GenAI can help ensure we derive the greatest benefit possible from all forms of inter-action, linking them together in iteratively enriching ways which generate intellectual rewards for everyone involved. In the last chapter, we saw how conversational agents can support our thinking just as readily as they can be used to outsource it. In this chapter, we explore how they can be used to support our collaboration, as well as what this means for what we can achieve together as scholars.

MAKING THE MOST OF YOUR TIME WITH COLLABORATORS

There has been a shift in the social character of knowledge production in which the inclusivity and flexibility of hybrid working are matched by less face-to-face interaction for many. This will have different meanings depending on personal circumstances. For those who experience the landscape of hybrid work as lonely in a way pre-pandemic academia was not, the introduction of conversational agents into scholarship could seem like a bleak substitute for social connection. However, instead of seeing GenAI as an alternative to human collaborators, we can approach conversational agents like ChatGPT as a support to the conversations and interactions that we have with these colleagues. They can help us make the most of the time we spend with our collaborators, minimising the organisational demands involved in working together and enabling us to realise the creative potential of the collaboration in enjoyable and effective ways. In the hybrid workplaces we now inhabit, there is a need to be reflexive about the time we spend with collaborators, both online and face-to-face. There are a number of ways in which GenAI can help with this.

For example, I have a weekly Zoom reading group with a media theorist friend. We work on a book at a time, ranging from Continental Philosophy to Internet Studies and Media Theory. There's no direct relationship to particular projects that we work on and this is one of the reasons why I value these meetings so much. We simply talk about the ideas we encounter in the books, as well as generally catching up when we live in different countries. As I'm guessing every reader will have experienced at some point, when you have sustained intellectual interactions with someone who shares your interests and knows where you are, so to speak, coming from, there can be moments of insight in the conversation that feels like you've grasped something hugely significant. It is easy to lose these as they emerge in dialogue, with insights arising that fall away again as the conversation progresses. Obviously, we could take notes in these conversations but my experience has been that this changes the dynamic, reducing the intellectual liveliness which makes these conversations so valuable.

This is where GenAI can be a powerful assistant to help you make the most of these interactions. It can record, summarise and analyse these conversations in order to allow the people involved to keep moving these ideas forward separately, as well as bringing them into future conversations. When I raised this idea in a conversation with ChatGPT, it suggested the phrase *digital scribe* to describe this role, and I think this is a very helpful way of articulating it. It suggests that the generative agent is a participant, albeit a passive one, in the conversation. This reduces the need to attend or record the points, leaving the participants free to engage fully in the discussion. It allows us to enjoy the spontaneity and dynamism of in-person conversation, safe in the knowledge that the digital scribe will be recording the ideas and insights which can be revisited at a time of our choosing. Far from replacing human interaction, GenAI can ensure we realise the full pleasures of our work together.

This record of the conversation can be much more than minutes from a meeting. We can use it as a prompt to further thinking, both individually and together.[2] It supports asynchronous modes of interaction, either between synchronous meetings or when synchronous meetings simply aren't feasible, such as when you are working with someone in a remote time zone. These notes can also be indexed, analysed and digested in further ways supported by automation. For example, transcripts produced according to a specific rubric which meets your needs can be stored in a Google document which can then be intermittently uploaded to ChatGPT or Claude in order to provide commentary or offer analysis of the discussion. I've found this particularly helpful as a way of providing an alternative perspective on the analysis we have undertaken together in a meeting. I discuss an example later in the chapter of what this looks like in the context of a research project, suggesting real, though limited, ways in which GenAI can be incorporated into empirical research. I would be hesitant about moving to every interaction being recorded by default, but there are specific conversations we have where the 'digital scribe' can make a valuable contribution.

RECORDING YOUR CONVERSATIONS WITH GENERATIVE AI

This functionality is rapidly developing at the time of writing, with summarisation built into platforms like Teams and Zoom, as well as being available through plug-ins and third-party services. In an obvious sense, it is an extension of the capacity to automatically produce a transcript of the meeting, which itself would have seemed like a remarkable innovation only a few years ago. The additional element is to summarise that transcript in order to extract information from it which is useful to people who participated in the meeting. The challenge with producing summaries is the judgements of relevance deciding what to exclude and what to merely condense. Not only will these vary between sectors and use cases (e.g., what be relevant in a legal meeting will be extremely different from an academic meeting), but they will vary within sectors as well (e.g., an exam board meeting vs a startup meeting for a research project). These limitations mean that human oversight will be necessary for the foreseeable future, even if just a quick scan of the summary following the meeting, in order to ensure the relevant points were captured.

---

[2] We should note these transcripts are still prone to unreliability at the time of writing. They can struggle with distinguishing speakers, as well as sometimes making mistakes about exactly what was said. While I advocate their use as a prompt for thinking, capturing and summarising conversations in a way that feeds into intellectual work together, I remain cautious about their use for organisational functions where there are issues of equity leading from the reliability of the transcript. This unpredictable weakness in the transcripts is distinct from the issues surrounding summarisation which I discuss below. Use them as a thinking tool in your work together but don't use them as a formal record.

However, it is easy to imagine defining roles and establishing parameters for the summaries in advance of a meeting or a particular series of meetings, in a similar manner to the effective use of a conversational agent. Exactly what these instructions should be would vary across meetings, for example, requesting a detailed minute taker for a formal record, a focus on the action points arising from the meeting or a record of the conceptual disagreements between researchers in a project planning meeting. The possibility of undertaking this for a series of meetings could be particularly fruitful, creating opportunities to cross-reference summaries across past meetings to check progress towards goals or even track the development of ideas. The role of the digital scribe could be even more active, if given proper guidance and con-textualisation, by continuing to refine and digest conversations in the meeting with a view to increasing their clarity and supporting progress to the relevant goal (Figure 5.2).

ChatGPT: Academics interested in using Generative AI (GenAI) to support collaborative work across geographical distances can benefit significantly from adhering to foundational principles designed to enhance efficiency, creativity, and communication. Here are key principles to guide experimentation with GenAI tools in academia:

1. *Define Clear Objectives and Roles*

Before integrating GenAI into your workflows, clearly outline the objectives of your collaborative project. Understand the specific tasks or problems GenAI can help solve and assign roles based on expertise and interest. This clarity helps in selecting the most relevant GenAI tools and approaches.

2. *Prioritize Accessibility and Inclusivity*

Choose tools and practices that are accessible to all team members, considering different levels of technical proficiency and accessibility needs. Ensuring that the GenAI tools used are user-friendly and offer support or tutorials can help in reducing barriers to effective collaboration.

3. *Ensure Data Security and Privacy*

When working with GenAI tools, especially those that process sensitive research data, prioritize security and privacy. Understand the data policies of the tools you are using and ensure they comply with institutional and legal standards regarding data protection.

Figure 5.2 Principles for Incorporating GenAI into Collaborative Work
Source: ChatGPT.

It is essential, for practical and ethical reasons, that this is something the group as a whole signs up for. If some find it a creepy imposition on their working routines which makes them uncomfortable, it is unlikely they will participate in an open-minded way, if they agree to participate at all. There needs to be a space for concerns and questions to be raised, including a discussion of how the data will be stored and transmitted. As we will see later, there are some GenAI collaborations assistants which rely on screen recording which make it disturbingly easy to record a video call without another person's knowledge or consent. If this is something you want to explore then it has to be something which the team reflect upon and make sense of collectively. This means being sensitive to whether people feel comfortable voicing anxieties and concerns, as opposed to feeling at risk of being regarded as a luddite if they resist this technological development.

It also has the potential to change how power works within groups and organisations. What the political theorist Steven Lukes (2005) describes as the second face of power, setting the agenda and establishing the parameters for discussion, could become unsettlingly opaque under these conditions. The system itself could become a black box with decisions about relevance and inclusion being immune to scrutiny within the wider group. This could be a deliberate exercise of power through controlling the automated system, hiding behind what Vallor (2016) calls technosocial opacity.[3] But it could also be those involved having not found a way to determine the choices made in the process of summarisation. As organisational processes are increasingly mediated by automated systems, the digital literacy of staff becomes ever more important to ensuring equitable outcomes. It is easy to see the possibilities for workplace surveillance, particularly when online meetings take place through platforms like Microsoft Teams and Zoom which are either configured internally or operated using organisational licenses.

While a snooping manager might not feel inclined to read the 5,000–10,000 words likely to be generated by a literal transcript of an hour-long meeting, particularly if there are countless such meetings happening each day within a large organisation, we could imagine how a system might be guided to provide summaries which highlight elements which management deemed problematic in some way during the meeting. As Pasquale (2020, loc 2653) observes 'ethical AI vendors may include language in their contracts that require employers not to pick on disengaged workers for failing to smile at the CEO's joke' but the 'business case for a firm to continually police uses of its products' remains unclear. The reassuring promises made by the developers are less important than the capacities which these systems enable. Even if there are safeguards what matters is whether these are enforced in practice.

NEW MODES OF COLLECTIVE DISCOVERY

For the last ten years, I've been an active participant in the Centre for Social Ontology's annual workshops. These meetings take place in January every year, involving a group of 8–12 theorists across a range of disciplines, coming together to work overtime on a project to tackle large conceptual issues of a sort which would be difficult to address alone. The first project involved a series of five books about the social ontology of social change, asking if there was a fundamental shift in how society was undergoing transformation and what the implications

---

[3]This is a real and worrying possibility but exercising influence by controlling the agenda is a pretty ubiquitous means of exercising power in pre-GenAI organisations. It's a new expression of an existing strategy, rather than the introduction of a novel threat into previously well-functioning organisations.

of this would be. The second project, producing four books, explored how emerging technologies might be changing the nature of the human being.

These meetings are the highlight of my academic year. They involve intense and rewarding, even if sometimes tiring, conversation, taking place through long days and extending into the night over dinner. For each meeting, a participant produces a paper in advance which is circulated to enable prior reflection. They then present this paper in a session of around an hour and a half to two hours, getting feedback from the group. After the workshop, the editor of each book in the series takes responsibility for collecting and coordinating the papers that have been further developed. Then, there is a series editor who ensures the coherence of the volumes over time and tracks our progress on the overarching project. I find this an incredibly rewarding way of working, which I look forward to each year, but it does involve a sharp contrast between the largely individualised working patterns on the project throughout the year and the intensity of our face-to-face meetings over the course of that week. This raises the question of how a digital scribe could be incorporated into the process in order to enrich and build on the intensity of those face-to-face interactions, as well as facilitate more extensive collaboration outside of these meetings.

There is a range of ways in which we might incorporate the digital scribe into these activities. It could *capture* and *filter* the ideas generated through the discussion, feeding these into our ongoing discussion through real-time identification of the most salient points and provocative issues which emerged. In our last meeting, we had a note taker for the first time, a talented doctoral researcher based in the host institution, but these notes inevitably took time to clean up and circulate following the meeting.[4] The possibility these could be real-time features of the meeting before the production of a condensed digest after the meeting, perhaps having given each participant a chance to reflect on the experience which could in turn be incorporated into the record. Automation would mean these could be captured exhaustively but with various levels of granularity depending on the purpose of our interaction with the record. This would be particularly interesting for highlighting areas of agreement and disagreement, supporting a more precise exploration of a shared agenda over the course of multiple meetings, without losing the spontaneity and dynamism that makes the collaboration so enjoyable and constructive.

The *archiving and searchability* opened up by this would be a potent resource in preparing for subsequent meetings, as well as supporting authors and editors in their contribution to each volume in the series. The result would be a knowledge base we coproduced through our intellectual work, offering a resource to individuals and the team which would be iteratively developed over time through our continued collaboration. The potential use of this resource would be as far beyond familiar tools of shared documents and shared folders as these were in turn beyond the emailed attachments and USB drives which preceded them. The point would not be simply to have a common point of reference or common outputs but rather to make

---

[4]However, as I observe below, these notes were superior to any that could be produced by a GenAI summariser and are likely to remain so, given the expertise he brought to the process, which the system unavoidably lacks.

knowledge production itself a process undertaken in common, with individual contributions iteratively contributing to an ever more complex shared resource. There are enormously valuable contributions which the digital scribe could make to the projects we work on together over time.

Knowledge base platforms such as Notion and Saga, or knowledge management services such as Roam and Obsidian, can be used to organise and integrate the outputs from these meetings. The transcripts can be filed alongside meeting summaries and initial responses from ChatGPT to provide a searchable index of meetings and ideas generated from them. These platforms have some GenAI functionality built into them at the time of writing but this operates mainly at the level of a writing assistant. In Notion's case, this is a relatively expensive ($10 per month) addition to an existing subscription for services which in my experience have little immediate value for academics.[5] We can expect that analytical functionality will be incorporated into knowledge bases in which GenAI can be used to summarise, extract themes and analyse trends within the information. The capacity to infer context from the information within the knowledge base, effectively learning from what you have shared with it, provides a sense of how this might develop over time. The note-taking software Mem is developing in this direction, offering you the possibility of conversing with your knowledge base. The archival software Rewind provides similar functionality which is dependent on recording your screen across devices,[6] even if the conversations don't yet live up to their promise in my experience. But the possibility that one could ask 'what new ideas emerged in the meetings I've had this week?' or 'did the arguments I made about relating to my new book project develop at all during this week's seminars?' is enticing.

However, it will remain reliant on either an archival practice which meticulously registers the relevant materials within the knowledge base and/or automatic record of meetings. The development of GenAI workflows in software like Office 365 or Google Workspace might mitigate this problem over time. Platforms like Slack and Teams can be used to integrate and coordinate work on the collective knowledge base. Their rapidly expanding GenAI capacities, likely to encompass Microsoft's Notion competitor Loop in the near future, could be used to automate these processes in agreed-upon ways. The point would be to integrate individual workflows into collective collaboration to the greatest extent possible.

The account I have given above is slightly optimistic at the time of writing. The difference between the talented doctoral researcher mentioned in the example above and the automated

---

[5]I suspect this might not be viable as a business model given the costs involved in providing the service, raising the question of whether commercial considerations might constrain some of the developments I talk about in this chapter.

[6]This is stored in a compressed form on the local device, rather than being uploaded to the cloud. This mitigates some of the privacy concerns involved but the invitation to record *everything* as default is still rather unsettling. The convenience of having this record inclines the user towards accepting the default setting, which I found uncomfortable enough to lead me to cancel my subscription. It suggests a worrying path towards ubiquitous surveillance as a precondition for individual and collective productivity gains.

system is that the former has existing domain expertise which contributes to the note-taking. If you understand the subject matter of the conversation, then you will be much better placed to make judgements about what to include and exclude. As discussed in previous chapters, automated systems have no understanding in this sense, in spite of their remarkable capabilities. This means that summaries can often be bland and general, built around features of the meeting (such as action points or points of agreement/disagreement) which can be identified through the structure of the conversation. This can be useful for functional meetings but is a real limitation on their capacity to parse the more abstract conversations often involved in the research process. In the future, we might see specialised services or add-ins to existing platforms which are customised to the particular character of academic conversations, in which case the automatic transcription could become more discerning. There is also no capacity at present to develop a sense of what's relevant over the course of multiple meetings in the way that a conversational agent learns over the course of the conversation. This might be available in future but at present, I can find no reference to this functionality being in development and it is easy to see practical, if not technological, obstacles to its implementation.

Therefore you need to be prepared to engage in interpretive work to make effective use of summaries and resist any temptation to rely on the system. In this sense, it is no different from the other forms of automation we have discussed, in which this reflective approach is necessary to negotiate the potential pitfalls of GenAI. There might be slightly more copying and pasting in this case, though this can be automated using Apple Shortcuts once you have settled on a stable pattern of use. Fathom tries to make human interpretation as straightforward as possible by encouraging you to identify 'highlights' in the discussion: these are coded using categories which can be customised and pulled out from the transcript. These are recorded from the point at which the current speaker began speaking, recognising how it is often not clear something *is* a highlight until someone is halfway through making a point.

My experience is that it is difficult to fully participate in a meeting while being responsive to these highlights. This suggests a role in the meeting which is not quite as detached as that often associated with the person focused on producing the minutes. However, it is a specific role which needs to be agreed upon which could be executed in expert ways with practice, identifying different highlights relevant for each kind of meeting and coding them according. Fathom pulls out questions which were asked during the meeting which can be extremely useful for identifying intellectual points of discussion alongside the inevitable action points in most academic meetings. It provides a helpful workspace for each meeting available at a sharable URL which brings together video, transcript, summary, highlights and questions. These can be shared individually or quickly exported which is useful for establishing the workflows described towards the start of this section, even if it involves more manual activity than might ideally be the case (Figure 5.3).

In its current form, the technology is far from perfect. But even the most superficial experiments can leave you with a sense of how inefficient existing practices can be within higher education. We often lose the insights which emerge in meetings or capture them in partial ways which fail to do them justice. The capture mechanisms we have can in turn introduce a stultifying

> **MC:** I'm writing about the notion of a GenAI 'digital scribe' who works within academic teams, operating as a general assistant to streamline their interaction, record it and maximise the creative enjoyment they derive from their work together. What might this look like in practice? How could it change their work together? Please provide a paragraph of narrative which summarises a fictional vision of how this might operate
>
> **Claude:** Here is a fictional narrative paragraph envisioning how a GenAI "digital scribe" could transform academic teamwork:
>
> Professor Sato's research team gathers for their usual Monday morning meeting, but this time, a new member joins them – Claude, their recently acquired AI assistant. As the scholars begin discussing their latest experimental findings and analyzing implications, Claude listens intently. It captures their dialogue nearly verbatim while instantly detecting cross-cutting themes and highlighting outstanding questions in the team transcript. When the hour wraps up, members open their inboxes to find Claude's skillful summary. By the afternoon, Claude has generated a timeline mapping how each researcher's independent pieces fit together into an integrated discovery process. It schedules check-ins on current roadblocks and automatically prompts the lead authors to storyboard presentations for an upcoming conference. Over the next weeks, Claude will continue learning along with the team - retrieving relevant archives, taking notes, coordinating schedules, and even suggesting creative new directions or additional experiments to run, all to maximize this team's collaborative scholarly potential.

Figure 5.3 The Implications of Collaborating with a Conversational Agent AI

formality into our interaction which constrains our capacity to do what matters. It can feel like we've reached a consensus at the end of the meeting, only for that to dissolve away as we disperse into our individualised patterns of working, leaving it needing to be reconstructed at the next meeting. There is a risk that introducing GenAI into meetings could amplify these problems by amplifying an instrumental approach to them. For example, Google Meet already offers an 'attend for me' function which sends a transcription agent along with some notes to contribute to the meeting. I discuss the opportunities and problems posed by this in Chapter 6. But there are real possibilities to have more humane and creative meetings, in which GenAI provides a scaffolding for meaningful human interaction rather than constituting an obstacle to it. It will be difficult to find the right workflows for this, not least of all because they are a matter of teams, organisations and cultures as much as they are a technological question.

USING GENERATIVE AI FOR COLLABORATIVE RESEARCH

We are likely to see significant growth in the use of GenAI for research. I have resisted including it here because I am concerned that large language models (LLMs) are unsuitable for these purposes. Their reliance on statistical associations means the inferences they make about data will be unavoidably precarious, as likely to hallucinate about the data as with any other domain of activity. The black box character of these systems means the reason for these results will always be opaque, creating difficulties for reproducibility as well as creating the need for human oversight which possibly negates any productivity gain. Furthermore, there is a conventional bias to their inferences reflecting their reliance upon training data. It would be too simplistic to say they will inevitably reproduce the past in their interpretation of the present. But there are reasonable grounds to assume the nature of their statistical inference will tend to squeeze out interpretations which don't fit with past trends.

While there could be ways to mitigate the negative implications of these tendencies in data analysis, the problem lies in the nature of the LLM itself rather than a contingent deficiency which can be overcome with better engineering. It's possible there could be services which supplement LLMs with additional approaches or techniques, such as Anthropic's use of Constitutional AI to regulate the responses of Claude, which could make GenAI tools more appropriate for analysis. However, I remain sceptical that a sufficiently reliable approach to data analysis can be built on these foundations. The exception to this might be the use of GenAI for writing code to work with data in computational disciplines. In these cases, the GenAI is likely to be automating a reasonably transparent human-led process, such as cleaning up a dataset, rather than substituting for human judgement. These were already routine processes in many cases, making it possible for the LLM to verifiably follow the series of steps which a human would but to do so more quickly and effectively. But these are complex issues which I cannot do justice to here. I suggest more specialised literature for anyone interested in the computational applications of GenAI while being wary of the possibility that enthusiasm for these new capabilities might lead some authors to be insufficiently attentive to their risks and limitations.

Even if GenAI cannot be used reliably for data analysis, it can still be included in the research process. Consider the many other tasks involved in managing a research project. GenAI could be used to refine and improve project documents using the techniques discussed in Chapter 7, for example, increasing the accessibility of participant information forms, producing summaries and optimising engagement materials. Perhaps more interestingly it can be used as a supplement to human interpretation, introduced at a later stage to refine and elaborate upon the analysis rather than being expected to perform it. For example, I recorded a meeting for a research project in which we talked about the secondary data we had analysed which had been presented in an interim report. It was a substantial conversation in which we talked through each aspect of the report, discussing the significance of each finding and comparing it to our expectations. It was an enjoyable meeting in which I came away feeling excited about the work and with a clear sense of the arguments which would feed into the paper we would soon start writing.

I then presented Claude with the interim report and explained the context of the project. I asked it to summarise the findings of the report which it did effectively, identifying the same elements which were the basis for our earlier discussion. The experiment became more interesting when I explained the analysis of impact case studies in the Research Excellence Framework (REF) 2021, the method by which research outputs of universities are assessed by the government in UK higher education, followed up on a previous study we had undertaken of REF 2014 where these impact case studies were first introduced. I uploaded the earlier paper to Claude to provide context and reinforce it through a series of prompts to indicate the relationship between the current study and the previous one. It was surprising how effectively it incorporated this comparison into the analysis and produced a series of claims which largely captured what we had talked about in the meeting. To test this further, I uploaded the transcript from the meeting, asking Claude to review its own analysis in light of the interaction we had during the meeting. It reported that our conversation included more nuance and complexity than it applied in its own analysis, which was rather reassuring. It identified particular points of complexity which could then be fed back into our conversation as a project team. Obviously, there would be huge ethical issues involved in sharing most, if not all, primary data with a conversational agent in this way. But these could be negotiated by compiling a summary document at a level of generality which respects anonymity, identifying themes and offering interpretations which could be the basis for the discussion.

I would not suggest that Claude could undertake the analysis on behalf of the research team but it can be used to review, challenge and prompt reflection in the iterative way described here. The point is not to replace human collaborators but rather to find ways in which conversational agents can productively enter into existing processes as meta-collaborators; like any collaborator, they will bring a balance of strengths and weaknesses to this undertaking. I would argue they could be incorporated into a team as an assistant to support a research project. This could be the narrow role of the digital scribe described earlier but establishing this context in itself creates opportunities for a more analytical contribution, albeit one which would be managed carefully and reviewed regularly rather than taken on faith. The outputs which a digital scribe generates can provide the basis for this collaboration through the generation of artefacts from team interactions which might otherwise be lost. Far from being a static archive, these can be incorporated into ongoing discussion in a way that is potentially rich, if not entirely without risks. I would be concerned that the conversational agent could become too familiar to the team over time, leading to diminishing scrutiny of the outputs particularly during busy times when collaboration is difficult. However, the key consideration is that its role is always a contribution to a process rather than something relied upon to produce the outcome of that process.

If we are going to compare feedback from ChatGPT to feedback from a human interlocutor, it's important that we do so in a way that recognises the real-world context within which both are taking place. I'm enough of a humanist to retain a commitment to the idea that a skilled human reader, immersed within your field of expertise, will always, in principle, be a better interlocutor than a GenAI system. The caveat for that is that this human reader needs to have the time, energy and care to respond to what you have sent them at the point where it is useful to you. These sociological conditions are ones which do not diminish the category of the human but do mean that, in practice, we ourselves and the people in our networks can rarely provide the support to each other that we would ideally seek to do so. Much as the limitations of your human collaborators will tend to be situational, reflecting the varied range of commitments they have at a particular point in time, the limitations of your meta-collaborator are epistemic. There are things it can do more quickly and effectively than any human colleague, but there are things it simply cannot do on methodological and epistemic grounds, even if that category will potentially shrink with time. Furthermore, it requires a level of oversight and guidance which would not be needed for a peer or even for a trainee, at least once the initial phase of introducing someone to a project or helping them develop a skill is completed.

THE FUTURE OF KNOWLEDGE PRODUCTION

Over the next year, I plan to experiment with these collective modes of working in every capacity available to me. This has to be treated carefully because academics tend to default to familiar modes of working, as well as assume the right to establish their own routine patterns. There is a parallel here to trying to use project management systems like Trello and Basecamp within research teams. My experience has been that it can lead to remarkable increases in efficiency which receive near universal approval from the team *if* we get to the point where everyone is routinely using the software. The problem is that unless everyone is committed there is a tendency to default to email over time, in spite of the fact that it is near uniformly experienced as a problem by those involved. My own enthusiasm for platform-based coordination comes from an early experience of organising a large international conference using Basecamp, with little to no email being sent within the team for an undertaking which might otherwise have generated hundreds of internal emails per week. It might, therefore, be difficult to effect a radical shift in collective routines even as these services become ever more automated, such that interoperability between the elements described above largely ceases to be something which has to be practically negotiated. Given the relatively early stage of development for the tools involved, it will be more effective to agree experiments with individual elements (such as meeting summaries) built on a clear case for how it could streamline collaboration and reduce the workload involved. These experiments can make the tools involved more familiar to members of the team, leading to more expansive uses of GenAI further down the line.

Even if we are still some way from the digital scribe, I have described it as a one-stop solution which can be easily taken up by research teams without established expertise in this area, the potential ramifications for how we work together are significant. Projects could become more ambitious as logistical constraints upon size and complexity melt away through the careful coordination and curation of the digital scribe. This opens up possibilities for more iterative and collaborative forms of knowledge production, in which the processual model of scholarship, introduced in Chapter 2, becomes a lived reality for a research team. The individual experience of creative augmentation which animates this book could become a *shared* process, not only capturing the vibrant sense of insight which often accompanies in-person collaboration but continually developing these connections, in a way which connects the creative work of the individuals involved with their shared undertaking.

There is a tendency for the technical infrastructure of knowledge production to fade into the background, at least within the social sciences and humanities. Consider the voice recorder which has been ubiquitous for qualitative researchers yet rarely figures into epistemological reflections as opposed to practical guidance for researchers in training (Back, 2012).

There is a suppression of the technological generated by this lack of intellectual curiosity about the devices upon which scholarship depends and the infrastructural conditions for scholarship being provided by the university. I have long been persuaded by the call Marres (2017) makes for a 'coming out' of technology within social enquiry, reclaiming a serious intellectual interest in this infrastructure and how we can better adapt it for our purposes. This means recognising that sociotechnical limitations often lead to epistemological constraints: *how we coordinate knowledge production technologically limits the kinds of knowledge we can produce*. It can be particularly difficult to improve forms of coordination in the humanities and social sciences[7] because of the rhythms of working together. When this happens it will often be in the context of funded projects which impose time cycles and obligations which reflect the imperatives of funders and concerns of the institutions hosting the project (Dollinger, 2020). It is tricky to develop more effective ways of working together if you have only come together for a demarcated period of time, often defined by the struggle of balancing your collective obligations for the project alongside your individual obligations. But unless we can find ways to exercise collective responsibility over the sociotechnical conditions of our work together, it won't be possible to improve this situation. The only way to find more effective modes of collaboration is to begin to try. The point I have made here is that isn't simply a matter of collective productivity or working together effectively as a team. It has epistemological implications for the kinds of knowledge which can be produced through this work.

My suggestion is that distributed forms of knowledge production intended to circumvent the limitations of traditional organisational modes within the humanities and social sciences could be radically expanded using GenAI, particularly with regard to the developments which are still on the horizon at the time of writing. These modes of distributed knowledge production are most developed within the digital humanities, where it has become routine for large teams in which each contributes 'domain-specific expertise that enables a research question to be conceptualised, answered, and then re-conceptualised and re-answered'. The diverse character of these collaborations represents the nature of projects which call for diverse forms of expertise which tend to be located within different units across the university, with 'authors' often ranging from 'professors and librarians to student programmers, interns, staff, and community members' in complex undertakings coordinated by project directors and technical leads (Burdick et al., 2012, pp. 49–50). The success of these undertakings led to calls for 'the massive expansion of the scholarly enterprise through a wealth of networks, information streams, and emergent communities of practice that produce and share knowledge and culture in ways that open up opportunities for participation, dissension and freedom' (Burdick et al., 2012, p. 60). The techniques suggested in this section represent ways in which GenAI can support such an expansion, by reducing the logistical demands and

---

[7] I talk specifically about the humanities and the social sciences here because sustained working in large teams simply isn't the norm in most places. Obviously, there are exceptions though, such as the collaborative cultures which are the norm within the digital humanities and vast multi-partner projects funded by the European Union.

increasing the intellectual richness of the interactions upon which distributed knowledge production inevitably depends. It could facilitate the expansion of these collaborative modes into intellectual contexts which lack the complex objects which inherently call for innovation in the organisation of knowledge production. There are new ways of working even for disciplinary research teams who might previously have remained comfortably within an established modus operandi, while dimly sensing or even occasionally discussing the epistemological limitations which flow from practical ways of working that prioritise the individual scholar.

Nielsen's (2011) suggestion of maximising the epistemic diversity of our collective undertakings easily lends itself to the inclusion of conversational agents, who epistemically contribute to that diversity directly in their own powerful but limited way, as well as amplifying the epistemic contribution of others who are engaged with them. In this sense, the techniques in the previous chapter for individual thinking with a conversational agent can be brought into our collaborations, with these individual practices of generative scholarship having the potential to combine with the collective deployment of conversational agents in powerful and exciting ways. In his reflection on the rise of 'networked science', Nielsen (2011, p. 28) argues that 'in creative work, most of us ... spend much of our time blocked by problems that would be routine, if only we could find the right expert to help us'. His point was that serendipitous encounters, in which we stumble across the right collaborator who can immediately move us through a problem we have struggled with, expand the range of problems we can solve. He saw this as a matter of digital platforms facilitating 'architectures of attention that go beyond what is possible in offline methods of collaboration': they make it far easier for relevant expertise to coalesce within networks orientated towards related problems (Nielsen, 2011, p. 39).

While the commercial imperatives which have driven the design of social platforms militated against this in ways which went unrecognised in these earlier phases of digital scholarship, he recognises that collaborative platforms were not designed by experts in collaboration but rather by people who were essentially amateurs (Nielsen, 2011. p. 29). The excitement which I felt about social media in the early 2010s rested on the sense that it would make new modes of collaboration which could prove intellectually enriching and practically effective. Unfortunately, this collective horizon was swamped by individual incentives and practice which meant this potential went largely unfulfilled, though of course research communities did emerge through these dynamics in spite of the algorithmic incentives towards reputation building at the cost of community building (Carrigan & Fatsis, 2021). The optimism that we can build platforms which are more adequate to collective scholarship, rather than outsourcing this need to commercial firms that emerged during the big tech boom of the late 2000s, feels particularly relevant at a time when Elon Musk's takeover of Twitter has driven a fragmentation of online academic communities.

Nielsen's (2011) commitment to a design science of collaboration suggests a way forward in which we can develop new modes of collective discovery, driven by but extending beyond the 'designed serendipity' he advocates to expand the range of problems we can solve, suggests how the incorporation of conversational agents into collective undertakings could be part of a broader impulse movement towards a deliberate and purposeful digital scholarship. This would recognise that we cannot rely on external corporate platforms or imagine that technology can solve problems in itself, but rather that we can deploy emerging technologies in careful and strategic ways in order to enhance and expand our collective capacities for knowledge production. The extent to which GenAI is dominated by the major technology corporations, either directly or through their investment,[8] poses a challenge to this vision. But the way to meet this challenge is for the sector to take responsibility for what could be the most radical transformation in the research infrastructure since the emergence of email and the web.

If GenAI could support the development of more coordinated and engaged research communities, overcoming the limitations of schedule and geography which constrain remote collaboration, it might act as a bulwark against a similar collapse of collective possibilities into individual instrumentalism. Imagine if the research networks which sustain your intellectual curiosity through intermittent meetings could work together in more coordinated ways without requiring unfeasible feats of scheduling or significantly enhanced workloads. Imagine if research collaborations routinely lead to the coproduction of searchable knowledge bases as a shared resource containing the collective ideas, insights and connections drawn through work together. Imagine if conversational agents were familiar participants in these interactions, with their weaknesses mitigated through careful strategies and procedures concerning how they are engaged with and how their outputs should be treated. The practical steps through which GenAI can be incorporated into distributed collaboration, a category which might include even those within the same institution given the realities of hybrid working, can be configured together to support agile and sophisticated ways of working together at a distance with the potential to transform scholarship.

LEARNING FROM EACH OTHER

In this chapter, I have ranged from immediate possibilities for collaboration through to an optimistic account of how GenAI could transform working together. There are reasons to be pessimistic about whether this vision could be realised in practice, building on the issues raised in Chapter 3. Even if much is outside of our control as a professional group, we nonetheless have a degree of freedom about the professional culture we seek to create around GenAI within higher education. This book is intended as a contribution to this project, arguing for a reflexive approach orientated towards realising scholarly values through GenAI rather than looking to these developments as a way of reducing the costs of scholarship. These issues are taken up at length in the final chapter. However, the possibility of developing a professional culture[9] relies on there being mechanisms through which we can reflect on what

---

[8]Despite being founded less than ten years ago, initially as a non-profit research lab, OpenAI's revenue had reached well over $1 billion by the end of 2023. While it still has less than 1,000 employees, this is not a small firm, even if it is tiny compared to its main investor Microsoft.

[9]I use the term in the singular largely as a stylistic choice. Obviously, there is unlikely to be *one* professional culture, as opposed to multiple overlapping cultures reflecting intellectual, disciplinary and geographical differences amongst myriad other factors.

we have learned about GenAI. This is how we order and filter our accumulated knowledge with a view to establishing norms and standards that guide professional practice.

One of the striking features of how conversational agents have been rolled out is the lack of support for end users or guidance on effective use. The speed at which are they being rolled out would make support materials difficult to keep up to date, suggesting a prioritisation of development over documentation. Underpinning this is a more interesting challenge concerning a lack of clarity about how to use these technologies effectively, with GenAI relying on the 'collective intelligence' of users experimenting in order to better understand how these astonishingly versatile systems can be used across different sectors. This has created a void that a plethora of influencers have rushed to fill, sometimes in effective and supportive ways but often with a get-rich-quick vibe in which their (presumably AI-generated) content is intended to capitalise on the hype and rapidly increase their visibility. This does not mean there is no value to be found in their work but unfortunately, it will be necessary to filter through a lot of hyperbole in order to find it. Finding a Substack newsletter which seems reliable and addresses topics in a way which is relevant to your interests can help enormously in this respect, enabling you to prioritise quality over quantity. But it can still be a challenge to find reliable sources of guidance which match your interests and are attuned to the practical realities of the field in which you are working.

There is a parallel here to the early years of social media. In their insightful platform biography of Twitter, Baym and Burgess (2020: 9) point to the public pedagogies which emerged as users reflected on their experiences and shared them with others:

> A form of public pedagogy emerged. Whether to help others out or gain attention as Twitter experts, bloggers wrote copious "what is Twitter, and how to use it" articles for at least the first few years of Twitter's existence. Those posts that circulated on well-read blogs got the most attention. This meant that from the beginning, the public conversation about what Twitter was and what it should be used for was shaped significantly by tech influencers—mostly white, a lot of them men, and with technical expertise and professional identities tied up with journalism, software development, and especially blogging.

This was particularly the case with a platform like Twitter given a format that often confused users initially because it did not easily match past experiences. There was a sense in which academics struggled to talk to Twitter much as (many) academics now struggle to talk to conversational agents. What made the difference was a willingness to jump in and experiment, ideally guided by orientating questions to help make sense of the experience and a baseline awareness of the underlying technology (Carrigan, 2019). The manner in which users responded to this challenge played a significant role in establishing the culture of the platform. The pedagogical culture which emerged (or failed to) reflected these individual responses but also channelled them in particular directions, as tweets, blog posts, podcasts, slide decks and videos collectively shaped how digital scholarship was conceived of by academics, whether they were early adopters or new to these activities.

Even with platforms like YouTube which were seemingly more straightforward, the pedagogical culture which users developed had a real impact on how the platform developed over time (Burgess & Green, 2018). Features which originated with users such as the convention of the hashtag have been incorporated into the infrastructure of platforms, showing how platform operators and users co-develop over time (Baym & Burgess, 2020). These conversations matter because they produce a sense of *why* and *how* a platform should be used which over time influences how that platform is seen and even how it is designed. The problem with public pedagogy is that it tends to be dominated by 'power users'. The people who are most committed, opinionated and influential on a given platform tend to be the ones whose opinions have the most visibility (Carrigan, 2022). This dynamic is particularly corrosive on social media where the influence of one's opinions tends to be correlated to commitment to the platform, in the sense that the more you post above a certain quality threshold the more influence you will tend to accumulate.

But it is a broader problem which we are likely to see with GenAI. In the act of writing this book, I mark myself as someone who has, in spite of my critical reflections in chapter three, in some sense swallowed the Kool-aid. Over the last few months, GenAI has become part of my working routines in a way which is unlikely to unwind over time. If the costs of access increase, as might happen given what we know at the time of writing about Microsoft's intended pricing for its forthcoming Copilot functionality, I am likely to pay them if this is feasible. In this sense, I represent a misleading guide to this terrain because the majority of academic users of GenAI are unlikely to immerse themselves as deeply as I have. For this reason, stories about personal use ought to be treated with caution. They provide useful illustrations of how technologies can be used (hence why I have included them in this book) but they risk creating a sense this is how academics *should* use them.

Here are some of the questions it is worth asking when confronting a potential practice, whether it is something you have discovered yourself, been shown by a colleague, encountered in this book or read about elsewhere:

1　Would this practice save you time? What else could you use that time for?
2　Would it be difficult to take up this practice? What new software, skills or equipment would you need?
3　Would this practice solve a problem? Are there easier ways to solve a problem?
4　Would this practice make you uncomfortable? Does this reflect a specific ethical concern or a vague intuition?

As I argued in Chapter 2 at least some experimentation is necessary because this is such a new technology. There are untapped domains of capability in these systems because of the inherent versatility of the underlying model. It can by its nature be deployed within any domain of activity to support, enhance or replace action which involves the use of text. The people who are best placed to work out how to apply this are teams who have worked together, towards a common goal which matters to them, with their own history and relationships. This might be teaching teams brought together within university departments to deliver education to students. But I suspect it's more likely to be research collaborators, working towards a common set of intellectual goals, possibly over a substantial period of time.

This does not suggest that research is more important than teaching. It would be easy to write a book on GenAI and teaching, excluding all other topics. The reason I've suggested research as a more suitable arena to explore the potential and pitfalls of collaboration through GenAI is that it gives us time and space away from the formalised responsibilities we have to students and how these are codified within teaching and learning bureaucracies. With the significant exception of research ethics and data governance, there is a much greater degree of freedom with how we choose to work together as researchers. This creates a space in which we can explore and experiment, in ways which might not immediately impact how we relate to our students but can certainly be informed by them over time.

6

COMMUNICATION

This chapter will:

- Explore the capacity of Generative Artificial Intelligence (GenAI) to support academics in managing the burden of digital communications, particularly with regard to the continued centrality of email within academic life.
- Discuss how conversational agents can be used to coach academics in writing more inclusive and engaging emails, with students and colleagues.
- Consider how GenAI can be used to support the 'translation' of existing work across different formats while respecting the expectation of originality and rigour.

What do you dislike most about being an academic? Even if email wasn't your first answer to this question, I suspect for most readers it would figure somewhere in the top five. The burden of email in higher education often feels crushing and at the heart of what Burrows (2012, p. 355) describes as a 'deep, affective, somatic crisis' which threatens to overwhelm academics. The hybrid working entrenched by the pandemic has further individualised working routines concerning who comes into the office, when and for what purposes. There are now online, hybrid and in-person meetings where once only the latter category was a regular feature of our lives. It is often unclear which meetings will fall into which category, contributing to the overall sense of flux while also requiring coordination for each particular meeting. How often do you ask, or are asked, the question 'are we meeting online or in person' in a given week? The mainstreaming of platforms like Teams and Slack, as well as the blurring of personal/professional boundaries in the use of messaging apps like WhatsApp, have further contributed to this expanding and mutating communicative burden. The fact that many now experience social media engagement, the subject of the next chapter, as a professional obligation only adds to the burden. There is a constant flood of messages across platforms combined with a lack of clear agreement about the norms surrounding replies and the expectations which we have of each other in the workplace. It is a complex and confusing landscape of interaction which has emerged so quickly that it can be easy to lose track of what a significant shift it has been.

The problem here is far from unique to higher education, and it predates the pandemic. Brubaker (2022, loc 2050) places the blame on digital media 'lowering the threshold for communication' which has led to a 'superabundant digital sociality' that can be a profound emotional and temporal burden (Brubaker, 2022, loc 2050). It is easier than ever to communicate across a vastly expanded range of channels, leading to the continual growth of interaction in a self-propelling spiral. Emerging expectations about when we should be in contact with others and how rapidly we ought to respond when they contact us reinforce each other, producing a sense of drowning under the weight of the messages we are sending and receiving. In the last couple of years, I've noticed people apologising for the lateness of their response when they're responding in the afternoon to an email I sent that morning. I certainly don't have an expectation someone will reply to me within a couple of hours. Do other people in higher education *really* have this expectation? Or have these apologies become a reflex when we feel continually behind on our communicative responsibilities? As Gill (2013, 12) has documented, email has become a profound source of anxiety for many academics, compounded by the spiralling channels through which academics now communicate on social platforms (Carrigan, 2019):

> 'Addiction' metaphors suffuse academics' talk of their relationship to email, even as they report such high levels of anxiety that they feel they have to check email first thing in the morning and last thing at night, and in which time away (on sick leave, on holiday) generates fears of what might be lurking in the inbox when they return. Again, inventive 'strategies' abound for keeping such anxiety at bay eg putting on your 'out of office' reply when you are actually in the office.

A common experience with other knowledge workers is the sense that email stops us from getting on with our 'real work' (Gregg, 2013, loc 1152). It's a continual drain on our energy and attention, leaving us with obligations that can never be finally met. There will always be more email, just as there will always be more communication to deal with through the other channels which academics now use. These problems only got worse during the pandemic, with the profound fatigue of endless Zoom meetings and the ambiguous norms of post-pandemic hybrid working environments, which sometimes feel like they combine the worst of in-office working and enforced remote working.[1]

This is the environment in which GenAI has emerged. I find it strange that the potential for automated communication has received so little attention within higher education, given it offers a potential means to solve a problem which so many of us feel crushed by. There are reasons to be cautious about an enthusiastic uptake of GenAI to ease these communicative burdens, which sap our energy and distract us from the things we want to be doing. There is a risk that a disorganised uptake of GenAI for communication within the sector could make the existing problems worse, leading some people to exploit their expanded capacity to communicate for self-interested reasons.[2] There will inevitably be a debilitating wave of GenAI-infused spam within the sector as well, the initial signs of which are discussed towards the end of this chapter. However, there are still real and immediate opportunities to make communication within universities easier and more effective.

The opportunities for internal communication are discussed in this chapter before the next chapter explores how this can be used for digital engagement. I illustrate these discussions with examples of how I've been using GenAI for communication myself, though I share these with a concern that some readers might object to these practices. If this is the case I'd encourage you to articulate what the objection is, why you see it as problematic and whether this is anchored in a sense of a harm being enacted. These are the conversations we urgently need to have as GenAI begins to drive a further transformation in our communications environment. This means grappling as a profession with the values we bring to these changes, as well as what they mean for how we take up or resist these new possibilities of organising our communication. It is far from clear in my own mind what the answer is but I am certain our existing communications culture is inadequate for the challenges we now face, let alone those which are coming soon.

---

[1] Suggesting the hybrid work culture we have is inadequate is not an argument for returning to the pre-pandemic norm. Eliminating the expectation that in-person meeting is the default has made a huge contribution to accessibility within higher education. The problem I'm pointing to here is how that hybrid work culture is planned and organised, rather than the fact of hybridity itself.

[2] There is a parallel here to the manner in which some academics realised that social media success is, at least in part, a numbers game. This brought short-term gains for their visibility but at the cost of ratcheting up the demands involved in being professionally visible as an academic on social media platforms (Carrigan, 2019, ch 6).

HOW COULD GENERATIVE AI CHANGE COMMUNICATION WITHIN HIGHER EDUCATION?

I suspect we will see a rapid expansion of GenAI for communication within higher education, even if the uptake has initially been slow while the sector's attention was diverted by assessment integrity. Email is too widely experienced as a problem and GenAI too enticing a potential solution for automated communication to not become more widespread. There is an obvious case to be made for freeing up the time we would spend on routine interactions, such as the occasionally mind-numbing process of finding a date which works for a meeting. Techniques which have developed to address this problem (such as using a Doodle poll, the Outlook scheduling assistant or simply offering three dates and times to avoid a wider discussion) can be seen as more primitive forms of automation. It replaces what would otherwise be an exchange of messages with a process which circumvents that exchange, accomplishing the same outcome without the quantity of interaction that was previously required.

If we accept that certain kinds of email interaction ought to be routinised in order to save time, why not explore more effective forms of automation? How widely should we cast this net in terms of interactions which should be automated? The fact my inbox is full of these logistical interactions leaves email feeling like such a Sisyphean undertaking that it often leaves me antisocial in the face of longer emails from friends and collaborators. While scheduling a call or a video chat with them is a way around this, it nonetheless leaves me aware of how one category of email (unenjoyable but necessary) leaves me unable to appreciate another category of email (enjoyable but unnecessary).

Could automation help free us from the former in order to increase our enjoyment of the latter? The main objection I can see to this concerns the evident capacity for this to go wrong. There are far too many examples of a lack of digital literacy amongst academics causing significant disruption, particularly when small mistakes aggregate within an organisation. Consider what happens when a particularly intense period of conversation on a previously defunct mailing list leads to people asking to be removed from the list. This in turn leads to people explaining that the person who subscribed will have to unsubscribe themselves. Everyone uses 'reply all' for every message, including the people complaining about others using 'reply all'. In the process the traffic spirals, leading more people to ask to be unsubscribed from the list, often without having read the earlier clarifications. Before we know it, we have an explosion of emails and mutual irritation, which could easily have been avoided if academics who subscribed to a mailing list had familiarised themselves with what that list is, how it works and how they can remove themselves from it; a process often detailed in the footer of every message sent to the list.

If academics cannot be trusted, at least en masse, to manage a mailing list, can they really be trusted with GenAI? The functionality which now exists to automate email responses, using a tool like Zapier to connect email accounts to ChatGPT, heralds a near future in which significant portions of communication will be undertaken by automated systems. The safest way to do this is to set up automated drafts rather than responses which leaves a prewritten email sitting in your inbox as a draft, presenting you with a reply which can be reviewed and modified before sending. However, imagine coming out of a meeting where you haven't looked at the email, only to find that an intelligent system has run amok and sent scores of incoherent or irrelevant emails to people who had contacted you. What harm could the hallucinations we discussed in Chapter 3 do to your interpersonal interaction if left unmonitored? Imagine what could happen if the address book became the medium for spreading this chaos, with emails potentially going to everyone you had ever contacted. Imagine what could happen if this system was compromised in some way, with the sheer range of malicious possibilities opened up by the integration between ChatGPT and your email. Obviously, these are things which a manual intruder seeking to either steal your identity or cause chaos could do in principle but GenAI could literally automate these malicious possibilities.

There is the potential for disaster at the level of individual systems but also in the interaction of these automated processes. For this reason, the incorporation of automation into organisationally sanctioned mail providers like Outlook or Google Mail will be key to mitigating the risks which could ensue through individual use. Yet despite these risks, we should not lose sight of what a significant problem email has become within the academy, as well as the possibility that GenAI might make the burden newly bearable. The question is not whether we should accept automated communication, it is already here in primitive forms and will inevitably grow as it is incorporated into email clients, but how to build cultures within universities that ensure we use the time freed up for creative and rewarding pursuits focused on high-quality interaction. Rather than simply sending more emails. The scale of the change coming could lead to a shift in how we communicate equivalent to the introduction of email itself. Hopefully, we can take this as an opportunity to build a more rewarding and less draining professional culture, in which we use email as a tool to support our work together rather than subordinating that work to keeping up with the demands of the tool.

USING GENERATIVE AI TO COMMUNICATE WITH YOUR COLLEAGUES

My instinct is that it would be deeply rude to your colleagues to outsource the responsibility of responding to their (presumably human-generated[3]) messages to a machine. The risks involved are significant enough that, for the foreseeable future, it would be a terrible idea even if you didn't think it was egregiously rude. But there are many ways to use GenAI to support communication which don't involve this wholesale outsourcing. Initially, I want to map out some of the ways in which it *can* be used before we turn to questions of whether it *should* be used in this way. These are just a few suggestions based on my experience integrating conversational agents into my working life over the last year. If you start to experiment

---

[3]If this assumption breaks down, we might see automated communications rapidly becoming normalised within the academy. If other people are doing it, why wouldn't I? This is an example of why professional conversations about these new technological possibilities are so important. Without them, individual decisions made out of convenience can rapidly aggregate into an institutional shift, through the process of 'network weather' discussed in the final chapter.

yourself in order to find ways to apply them, you will reliably discover things which I've not discussed in this chapter. The discussion later in the chapter provides principles to help you evaluate such discoveries and consider whether they are things you feel comfortable integrating into your working routines.

Getting Feedback on the Clarity of Your Messages

How clear are your emails? I have colleagues whose emails consistently embody an admirable clarity, laying out what it is they are raising in a friendly and easily digestible way. My natural emailing style in contrast is quite different, often brief and careless in spite of my intermittent attempts to improve it. As I've taken on leadership roles, I've realised there are certain points at which this just isn't viable, for example, sending a list of updates to a teaching team mid-way through a busy semester. This realisation hasn't changed my style of emailing though, it's simply led me to demarcate the emails where I really have to try from those I answer in my usual off-the-cuff way. It's made me a better colleague but the manner in which these end up on my to-do list, as a consequence of no longer doing them reactively, nonetheless adds to my workload.

If like me information doesn't come out of your mind in a way which is easily digestible to others, conversational agents can help you improve the clarity of your communication. In contrast to the rambling emails I would once have written in which I worked out the points I needed to cover in the course of writing them, I now map out the points I want to include in a conversation with Claude prior to writing. I often share the email I subsequently draft in order to get feedback on clarity and suggestions for improvement. I keep these dialogues in a single thread which means that Claude develops expectations of what I take a clear email to be, as well as the support I need in writing them effectively.

The first part of this is obviously something I could have done with a notepad or a blank document if I had been sufficiently motivated to do so. It might simply be a lack of imagination on my part that it didn't occur to me to do this until I was working with conversational agents. But the fact it is a *conversation*, in a genuine sense hopefully realised in your own experience by this point in the book, changes the character of this planning. It provides an occasion to explicate the task in a dialogue which gives it an energy which is hard to recreate in a monologue. This then feeds into review and feedback of what you've drafted following the planning, in what rapidly comes to feel like an organic process even if it might initially feel stilted and strange. The contribution this makes to your working life isn't revolutionary, nor should you expect it to be. It's one of many simple ways in which GenAI makes it possible to insert supportive interlocution into processes that were formally isolated monologues. It's like having an academic coach on hand to support you whenever you need their input. Not a replacement for colleagues, collaborators and mentors but a useful supplement to the support they can provide.

Analysing Communicative Dilemmas

I remember in the early stages of my PhD when I would frequently find myself unsure about how to reply to someone. It might be there was something in the email I didn't understand or I was unclear about what was expected of me in a particular situation. It is startling to remember how much mental energy could be consumed by a single email. In contrast, I now dash off scores of one-line responses on a daily basis, often from my phone while commuting, rarely stopping to reflect on the interaction in any depth. I'm not alone in this tendency but the thoughtlessness which easily creeps in often worries me. It nonetheless feels like a necessary adaptation to communicative load: it's better to be brief and ensure a rapid response than be expansive and leave them waiting for days.

However, there are emails which I'm not sure how to respond to. Occasionally, this is a consequence of something outside the message itself, such as when a senior manager accidentally cc'd me on an email to other senior managers, and I couldn't work out whether I should acknowledge the mistake or ignore it.[4] It's more frequently because there's something in the message which I'm unsure how to interpret or respond to. It might be that a particular passage seems ambiguous or I can't shake the feeling there's an implicit judgement lurking behind a phrasing. In these cases, Claude can be a really helpful support, reflecting what I experience as its greater acuity with language and stronger privacy safeguards relative to ChatGPT. The process of describing the dilemma can help clarify matters, leading you to put words to a worry which can in turn help map the options available to you going forward. I've found it helpful to better understand the situation in this way, before mapping out potential actions and then discussing the relative merits of each of them.

In my experience, you can outline the dilemma in a way conducive to a response without sharing any confidential information. Simply explaining the issue in broad terms can itself be clarifying, helping you understand what is at stake in the choices available to you. The conversational agent builds on this clarity by illustrating the potential costs and benefits attached to the options you are considering, as well as expanding the scope of the perceived choices available to you. In most situations, it would be better to discuss with a friend or colleague but how often are they available to help you make sense of a minor situation at short notice? If it's a significant problem with potentially upsetting consequences for you, it might be best to wait until a human interlocutor is available. But the use case I'm describing here refers to those trivial, though energy-sapping, communicative dilemmas which inevitably occur in electronically mediated workplaces. Rather than getting stuck on an issue and working out what to do, Claude can immediately provide a sounding board through which you can work out the best path forward available to you.

Each of these dilemmas might have minor implications for your well-being but their accumulation over the course of a week can be a draining experience. Claude provides a way of immediately taking action and working out what to do so that you don't get stuck. If you were to measure the time/energy involved in being stuck, unsettled and preoccupied by an issue that has emerged, it might seem trivial when considered in isolation. But this is a broad category when considered in terms of the working week, months and year. In helping us maintain our poise through the many small challenges we encounter, conversational agents

---

[4] It was a relatively positive message in case you're curious. The deliberation would have been even more fraught if it had been a critical message.

can make a significant contribution to reducing the psychological and emotional costs of our work. They can't solve structural problems but they can make a small contribution to helping reduce the impact which these problems have on our well-being.

USING GENERATIVE AI TO COMMUNICATE WITH YOUR STUDENTS

Over the last decade, there has been a shift in the role of learning materials within education. As Weller (2020, loc 398) observes, the use of the web to disseminate information led to the growth of an 'infinite lecture hall model' in which large numbers of students could be taught cheaply because the content could be delivered to 10,000 students for largely the same costs as delivering it to one hundred students. The problem with such a view is, as he points out, the broadcast assumption underpinning it. It imagines learning in terms of the transmission of content from the teacher to the students, with teaching being the mechanism through which that transmission takes place. As Watters (2016, loc 118) points out, these assumptions can be seen as far back as the 1910 World's Fair, in which a print by the French artist Villemard as part of a series imagining life in the year 2000, shows a 'teacher stuffing textbooks—L'Histoire de France—into a machine, where the knowledge is ground up and delivered electronically into the heads of student'.

Unfortunately, GenAI easily lends itself to a preoccupation with content. The category itself is defined in terms of the automated production of content text, images, audio, video and websites. The immediate experience which many users have of GenAI is the ease with which content can be produced, suggesting possible economies in which one person could create content for many. Rather than the 'infinite lecture hall' we might instead confront the 'infinitely productive lecturer' in which a small number of individuals (perhaps even non-specialists) are expected to produce the learning materials for a range of subjects. The parallel in journalism would be the rise of the 'AI editor' who is expected to produce hundreds of articles per week.

The reason I'm invoking these slightly dystopian scenarios is because they help us understand how the choices we make about GenAI might have unintended consequences. There is a risk that using GenAI to save time when preparing for teaching could escalate into a teaching culture in which automated systems substitute for professional judgement. The tendency for institutions to ask staff to produce more in the same amount of time, reflecting financial pressures and the need to expand recruitment, encourages this destructive use of GenAI. The hard limits beyond which staff cannot be pushed without an immediate and measurable impact of standards might be more difficult to discern in the near future, as GenAI makes it possible to keep going in a seemingly effective way while risking problems which might not be immediately recognisable (e.g., hallucinations in information shared with students) and contributing to a professional culture which makes the restoration of standards difficult to achieve in the future. As I've argued throughout the book, we should tread carefully when it comes to the use of GenAI to increase productivity, even if doing so solves an obvious short-term problem.

In contrast, there are ways in which we can use GenAI to work with our students which are either neutral or positive when considered through this lens. There is an exciting opportunity to use these systems to ensure inclusive practice becomes properly mainstream, with GenAI expanding the range of potential interventions while also making them easier to incorporate into all aspects of existing practice. I talk later in this section about how we can use conversational agents to support more inclusive practices of communication, particularly with international students. But before that, we should consider how these systems can be used to support inclusion through practices such as captioning videos, producing text descriptions for visual content and providing transcripts of recorded lectures. In many cases, there are already technological means to support these interventions. What GenAI brings is a shift in the quality of the output, as well as the speed and ease with which it can be generated. These can now more easily be incorporated into working routines, creating an environment where we could realistically expect near-complete compliance with best practice in the not-too-distant future.

I have urged caution about solutions like Microsoft Copilot in recent chapters because of their reliance on pre-defined formats rather than expecting the user to make requests. However, there is a vast potential for these systems to ensure accessible practice is the norm, by ensuring that resources like transcripts and alt-text are offered as automatically generated for each document. For example, the alt-text automatically generated by Microsoft PowerPoint has got progressively better, even if it still needs manual review, particularly if there is a feature of the image you wish to emphasise that the automated system might not recognise. High-quality transcripts can be quickly produced within Microsoft Word by uploading an audio file under the 'dictation' item in the menu bar. In future, the user might define a particular template of styles which are relevant to their work or the student group they are working with, and then the system would include these as standard on everything they produce. The same functionality could easily be incorporated into learning management systems, building on the existing accessibility checks which are offered in a system like Blackboard. The intention would not be to make this an entirely automatic practice, as opposed to streamlining the process in order to make this a feature of existing workflows rather than an additional task which can too easily be neglected. There are likely to be rapid developments in the near future with enormous promise for accessibility if universities invest in training and supporting their staff.

There are also important opportunities to work more inclusively with international students. I explained in the first chapter how I originally came to this topic as the programme director for a large postgraduate programme with an almost entirely international student cohort. Our team was increasingly aware of the ubiquity of students using translation and paraphrasing software in order to prepare their work and in interactions with the teaching team. One of the most striking instances of this has been in students seemingly relying on conversational agents[5] to send formal emails, particularly when it comes to sensitive matters

---

[5] I say 'seeming' because in the absence of, say, a student accidentally including their prompt or the conversational agent's formatting in the email then it is difficult to be sure. But there is an overly expansive, stylistically generic way of writing a formal email which I take to be a red flag for GenAI, particularly when it's an obvious departure from the student's previous writing style.

such as contesting grades or making complaints. There is a risk of being overwhelmed by detail here, with the capacity to easily generate extensive and detailed arguments creating a sense of overload in staff who feel obliged to read and respond in an entirely human manner. It is easy to see how problematic norms and standards might become embedded in staff/ student interaction within higher education.

However, I can certainly see why a student writing in a second or third language might want to use a conversational agent when writing an email to their programme director about a sensitive issue. The problem is not so much any individual act of reliance on GenAI, but rather the consequences which accumulate if particular modes of reliance come to be normalised. Under certain circumstances, it's not only understandable but possibly desirable for students to assist their drafting of a formal message in this way. The problem is if that reliance becomes ubiquitous, leaving students unable to express themselves effectively without that support and changing the nature of the professional relationships with the sector. This is why recognising the practice and addressing it is so important. Unless we name it, making it the basis for a discussion, we cannot hope to exercise an influence over how the practice develops over time. It remains an individualised and privatised matter, confined to the sending and receiving of emails between individuals, rather than something we discuss in terms of what should at least in principle be a learning community.

I have used conversational agents to support group emails to our students. It is not a practice which has saved me much time, but it has certainly improved the quality of my communication, adapting it to the needs and preferences of the cohort. There are features of my writing which were ill-suited to communicating with international students, particularly in the early months of the single year they would spend with our programme. Even though I understood intellectually that the use of idiom was unhelpful in such communication, I was still prone to using it in my communication, particularly when I was in a rush. Furthermore, there were things which I didn't actually recognise as idioms because they were so familiar to me. There are expressions which I realise are too convoluted for me to reliably use when I'm communicating with students, particularly when I'm attempting to convey institutional information in a way that helps them understand the decisions they need to make and steps they need to take. These might be fine with colleagues but they are not suitable for students, particularly with the international cohort I am working with. Through the course of sharing my communication challenges with Claude, I have improved my own writing, deepening my awareness of features I was already vaguely aware of and identifying aspects which entirely escaped my notice. In this sense the conversational agent has supported my agency as a writer, effectively acting as a writing coach in these initial exchanges. I continue to draw on it as an editor, particularly when I have a message to write which needs to strike a precise tone.

For example, there was a lot of anxiety amongst our students after a miscommunication over expectations of progress with their dissertations. There were a number of emails I needed to send which sought to reassure students, which could only be achieved by identifying the misunderstanding and addressing it in an informative way which simultaneously helped alleviate their anxiety. These messages obviously require careful thought because dashing them off in a hurried fashion risks compounding the problem by amplifying the misunderstanding.

Talking to Claude about the message provided a focal point for this thought, ensuring that it didn't spill over into my internal *monologue* throughout the day by making it possible to sit down for a detailed (though time-limited) *dialogue* with the conversational agent. It provided practical suggestions to aid the writing of these messages, including commenting on drafts informed by an understanding of what I was trying to achieve. It's a practical example of how conversational agents can support you in saving time, communicating more effectively and helping ensure problems don't spill over into our personal lives because we are not sure what to do about them.

In this discussion, I have focused on how conversational agents can help negotiate some of the intercultural communication challenges which can be encountered when working with international students. There are intriguing possibilities for GenAI translation which operate at this interface by enabling materials to be produced in other languages. For example, services like VEED can translate videos into another language. The quality of the automatic dubbing is remarkable to the point of being eerie. It is not simply that it sounds like you are speaking another language, even the movements of your lips are synched with the new soundtrack. If you have never seen one of those videos, I recommend producing one with a teaching video in order to produce the full effect of recognising how odd this experience is. These services are relatively slow and expensive at present, at least compared to the immediacy with which content can be produced with other services. However, it is easy to imagine how they could be made more accessible with time, particularly if they offer organisational subscriptions or integration into other platforms. What if this translation were to be accessible to everyone working in your university? What if it was integrated into your learning management system? Under what circumstances would this be a beneficial offering to students previously expected to work in their second or third language? These are enormously complex questions which we will need to explore collectively in universities over the coming years.[6]

Even if international students do not figure as prominently in your working life as mine, the techniques I have shared in this section can still be used with students. Dialogues with conversational agents create an occasion to reflect on your own communication practice. They offer a way to slow down and get feedback, sharing examples with a view to improving how you communicate with students. They provide a forum in which you can identify the assumptions you are making about your students, their preferences and needs, in order to reflect on these to develop a more robust understanding of who you're teaching. This might sound time-consuming, but it's a practice which has the potential to save you time in future by ensuring your communication with students is smoother and more effective than it is at present. If using Claude as an ongoing coach in the way described here doesn't appeal to you, it could still be used to conduct occasional audits of your communication: describing your students, sharing examples of your messages to them[7] and asking for feedback on the

---

[6]In the system I work within, where a broken funding system creates a financial reliance on ever-expanding international recruitment, this will be particularly complex.

[7]Please note I'm suggesting you have the right to share *your* messages but should think carefully about the ethics of asking for feedback on the student responses.

suitability of your communication and how it could be improved. It is far from foolproof. Even if there is little practical pay-off, it can still be helpful to articulate and review these assumptions which otherwise lurk in the background of our communication. Furthermore, I suspect you might be surprised to discover what an insightful editor Claude can be if you take the time to describe your intentions and the context in sufficient detail.

THE ETIQUETTE OF GENERATIVE AI

While etiquette might seem like a strange term to invoke in this context, the situations we are confronting are at times simply a question of what is appropriate and inappropriate behaviour. Under what conditions might it be appropriate to send automated responses to emails? At what point does using ChatGPT to refine a communication become using ChatGPT to author a communication? Can we legitimately expect that people would pay the same care and attention to a communication written by an automated system that we hope they do to one they know is written by us? These are complex questions for the simple reason they reflect possibilities that were a matter of science fiction until relatively recently. They are questions that risk lurking beneath the surface until we reach a tipping point because until there is widespread awareness of the use of GenAI in professional communication, these will operate at the level of sneaking suspicions and vague intuitions rather than explicit questions about how we interact with each other within the university.

This is particularly true when these issues are filtered through hierarchies within the workplace. I remember the discomfort I felt as a research assistant years ago when my line manager would routinely ignore my emails, even those for which I needed a response, while expecting I would respond promptly and at length to their emails. There are legitimate reasons for this, as annoying as I found it at the time. I had one core responsibility while they had many, I received comparatively little email while they received torrents of it and their role was to strategically direct the project while mine was to enact the instructions. Certainly, it would have been helpful if they had more reliably recognised the points where I needed specific information and guidance. But there are nonetheless practical realities underlying the asymmetries we experience in communication with people who are senior to us in the workplace. But imagine how the use of GenAI could be filtered through these hierarchies and what that might mean for workplace culture. I have taken email as a lens through which to explore the potential implications of how we might relate to each other in a system saturated by GenAI. But there are many areas in which once speculative scenarios are plausibly on the horizon.

When is it acceptable to send a GenAI tool to a meeting on your behalf? If your role in the meeting was to listen to other people, identify key issues and be given action points, why not have the tool summarise that meeting on your behalf? If you intended to deliver a brief message and answer questions within a narrow remit, then could a conversational agent do that on your behalf? It is much easier to imagine a senior professor or university leader feeling entitled to do this than it is to imagine a junior lecturer or precarious researcher. What happens if online meetings come to be composed of automated systems sent to record an interaction between a small number of humans who are expected to be there? Could a conversational agent trained on your publications be made available for speaking engage-ments in lieu of your actual attendance? Would it be ok to make this agent available to your students for enquiries and restrict interactions with the 'real' you to special occasions? Could you open up your automated knowledge base to a potential collaborator in lieu of an initial meeting with them to explore possible overlaps in your work?

Over the coming years, we will encounter an increasing range of scenarios involving automation for which we lack a clear sense of what is acceptable and unacceptable behaviour. There will be varying intuitions about what is and is not acceptable in these situations, with the potential to make the debates about 'professional' online behaviour look straightforward in comparison. If we want to prepare for a university in which GenAI is ubiquitous, we must begin debating the appropriate norms immediately. I explore this challenge at greater length in the final chapter while recognising there is a limited contribution this book can make to the undertaking. What it can do is support you in identifying and reflecting on your own intuitions. If you are clear about your own views, it makes it easier to contribute to these debates about professional practice over the coming months and years.

TRANSLATING YOUR WORK BETWEEN FORMATS

My focus in this chapter has been communication in the sense of writing and sending messages. This is a focal point for stress and anxiety within higher education, as well as an obvious place where GenAI can make an immediate positive contribution. However, there are many other ways in which academics communicate, between themselves within the academy and with the external audiences we discussed in the next chapter. The extent to which we communicate by translating our work between formats might seem less intuitive at first glance. But if you prepare a lecture tied to a book you have written, write a blog post about a journal article or develop a briefing note that summarises your in-progress research you are engaged in a communicative act.

Each of these examples involves taking knowledge which is one form (the book, journal article and research notes) and translating it into another (the lecture, the blog post and the briefing note) that better meets the needs of the audience in question. In fact, once you start examining the tasks you're involved in, I suspect you'll find that a surprisingly large amount of your hours are taken up by what are essentially translation tasks of this sort. They don't usually involve developing new ideas, elaborating on existing knowledge or drawing new conclusions. But they do involve translating ideas, knowledge and conclusions you currently have lodged in one format and preparing to deliver them in another. This can occasionally be a thought-provoking task in which you gain new insights by translating your existing findings for new audiences. For example, I didn't teach for a long time while I was a postdoctoral researcher and I really missed how preparing a lecture or seminar can clarify your under-standing of your own work. But it can also be a slightly tedious undertaking in which you spend a few hours preparing slides without any additional inspiration entering into the process. The many occasions on which we are expected to explain what we *will* do (e.g., preparing abstracts) or report on what we *have* done (e.g., a post-project report for the funder) only add to this burden, subtracting from the time and energy we have available to us to do original work.

If we minimise the former, can we maximise the attention we have for the latter? This is exactly why we must ensure that using GenAI in such activities does not become a mindlessly automated task, as opposed to using conversational agents to handle the mundane elements so you can focus on creatively reviewing your ideas. This is not an argument for dispensing with human oversight but rather ensuring that oversight is directed towards creative engagement with the task at hand. By drawing on conversational agents as a research assistant, it becomes possible to focus on the intellectual aspects of the process where you can learn from what you are doing and generate new ideas. I would suggest the closest parallel here is working with professional editors or research assistants who can collaborate with you in preparing documents, without detracting from the originality of the work which is being undertaken. There is a need for clear guidelines and professional norms to govern the collaborations I am proposing here, but this is exactly the conversation which my book is trying to initiate.

An example could help illustrate the point. There's a conference I would like to attend which asks for a detailed submission form with multiple sections. I have the project proposal I initially wrote, as well as an overview written for potential stakeholders. If the aim was to complete the task as quickly as possible, I could ask Claude 'please use the attached document to write a short abstract for a conference where I will share provisional findings from my research'. The results would inevitably be uncertain because of the missing context. While the two documents provide detailed information about the project, information about the event I am submitting this form is lacking. In contrast, I could write a much more detailed prompt in which this tacit knowledge is made explicit.

> **MC:** Hi Claude, I need to submit a detailed form for a conference where I plan to present my research findings. I have attached my original project proposal and the expanded overview written for potential stakeholders. Can you please draft a concise abstract for the submission? In the abstract, include the main objectives of my project, the methods, and the provisional results I've achieved so far. It's important to consider that the abstract should be tailored to align with the conference's themes and objectives, which I have attached in an additional document. Let's ensure that the abstract conveys the significance of the research and how it contributes to the broader field, as understood by the context of this specific conference.

Figure 6.1 Using Claude to Help Draft a Conference Abstract.

It can seem more complex to write this 119-word prompt rather than the 27-word prompt initially suggested. Not only is it longer, but constructing it requires more thought. It was necessary for me to think about the timeline of our project, and the date of the conference and consider the range of ways in which the two might interact in practice. I needed to think about the conference in order to prompt Claude, including what we wanted to achieve by presenting at the conference. It would be easy to have produced a one-sentence prompt which merely instructed the system to 'write this abstract for me' and with sufficient contextual information provided through the documentation it would not have been a *terrible* output. But in writing an extended prompt I was forced to clarify aspects of what we were doing which had previously been implicit in my own mind. It is a work-in-progress presentation which is intended to stimulate discussion about the finding. Furthermore, at the point we were submitting the proposal we were uncertain about the timeline which has implications for what we promised to share in the session.

There was a degree of clarification achieved through the simple fact of explicating this in the prompt. It is useful to have explicitly noted these aspects of our proposal, even if they were already implicit in my mind. However, it was crucial to provide a context to influence how the attached documents would be drawn upon by the system. My experience is this guidance is even more important than usual when you are uploading material which you are asking a conversational agent to repurpose in some way. If you provide it with multiple pages of input, then your prompt needs to convey what it is you expect to be done with these. It is particularly important with multiple documents and/or multiple outputs that you clearly establish the relationship between them when making your request. Establishing the parameters in this way is exactly what the template-based systems we discussed in previous chapters tend to preclude. If you don't specify the task in a precise way, which explains context and expectations, the conversational agent will default to inferring this intention from the brief prompt you have provided. It might be inferred in this case that I wanted to simply summarise the documentation in ways which fit within these categories. It might have still produced something usable, but the amount of labour involved in writing over and correcting this partial result would vastly outweigh the time I spent writing this longer prompt.

In this case, I spent around fifteen minutes reviewing and rewriting elements of the output before I submitted it for the conference. Claude helped map out the information I eventually submitted but it was not responsible for the final text. It was a device which enabled me to stitch together our existing materials in a way which helped me focus on the creative questions which required intellectual scrutiny. It also helped clarify the practical aspects of the task at the earliest possible stage, leaving me with a useful note when it came to planning our presentation nearer the time. It saved time relative to how long it would have taken me to write the statements from scratch. It also saved mental energy. Over the last year, I have become increasingly aware of how much attention was taken up in my working life by tasks which essentially involved rewriting material from one format to present it in another. As we have discussed, this can provide an opportunity to review your work, deepening your understanding of it as you articulate it in a new format. However, it can also frequently be a time-consuming chore, in which reporting on things you have done substitutes for doing new and interesting things. In fact, the reporting often gets in the way of the reviewing, which is exactly the practical challenge I'm arguing conversational agents can address.

I would distinguish between *functional* documents which describe, summarise and present your work from *expressive* documents in which your work is being shared in a voice that is implicitly presented as your own. It could be argued this is a spectrum rather than a binary. However, I would suggest that unless the ideas you are expressing are contained *entirely* in something you have already written, then you are writing an expressive rather than a functional document. What I'm talking about here is using GenAI to 'remix' existing work, in a way conducive to maximising your creative contribution, rather than using it to create new work. I am comfortable with including GenAI text in the former while it feels extremely important to me that we establish the professional standard that it should *never* be included in the latter.[8]

Obviously, it will still be necessary to review and write over the text, even in these functional cases. It is also good practice to ask the system to preserve your style, tone and voice to the greatest possible extent when doing these translational tasks. It might surprise you when you start looking at how many examples you find of tasks which effectively involve translating work lodged into one format into another format:

- Designing lecture slides for students which build on a published paper
- Writing a conference abstract based on a work-in-progress paper
- Compiling a series of blog posts for a conference presentation
- Producing a podcast script based on a published paper
- Turning a set of long-form notes into a briefing paper for collaborators
- Summarising the chapters in an edited book for the introduction

These are just examples which I have either tried myself or discussed with other academics. They will always involve prior thought in order to specify the task, as well as subsequent review in order to ensure the quality of outputs. This quality control constraints how much time can saved through this translational work. However, it's still possible to save a great deal of time and energy over the course of the working week, while retaining the reflection on your own work which this activity entails. In fact, I argue the approach I advocate can actually support a *more* reflective approach than would be possible when time-intensive tasks pile up in ways which leave us rushing through our obligations, too often neglecting the creative opportunities which can be found throughout our working day.

---

[8]I would suggest that some presentations would fit in one category, others in the other category. For example, I'm comfortable including GenAI text that summarises my publications in slides I use with students or when I am repurposing work which I have presented on many previous occasions. Obviously, **I will review and write over the final text** but there is still a significant GenAI input. Whereas I would be reluctant to use GenAI text in slides which present a project for the first time, even if this has a basis in the text I have already published because this feels like it would be substituting the system's voice for my own. There is an element of personal decision about these issues but it's important that we find ways to discuss our contrasting intuitions, in order to enable professional norms to coalesce. In that sense, I am trying to model transparent practice in this book, even if I have a vague anxiety that some readers might be appalled that I'm submitting conference abstracts which were even partially supported by an automated system.

THE COMING DELUGE OF GENERATIVE AI SPAM

I received a curious email in the final stages of writing this book. It initially seemed like another message which referenced a journal article I had written, inviting me to pay a company money for them to help me promote this. These arrive on a regular basis alongside similar messages inviting me to conferences and to publish in predatory journals.[9] It only takes a moment to flag them as spam but they annoy me in their cumulative impact on my attention. Even if each one only takes a few seconds, they are a collective distraction which I would rather avoid. What made this email so striking was that it included a list of questions about my (open-access) articles. These were not trivial questions. They raised relevant issues which seemingly reflect an understanding of the analysis contained in this paper. If I hadn't been immersed in writing a book about GenAI, I might have inferred that someone had actually read the paper in order to prepare them, implausible as that seemed for what was otherwise a clearly templated message.

Only week a before this came a more sinister email. It accused me of violating copyright through an image I had used in a blog post a number of years ago. It insisted that legal action was imminent unless I included a link alongside the image.[10] The email purported to come from a Boston-based law firm which had a site that looked impressive at first glance. It was only when I looked further that I could see the site was filled with patently GenAI-produced content including images of the firm's staff. There was no evidence of the firm's existence beyond the site, which was implausible for a company that claimed to have been operating for years. I then checked the two domain names cited which had both been registered in the last few months and were registered in Iceland rather than the United States.

The profile photos on the website were eerily similar, suggesting the use of GenAI to generate them en masse.[11] The associated blurbs were unconvincing, using phrases like 'corporate expert' as if these had professional meaning and being supplemented with vague and sometimes meaningless descriptions. It rapidly became clear to me there was no risk of getting sued by what was likely an individual with a laptop trying to manipulate bloggers into including a link to his client on their websites.

The ease with which someone could generate a website which, at least at first glance, looked professional was arresting. For a lecture on digital literacy, I tried to put together my own

---

[9]If you don't receive messages like this then check your spam folder! My employer's mail service is surprisingly bad at filtering these messages and I'm jealous if yours is more adept at keeping them out of your inbox.

[10]This was a particularly pernicious form of black hat search engine optimisation (SEO), i.e., using unethical and/or illegal tactics to increase the prominence of a website in search results. If a fraction of the people who received these (mass) emails added the link which was demanded, it could significantly increase the ranking of the site.

[11]One telltale sign is whether the orientation of the photos is consistently left, centre or right without the variation which characterises real photography, even if done by a professional under controlled conditions. These are the options offered by a popular GenAI face generation service. Once you've seen what these parameters look like in practice, it is much easier to spot them.

parallel fake law firm website and it was startling what I could produce in the space of ten minutes. In fact, it was striking in retrospect how amateurish the fake website I was sent was, leaving me with the sense I could generate a much more effective one myself if I tried. In other words, early attempts to use GenAI to mislead and manipulate only give us a vague sense of how insidious the practices could be in the future, particularly if these are taken up in more organised and professional ways. This was a trivial attempt to manipulate people at scale in order to improve the online visibility of corporate clients. What's more worrying is how the same kind of intervention might be used for less mundane purposes. I'm completing this book at the start of a vast year of elections around the world, with a radical expansion in misinformation capabilities having emerged at what could be the worst possible moment. The perception of weaknesses within the digital public sphere could have vastly increased by the end of this year, particularly if we see GenAI-produced misinformation (real or alleged) playing a role in political violence.

MC: I am writing a guidebook for academics about using generative AI in responsible and professional ways. I want to indicate the political significance of GenAI capabilities having advanced to the extent they have during a year (2024) with an enormous number of elections taking place around the world. What are the three issues which someone unfamiliar with this topic should consider in order to understand the social and political implications of GenAI? Please write a paragraph which briefly summarises these issues for this reader.

ChatGPT: In 2024, a year marked by an unprecedented number of elections worldwide, the advanced capabilities of Generative Artificial Intelligence (GenAI) bear significant social and political implications that merit careful consideration. First, *information integrity* emerges as a critical issue, where the ability of GenAI to produce highly realistic misinformation could undermine the democratic process, sway public opinion, and manipulate election outcomes. The ease with which GenAI can generate convincing fake news, deepfakes, or tailored propaganda poses challenges to discerning truth from fabrication, necessitating robust verification mechanisms and media literacy. Second, *privacy and surveillance* concerns are amplified as GenAI technologies can be utilized for sophisticated data analysis and profiling, potentially leading to invasive tracking of individuals' behaviors and preferences for political targeting and manipulation, raising ethical questions about consent and personal freedom. Lastly, *the digital divide and accessibility* issue highlights how disparities in access to GenAI technologies could exacerbate existing inequalities.

Figure 6.2 The Social and Political Implications of GenAI Being Used in Strategic Communication. *Source:* ChatGPT.

The proximity of the two emails left me preoccupied by the deluge of GenAI spam likely to be on the horizon, as well as the broader ramifications beyond the sector we work within. There's already a well-developed shadow economy within international higher education taking the imperative to publish, discretionary budgets and pervasive anxiety as its foundation. Consider predatory academic journals which demand significant article-processing charges for guaranteed publications, scholarly publishers whose lack of editorial controls slide into vanity publishing and transdisciplinary conferences which exchange a guaranteed speaking slot in return for payment. The more obvious examples of this can be spotted by many academics, but there's a more difficult grey area in which ambiguous messages seem to operate on the borderline between illegitimate and predatory. Given my interest in digital engagement, I've been particularly attuned to communication firms which offer to support academics in promoting their work for a fee. The output can often be of reasonable quality, such as a short profile featuring your research. But the promise of promotion is rarely fulfilled, with these profiles published on a general website with little sign of a dissemination strategy. It is easy to imagine how such firms might scale up their operations using GenAI. Not only would lowering costs have no inherent positive impact on the circulation of the output,[12] but it might also even detract from it by leading to a glut of mediocre academic profiles without any obvious audience for them.

What I'm flagging here concerns the *communications environment* rather than your own communications practice. But this is the environment we will soon be working within. One in which there will be continual waves of GenAI spam and fraud, which automated defences might temporarily catch up with but never overcome in a sustained way. My intuition is the human quality of communication matters more than ever under these conditions: the time we take to reflect on what someone is saying and what we say to them in turn. The expressions of personality, however small or trivial, which the messages we send are inevitably marked by. The capacity for someone else's need to break us out of our working routines reflects the way in which our colleagues matter to us. I've suggested we need to be realistic about the time and space which many of us have for these human elements, amidst a background of escalating communication and intensifying workloads. We shouldn't romanticise the messy, rushed and sometimes passive-aggressive reality of pre-GenAI professional communication. But recognising those limitations should not lead us to dispense with the human in pursuit of an automated solution which might cause more problems than it solves. There are strategies I've suggested in this chapter for automating *elements* of our communication in order to improve the outcomes within our working lives. But we should be cautious as we implement them, watching how they feel and how our teams change as a result. These strategies could at their best free up time and energy to attend more to the communications which really matter. But they also carry the potential of setting into motion a cycle of automation which would further strip what is human within an often alien (and alienating) university system.

---

[12]The limited way in which these services actually promote the work they produce doesn't suggest there must be an intention to mislead academics. It's simply hard to achieve visibility for academic work, particularly without a bespoke strategy which necessitates domain expertise.

7
ENGAGEMENT

This chapter will:

- Consider how recent changes to social media platforms create challenges for academics, particularly with regard to the time commitment involved in engagement.
- Identify practical strategies through which Generative Artificial Intelligence (GenAI) can be used to support digital engagement, with a focus on maintaining the integrity of academic voice.
- Discuss how the public role of academics has changed in recent years, as well as the significance of academic participation in the public sphere given the social and political challenges likely to be posed by GenAI.

I remember sitting in a meeting in 2010 where the prospect of an organisation launching a blog was discussed. 'Why would we want a blog?' sneered a senior academic with incredulity. The same year the BBC's senior political journalist Andrew Marr opined that 'A lot of bloggers seem to be socially inadequate, pimpled, slightly seedy, bald, cauliflower-nosed young men sitting in their mother's basements and ranting' (Plunkett, 2010). It was a febrile time for digital media's place within society, with overblown rhetoric of 'Twitter revolutions' co-existing with unthinking disdain for the possibility that social media and blogging could ever have a significant role within institutions. It was intruding from outside the academy and divided opinion, often in hyperbolic ways that look silly in retrospect. As the educational technologist Martin Weller (2020, loc 1493) admits, 'everyone (including myself) is now rather embarrassed about the enthusiasm they felt for Web 2.0 at the time' though stresses how 'it contained within it some significant challenges and opportunities for higher education'. At the time I was drawn into supporting the use of social media within higher education, reflecting the enthusiasm I shared with Martin as well as the practical requirement of finding a way to support a part-time PhD, leading to two editions of *Social Media for Academics* (Carrigan, 2016, 2019) which I wrote alongside extensive training and consultancy work.

I witnessed a remarkable transition in which social media went from being something which many academics were disinterested in at best, or suspicious of at worst, to a routine expectation within academic life. Social media has become synonymous with external engagement, such that online visibility stands as a proxy for the capacity and willingness to make a wider impact with your research (Carrigan & Jordan, 2021). There are real and meaningful ways in which social media can be used to build relationships with and influence, the practice of groups outside the academy. But the dominant tendency is to see it as a black box through which impact can be achieved, imagining the accumulation of followers is a sufficient condition for influencing wider society. In reality, social media works most effectively when combined with other forms of engagement, using it as a means to build relationships with external stakeholders which extend beyond the digital (Carrigan & Fatsis, 2021).

The problem with the pursuit of online visibility as if it were an inherent good is the limitless time and energy which can be channelled towards this goal. While a small minority of scholars might willingly become influencers in Hund's (2023) sense, with an online identity which reflects the specific incentives of their sector, this is not desirable for many. Unless we are willing to embrace the role of the influencer, we are faced with the challenge of combining digital engagement with other demands of teaching, research and administration, alongside having a life outside work which isn't constantly interrupted by the impulse to check social media.[1] There are real opportunities to make a difference in wider society but

---

[1]Mark (2023, loc 1637) found that 41% of research participants checked their email without notification, rather than waiting for an external signal, i.e., they self-interrupted rather than responding to an external interruption. I'm unaware of comparable research for social media but my experience of talking to academics about their use of social media for 15 years suggests this figure could possibly be much higher for social platforms.

realising them requires satisfying and sustainable practice. This means finding ways to ensure your visibility, make yourself discoverable and convey the core of your work in a manner well suited to the intended audience. It also means doing this in a way which doesn't take over your working life.

Shifts within the social media landscape make this harder than ever to achieve (Carrigan & Jordan, 2021). Elon Musk's controversial takeover of Twitter (now X) has led users to scatter across a range of platforms: LinkedIn, Mastodon, Bluesky and Threads being the most prominent examples. Even when people retain their Twitter account, they often engage much less than they used to, reflecting a widespread experience of the quality of the service degrading over time. Engagement split across multiple platforms inevitably takes longer, particularly if you are judicious about adjusting to different norms and audience expectations. The introduction of subscription charges for Twitter has effectively penalised non-subscribers by prioritising the posts of paying customers in feeds and replies.[2] This fragmentation of text-based platforms comes after the continual growth of image and video-based social media platforms (YouTube,[3] Instagram and TikTok) which are more difficult for academics to use effectively. There are many cases of academics using these platforms successfully but my experience has been that the learning curve is much higher than for more text-based media.

This landscape has the potential to be immensely time-consuming, with academics caught between the expectations of their employers and their own motivation to make a difference with their research. In this chapter, I consider how GenAI can be used to support digital engagement in order to reduce administrative load and increase the effectiveness of your activity. It is not a comprehensive guide to social media, such as Carrigan (2019), instead, I outline different areas where GenAI can support what you are doing. Even if there is a time-saving focus here which I avoid in other chapters, I urge you to approach these activities with the reflective orientation you would for other uses of GenAI. There are easy wins but there remains the risk that careless use will lead to problematic or unreliable content that has the potential to cause harm, to yourself and to others. In the final section, I consider how the role of the academic might change as the digital public sphere comes to be flooded with GenAI-generated content. The values which inform scholarship will become increasingly important in this context, which is why it's so crucial that we don't let a careless embrace of GenAI undermine them.

---

[2] If you intend to use Twitter in a serious and strategic way for engagement, it's probably necessary to pay the subscription charge even if you find it as distasteful as I do. It will simply be too hard to cut through in the current environment, unless you have an existing platform.

[3] Obviously, YouTube is not a new platform but its global user base has grown from 608.64 million in 2020 to 933.39 million in 2024. The pandemic was very good for immersive video-based platforms and the evidence suggests this growth hasn't receded with the return of pre-pandemic life.

USING GENERATIVE AI TO SUPPORT ENGAGEMENT WITH WIDER AUDIENCES

In the early 2010s, I worked on a public engagement project with the photographer Holly Falconer, integrating photograph and biographical portraits of members of the asexual community. This built on my sociological research on asexuality with the intention of conveying a sense of what it is like to be asexual, something which allosexual (non-asexual people) often struggle with even when they are keen to understand. There was a popular website which expressed an interest in the project and invited me to submit an article alongside Holly's photography. Having conducted a large project on asexual experience, leading to a series of journal articles, I brought a lot of academic work into the project which raised the obvious question of how to translate that for a wider audience. Media interviews I had done about my research meant I had some practice in talking about it to a non-academic audience. However, a good interviewer will be adept at getting academics to speak in more everyday language, using the framing of their questions to invite suitable responses from their audience. It was an issue I had spent time reflecting on as someone who trained academics to use social media (in part for public engagement); also in part prompted by having rambled at length about 'ontological emergence' in the first media interview I ever did. I understood the problem, I felt, even if I knew it would take time and care in order to act on it properly.

I scrupulously expunged any academic language from the piece, reminded myself not to assume prior knowledge on the part of the reader and tried to ensure I foregrounded the experience of the participants rather than my analysis. After a great deal of work for a relatively short piece, I was proud of what I achieved. I sent my piece off to the editor, curious to see if I had cracked the art of writing an engaging article for a wider audience. My heart sank when every single sentence in my returned document had been rewritten. The problem was not technical terminology or the assumptions I was making as much as the syntax of the writing. I had been unaware of how prone I was to using an endless sequence of subclauses, nesting statements inside each other in a manner which serves no real purpose, as well as just seeming strange to the non-academic reader; made worse by the fact I had convinced myself that semicolons somehow made writing more accessible.[4] With hindsight, the editor was not being negative about the article itself, but it stuck in my mind as an example of how I could be oblivious to a structural feature of my writing. I had correctly identified the elements which limited the accessibility to a non-academic audience but it had never occurred to me that how I pieced together sentences and structured paragraphs could itself be a problem.

I have not written much for wider audiences since then, mostly because my subsequent research has not attracted non-academic interest in the same way. But I came away from working with that editor with a clearer understanding of how I could write better in contextually appropriate ways. There have been other occasions in which editors have improved my writing in lasting ways by pointing out aspects previously opaque to me. These editorial experiences not only improve individual pieces but also can lead to ongoing improvements in how you write for particular

---

[4]Time has not cured me of this tendency.

audiences. My suggestion is that conversational agents can provide continual support in a manner analogous to working with a skilled and experienced editor. Even if the quality of the editing will not match that of a person it can come surprisingly close, with its limitations made up for by the ongoing interaction. The political economy of publishing means that the imperatives of the publisher drive access to editorial feedback, whether this is expert readers at the proposal stage or copyeditors at the production stage. In contrast, using a conversational agent can provide access to editorial support driven by your own writing needs.

This has the potential to make a huge contribution to writing for wider audiences, particularly given how academics are trained to write for specialised intellectual communities. As Billig (2013, p. 11) rather acidly put it, our 'bad writing ... has not been produced by too little education' because 'you have to study long and hard to write this badly'. His point can be overstated and technical jargon facetiously construed as a form of elitist obfuscation. This does not seem to be Billig's view, even if I do think his claims are exaggerated at points. However, it is one frequently suggested in the grey literature of blogs and podcasts on writing for wider audiences. It is unhelpful in its refusal to recognise how specialised terminology serves a purpose in simplifying and accelerating conversations between specialists. It is the mirror image of the academic conceit that simple writing is necessarily simplistic and thus one cannot engage in it without doing a violence to the sophistication of your research. The semantic populism which denies any legitimate role for specialised terminology suggests that the only reason for writing not to be simple is elitism. Both positions are extraordinarily counterproductive in helping academics engage in the translational work necessary to move from writing for a specialised audience to a more generalised audience.

It is the audience which matters rather than some imagined moral qualities of simple or complex modes of writing. Who are you writing for? What will they expect from your writing? How do you want to influence them? What's the best way to do this given what you know about them? The degree to which academics are professionally socialised into a particular genre of writing[5] can make it difficult to ask these questions. As an editor of various academic blogs, it was always obvious if someone was writing their first blog post because they approached it like a short journal article. It was fascinating to see the different speeds at which academics learned the practice of this new genre. Some grasped it after their first round of feedback, for others there was a continual process of editing these micro-articles into something better suited to a blog post. It left me with a sense that reflexivity about academic writing is often lacking. This is unsurprising when you consider how strongly we receive the message that the only form of writing that matters is for peer-reviewed journals and perhaps monographs.[6]

---

[5]See Agger (2000) for a compelling account of scholarly writing as a particular sort of literary genre, even if it does vary across fields and disciplines.

[6]I still struggle with this 13 years after I wrote my first paper. I have a blogging voice which manifests itself when I write books like this one. It's overly florid at points and prone to meandering but for the most part it's conversational, clear and engaging. In contrast when I write a journal article, I immediately revert to a stilted pastiche of my PhD supervisor's voice mixed with unconscious tributes to a few other academics I admire.

How would we develop a multifaceted voice under these circumstances? How could we introduce an awareness of a range of audiences into our writing, if we're told that only one matters? What if we're told that we only matter to that narrowly professional audience if we write to them in the correct voice? As Sword (2017, loc 162) observes 'Successful writers seldom work entirely in isolation; even in traditionally "sole author" disciplines, they typically rely on other people – colleagues, friends, family, editors, reviewers, audiences, students – to provide them with support and feedback'. It might be that you have a network like this which can feedback on your formal academic writing, but do you have one willing and able to support you with your public writing[7]? This is much rarer, at least in part because writing well for external audiences is still a minority pursuit amongst academics. In the absence of support, it is difficult to sustain an approach to public writing which embodies the sense of 'an artisanal activity that requires ongoing learning, development and skill' that Sword (2017, loc 166) argues successful academic writers bring to their craft.

This is what conversational agents can provide. They might not match the insight of an experienced editor looking closely at your work. But they are continually available in a way that such a figure simply won't be, no matter how supportive. It may surprise you how incisive they can be with their editing if you establish expectations with them in an effective way. This discussion focuses on writing blog posts or op-eds but the same approach can be taken with shorter-form content. In fact, trends on LinkedIn and Twitter are moving towards longer-form posts which are a good fit for academics demonstrating expertise.[8] What matters is clarity in the prompts you use.

> **MC:** I'm a sociologist who does research on how generative AI is likely to lead to change in education systems. I'm writing an article for secondary school teachers in the UK which presents some of the key issues from a sociological perspective. I'm not sure of the right balance to strike with the level of detail and accessibility. I'm not sure what will be the most salient issues from their point of view. Please suggest some questions which can help me clarify my approach to this task.
>
> **ChatGPT:** Crafting an article for secondary school teachers in the UK about the impacts of generative AI on education systems requires a nuanced approach, balancing depth of analysis with accessibility. To clarify your approach and ensure that the content is relevant and engaging for your audience, consider exploring the following questions:

Figure 7.1 Planning an Engagement Strategy Which Matches the Needs of Stakeholders
Source: ChatGPT.

---

[7]The manner in which academic blog editors, whether academics or communications professionals, perform this role is the strongest argument for recognising and supporting their labour. They are repositories of expertise about how to write for public audiences, informed by accumulated knowledge about the audience for their own blog.

[8]Though the attentional burden of these short-form platforms being increasingly filled with long(er)-form content creates a pressure to ensure these texts are attention grabbing and well written.

Even if you're unclear at this stage about the right approach to take, you should convey this fact in your interaction with the conversational agent. What exactly are you unsure about? I've found it helpful to share a short description along with a request for questions which can clarify my approach. ChatGPT and Claude can both support you in undertaking a rough and ready stakeholder analysis to help you plan a particular intervention or a broader project. If you have access to a research communications practitioner they could likely provide you with greater insights in a more systematic way. But most of us don't have access to this expertise. The conversational agent supplements rather than replaces human expertise, with their accessibility outweighing the lack of relative depth.

While the conversational agent can help you think through the issues, I'd caution against relying on them to provide answers. This is another example of co-production in which the interaction provides a framework to clarify your own thinking and reach your own answers. It's a way of scaffolding a planning process which might otherwise have been rushed, overly reliant on unexamined intuitions or not undertaken at all.

I asked ChatGPT to identify elements from the opening section of this book which might usefully figure in an article written for a wider audience. I asked it to provide explanations as to why these elements could be interesting to non-specialists. It offered a list of nine points from a three thousand-word section with explanations ranging from 'an attention-grabber for the audience' to 'a relatable personal experience' and 'provoking curiosity about what's next in the world of AI'. It is a typical example of how GenAI can rearrange your ideas to support your own more thorough and sophisticated reordering. The limitation here is that 'non-specialised audience' is a hopelessly broad category. Any public engagement practitioner would tell an academic to think more deeply about who they were trying to connect with and why. I revised the prompt to ask for suggestions of topics to include for a piece aimed at 'university administrators with an interest in the implications of generative AI for higher education, including those with direct responsibility for issues related to AI in areas such as assessment and those without such responsibilities but with a general concern for how it will impact the sector'. I could then explore the assumptions made in its response by asking for clarification about the areas of responsibility of university administrators and how they match up with the potential impacts of GenAI.

The process of talking to ChatGPT about what I was trying to do helped clarify my understanding of my ambition, rather than it simply being a one-off task outsourced to an automated process. This clarification should be a reflexive dialogue in which you confront your own assumptions against those the conversations agent is making, revising one or both in the process. For example, there was initially a bias towards the American system in the areas of responsibility listed, such as 'Academic Affairs', which prompted me to specify my essay was intended for a UK administrative audience. This led to a dialogue about the specific issues which the latter system faced with regards to GenAI, with ChatGPT insightfully raising points like Brexit given 'generative AI potentially changing the landscape of distance learning and cross-border collaboration' which had not occurred to me previously. This is an example of how mutual learning takes place in a dialogue which is simultaneously a matter of reviewing and correcting the outputs of an automated system which will always have epistemic limitations, as discussed in Chapter 2. This reflective approach means never taking the GenAI outputs as a given but using critical review to reflect on your own assumptions, creating opportunities for learning that the conversational agent can then in turn support.

This works best in a real-world setting. It is hard to get a feel for these dynamics in the abstract. The area I have found most useful is re-examining existing material in order to plan engagements with non-academic audiences. To give an example, I've been blogging regularly over the last year for outlets like the LSE Impact Blog about the impact of Elon Musk's takeover of Twitter on the use of social media by academics. This topic is primarily orientated towards those within higher education but I was surprised to receive media requests from journalists who wanted to link up the implications to wider societal issues. I thought those interviews went well, but nothing came of them, and it occurred to me afterwards that I was still operating with reference points geared towards the internal politics of higher education and the interests and experience of academics.

When I next prepared for an interview like this, I took some of the writing I have published on this issue and explained to ChatGPT that I was trying to identify the most salient features for someone examining higher education from outside the sector. I took a recent blog post suggesting that there was a significant shift in the business model of social media underway to which academics needed to adapt. It was a piece that was distributed quite widely and seemed to strike a chord, arguing that higher education was locked into an outdated model of social media training. I asked ChatGPT to examine the piece and suggest which elements of the argument were likely to be most interesting to someone whose primary focus was on how academics engage with society, politics and the economy through digital means. I also asked it to prepare me an elevator pitch summarising my argument without technical jargon, in a succinct and powerful way likely to attract the interest of someone working outside the sector. It immediately sidelined the focus on social media training which was at the forefront of my thinking, instead prioritising the shift in the platform economy and the societal questions that it raised:

> Twitter's shift to a paid visibility model under Elon Musk's ownership is altering the way academics engage with the public. The narrowing of organic reach and prioritisation of paid content creates a chasm, possibly diminishing the voices of those who can't or won't subscribe. Amid the socio-economic changes impacting the tech landscape, this raises important questions about access to knowledge, diversity of voices, and the role of academics in public discourse.

It then provided me with a list of talking points representing topics I could cover in the interview. It was interesting how training, guidance and career considerations figured prominently but were framed far more in terms of wider societal implications than I had tended to, and were lower down the list away from the headline points. In this sense, the conversational agent supported a reframing of my arguments for a wider audience, as well as helping me prepare for the interview based on my past work. I used a short blog post here but there is no reason such an exercise could not be informed by a much wider corpus of your past work, including media engagement which you judge as having gone well.

The possibility of making a difference in wider society has been a motivation for many of us to undertake our research in the first place. Even though the 'third mission' of the university is more prominent than was once the case, often this is not matched by the time, support or training necessary to undertake this work effectively. While GenAI cannot solve this problem it can act as a versatile and ever-present assistant in a range of ways. It is even more crucial to critically review the output and avoid overreliance on these systems, given the role of academics as experts when relating to wider society. But it can be a constructive editor and interlocutor.

TRANSLATING AND REPURPOSING ENGAGEMENT MATERIALS

Using social media as an academic fundamentally involves *making* things for which we have rarely been formally trained. Blog posts, tweets, podcasts or videos (digital scholarship) are substantially different forms of production from the articles, chapters and books (legacy scholarship) which are the focus of professional socialisation. Burdick et al. (2012, p. 10) observe how this often entails 'what Roman rhetoricians called the *multum in Parvo* - the aphorism, the short form, that which distils the long and the large into compact form' reflecting the 'varied, extensible and multiplicative' character of digital media. This creates an environment in which 'argumentation must be able to expand and contract as a function of shifting constraints and technological affordances' (Burdick et al., 2012).

These practices are now mainstream, in part because academic journals, scholarly publishers and universities have encouraged their uptake with a view to increasing the visibility, salience and impact of academic work. For example, producing a blog post which summarises the findings and links to a research article. The blog will circulate more widely than the paper, assuming it is placed on an existing blog with a relevant audience, disseminating the findings while giving interested parties an opportunity to explore the original source. It has become common for journals to ask authors to produce video abstracts for their articles. The range of things we are expected to make has grown even more significantly since the pandemic. The emergency remote teaching required by the crisis was the first experience many academics had with producing short-form video content and digital materials (Nordmann et al., 2020). The period of complete reliance upon digital media for academic interaction suggests a parallel emergency digital scholarship in which many academics were forced to engage with digital media to a greater depth than before. These experiences are sticky with many academics more ready to consider new forms of engagement than prior to these experiences.

These examples illustrate the 'expansion and contraction' involved in digital scholarship, which can be supported by GenAI. If used effectively it can be a powerful assistant in working with material on a *rhetorical* level to smooth a time-consuming process of transitioning between formats, genres and audiences. In this section, I explore how it can be used more directly in *making* materials for purposes of engagement. There is inevitably a degree of overlap here as this involves similar questions of translation and repurposing. However, aspects of the engagement process can be automated thoughtfully and carefully.

Automation is already widespread in digital engagement within higher education. Software like HootSuite or Buffer is widely used to schedule social media posts in advance. This makes it possible to have a regular stream of posts without the distraction of having to post each one directly. When personal academic blogs were more common many academic bloggers automatically shared new posts on Twitter and other platforms. It was a useful and simple process to set up and a minor time saver.

It can feel strange to automate personal communication in this way. Even when I used social media scheduling software regularly, it only felt natural for project-based accounts. When used on my personal Twitter feed it just felt weird. These were public statements tied to my name and image which reflected what I *thought* people would be interested in, rather than what I *wanted* to say. This disconnect made me profoundly uncomfortable. These were tweets I was writing but in a way that was instrumental rather than expressive, intended to bring about an effect rather than put something into the world. While I have yet to find a research study which explores this, I have learned anecdotally that other people have similar experiences. However, if you are doing engagement for organised undertakings like research groups, networks, projects or journals this scheduling can be enormously helpful. It makes it possible to keep a continued stream of content across platforms, without logging in many times each day. Instead, engagement becomes a slower process of producing and scheduling content on what could be a weekly basis, coupled with light touch monitoring to watch for replies and any issues which have emerged from them.

Even if this practice has been marginal amongst academics it is mainstream amongst digital communications practitioners. As digital engagement is a numbers game, requiring a certain volume of posting in order to be 'heard above the din' (Beer, 2014) which means that automation of at least part of the process is a necessity. The fragmentation of social media into multiple platforms with their own forms and expectations means that academics who want to pursue digital engagement in a serious and strategic way will need to professionalise in order to make it manageable. Fortunately, GenAI provides a series of capabilities which can help enormously, particularly when combined with the effective use of scheduling software.

Generating Engagement Materials From Your Published Work

Increasing engagement with your publications is a major motivation for academics using social media. Their concern might be other academics in their field, the status of their work within the wider discipline or stakeholders beyond the academy. But the challenge of making published research *visible to* and *engaging for* audiences is one which academics increasingly feel the need to take on themselves, rather than assuming that simply being published will ensure it can be found by the relevant audiences. The word publish has its root in the Latin *publicus*, meaning 'of the people', with the implication that publishing involves bringing something *to the people*. This is what journals once did with limited audiences, in contrast to the promise of social media to bring our work to much wider audiences. Social media has changed the *range of audiences* we can (potentially) bring our work to and the *range of channels* available. Doing this effectively means being clear about who our audiences are, where we can find them and what constraints this imposes on how we communicate with them. Possible scenarios here include:

A. Engaging with one audience on one platform
B. Engaging with one audience across multiple platforms
C. Engaging with multiple audiences on one platform
D. Engaging with multiple audiences across multiple platforms

The appeal of pre-Musk Twitter for academics was the presence of multiple relevant audiences on a single platform. Other academics were there too, creating the risk that academics would imagine themselves to be undertaking public engagement when they were largely talking amongst themselves. But there were also policymakers, journalists, creatives, activists and many other groups who academics routinely try and build external relationships with. The co-existence of these groups in a fragmented yet singular space could create problems, as a result of what internet scholars call 'context collapse': the tendency for messages which make sense in one context (e.g., amongst academics) to circulate beyond that context, with potentially unpredictable results for how they are interpreted by others. But it also created opportunities to build connections in unpredictable and organic ways, as well as cementing existing connections through the ambient knowledge which comes from following and being followed on social media.

Unfortunately, the changes at Twitter now mean that (A) and (C) are much less viable strategies than they once were. Even if you're engaging with a single audience they are likely to be split across multiple platforms. If you are engaging with multiple audiences it becomes even more complex: policymakers, practitioners, journalists, activists and artists might now be found across a whole range of platforms. Before we turn towards how GenAI can save time in generating engagement materials and coordinating engagement, we need to be clear about how you will engage. Developing a strategy is important to ensure that you use time prudently. Without this, it is easy to spend time on efforts which don't advance your goals, or which aren't adequately addressed to the particular audiences you are seeking to engage with. There are four clusters of questions which I've worked through when advising academics about planning their digital engagement: **who, what, why and how**.

- Who are your potential followers and readers? What do you know about them? How can you learn more? What can you learn *from* them? Who are the key gatekeepers?
- What social media platforms do those people use online? What interactions and connections are possible on those platforms? Can you use a similar approach to reach all of those followers? Or do you need targeted appeals?

- Why will they be interested in connecting with you? What can you help them understand? What problems can you help them solve? Would participating in your project matter, or be useful, to them?
- How much familiarity do you have with various platforms? How much time do you have each week for social media? What existing connections do you have to the people you hope to reach? What existing activity or content can you repurpose to connect with more followers?

These were originally published in Carrigan (2018), Carrigan (2019, ch 5) and Carrigan (2022), which offer a more detailed exploration of these issues. I've often found that academics feel uncomfortable trying to answer them. Perhaps because it makes them feel like marketing professionals in a way contrary to their self-conception. It feels slightly icky to be this strategic about communications. However, I suspect the more significant reason is that we only have vague intuitions about this activity, existing at a slightly contentious intersection between the ambition to 'make a difference' with our research and the institutional pressure to 'demonstrate impact'. This is why workshop discussion can be extremely helpful. It provides a forum in which academics can tease out intuitions, discuss and refine them. Using a conversational agent to explore these issues is not a replacement for these workshops but it can be a useful supplement. For example, here's a prompt I shared with Claude to help me map out initial ideas for an upcoming collaborative project.

> **MC:** I'm an educational researcher working on a project exploring how controversial and contentious 'culture war' issues are taught within university classrooms. The intention of the project is for myself and my collaborator to support lecturers in negotiating associated challenges in confident and effective ways. This means that lecturers are our primary stakeholder group but the project is potentially relevant to other groups as well. The fact that individuals might already have 'stances' in relation to culture war issues complicates our engagement with these questions. Please help us undertake a stakeholder mapping for the project, with a view to better understanding how we can plan co-production activities with these stakeholders, as well as demonstrating the findings in a way which they will find useful and could meaningfully claim to make a positive impact on practice.

Figure 7.2 Using Claude to Map the Different Stakeholders Relevant for a Project

I then shared a refined version of the initial mapping with ChatGPT in order to produce a visual representation of the stakeholder mapping. This is a project in the earliest stages of planning but the immediacy with which I could conduct this analysis prepares us for more detailed work further down the line. It also provides useful textual and visual resources to inform our planning, as well as share with interesting colleagues. The fact we have the ambition of undertaking co-production means that we will conduct in-person workshops as the project progresses, including planning workshops which map out the contours of this face-to-face work. There is no reason this must be at the *start* of the project. It can be at any stage in the planning process to inform and refine what you are doing. Almost like a bespoke mini-workshop conducted at any time with a framing of your own choosing.

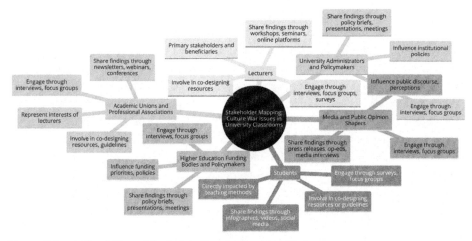

Figure 7.3   A Visual Map of the Stakeholders Involved in a Project

Translating Your Engagement Materials Between Formats

MC: I'm a sociologist studying how generative AI is used in higher education. I've attached a blog post I've written for a popular blog which is intended to reach a wide professional audience with a shared interest in higher education. I'm conscious that I'm writing as a sociologist for audiences who are not trained in my discipline and who will not share my intellectual starting points. Please offer actionable advice for making this post more accessible for a broad professional audience within higher education, without simplifying the argument.

Claude: Here are some suggestions to make your blog post more accessible to a broad professional audience in higher education:
Provide a clear and concise introduction that outlines the main topic and purpose of your post. This will help readers understand the context and relevance of the issue right from the start.

1. Break down complex ideas and jargon into simpler terms. While you don't want to oversimplify your argument, explaining key sociological concepts in plain language will make your post more understandable to non-experts. For example, you could briefly explain what you mean by terms like "path dependence" or "quantified academic world".

2. Use subheadings to divide your post into clear sections. This makes the structure of your argument more apparent and allows readers to easily navigate to the parts most relevant to their interests.

3. Illustrate your points with concrete examples that your audience can relate to. For instance, you could provide specific hypothetical scenarios of how generative AI might be used in different academic disciplines.

Figure 7.4   Using Claude for Advice on Making Blog Posts Accessible to a Wider Audience

We explored in the last chapter how GenAI can streamline the process of translating existing materials between formats. This could be a matter of drafting lecture slides based on a paper you have written, writing a conference abstract based on a research project that is in progress or summarising notes to support a conversation with collaborators. There are many things we do in higher education which involve taking ideas in one format and translating them into another. The same challenge is frequently encountered in engagement activity, with the added complication that external audiences will have different requirements. This is why being clear about your audience will always be important to engagement activity as you can specify the characteristics of the group you are engaging with in order to adapt your engagement materials accordingly. For example, I wrote a theoretical article about how digital platforms are leading to fundamental shifts in the socialisation process which I believe has significance for teachers. But a 9,000-word article written in terms of social ontology is unlikely to be of interest to practitioners. Furthermore, it is difficult to translate such an article once you have written it because your engagement with the subject matter is entirely abstract. This is where conversational agents can help, either through mapping out key issues to raise with the community you are engaging with or directly translating material into another format. I have included examples of prompts for both of these on the previous page, drawing on the example I have shared here.

Two broad approaches can be used here: planning an engagement strategy for a particular piece of work (ideally informed by your prior stakeholder mapping) or helping you draft the translated outcome. As with other GenAI contributions, this should only be part of the process. If you attempt to outsource the translation entirely you will likely produce low-quality engagement materials, even with careful prompting. Claude in particular is adept at helping you adapt your writing for specific audiences, if you provide it with sufficient detail. If you aren't clear about their interests and outlook, it can help you work towards clarity in the manner described earlier in the chapter. You have to intellectually drive this process. It can save time but the real value comes from the greater clarity you can achieve through such co-production. It not only helps you understand how to plan engagement which meets the needs of a particular group, but can also help you understand what this looks like at a granular level with potential lasting improvements in your writing. It's like working with a public engagement coach at every stage of the process. If you have access to a research communications professional then I'd suggest prioritising working with them. But most of us only have such access sparingly, if at all. Even if you do the two sources of support can be combined, helping you to prioritise acting upon the higher-level insights of the human expert to ensure you are making the most of the time you spend working together.

The format through which you are engaging matters, e.g., planning a podcast involves different considerations than writing a blog post. It is vital that you understand your audience(s) and that you put this into a dialogue with your knowledge of the given format. If you are unsure about this then articulating it to the conversational agent can help. Explain the challenge as you would to a human interlocutor. As an academic who has been podcasting for a long time, I've spoken with many colleagues who are seeking advice about getting started. These conversations typically open with 'I'd like to make an academic podcast but I'm not sure where to begin' leading me to ask *who* they want to engage with, *why* they think a podcast is a good fit and *what* they imagine the end result might look like.

Claude can facilitate a similar conversation. If you are uncertain that's fine: voice your uncertainty, ask questions and use the responses to guide the conversation in a way which can support you in achieving clarity. This can be about the strategy, but it can also be about the conventions and limitations of a particular format. As with any use of conversational agents to address factual questions, the answers should always be treated carefully but they can be a starting point for further reasoning. It is crucial to begin the conversation in a way which can help you turn an inchoate ambition into a practical plan. This might involve formats which you hadn't previously considered, particularly given how other GenAI tools can reduce the workload in producing engagement resources which might have formerly required additional expertise.

For example, it is now possible to quickly generate attractive websites based on existing documents. There has been growing use of services like Microsoft Sway or Adobe Spark (now part of Adobe Express) to produce micro-sites to support a project or initiative. Such services are likely to have in-built GenAI capabilities in the near future. This creates the possibility of quickly producing engagement materials based on existing documentation, with potentially minimal prompting. Gamma is the most fully realised service available at the time of writing, though competitors will likely emerge. It enables presentations, documents and websites to be created quickly based on text, prompts or an imported file. In my experience, the imported file is the best option here, using it to create an outline of engagement materials which needs to be manually reviewed and edited thoroughly in order to be fit for purpose. It suggests prompts can be as brief as one line, but these results tend to be so generic that I struggle to see the value of it. If you want to use GenAI to generate content then I'd suggest producing it in Claude or ChatGPT before pasting it in. The real value for academics lies in the ease with which you can produce presentations or websites based on existing materials. For example, Gamma could be used to create an attractive website for a workshop rather than distributing a PDF to participants or the workshop report could be produced in near real-time and distributed immediately after the session.

The risk in such a service is that we outsource creative reflection to the system, as Gamma worryingly seems to encourage with its suggestion that a one-sentence prompt could create meaningful materials. It is easy to see how these services might lead to a proliferation of low-quality digital artefacts by people who see them primarily as a way of making things without putting effort into the process. I wonder what this could mean for how the brand is perceived if this becomes a widespread use. If you pay for a premium subscription the 'made with Gamma' badge can be removed. This is far from unusual with online creative software, but it does highlight how not making it obvious you used GenAI is a desirable user feature. The real value comes from automating the formatting in order to enable you to focus on the creative process. The possibility we will soon be able to describe the website we want in natural language is an evocative one, even if the services are not there yet and there will always be tidying up required afterwards.

However, there are urgent issues raised by the immediacy with which professional-looking websites can now be produced, with content that requires nothing more than general direction from the producer. We are already seeing a wave of GenAI spam and misinformation which threatens to engulf the academy and wider society. While I've not encountered Gamma being used in this way, this process creates obviously possibilities for misuse. But such services are nonetheless extremely useful in their capacity to immediately produce visually satisfying and textually coherent engagement resources based on minimal prompting or existing documentation. If you are producing engagement materials, experiment with these services to familiarise yourself with their capabilities. Even if their uses at present might be too limited for more specialised purposes, we are likely to see rapid developments in this space because it's such a persuasive and concrete use case for GenAI.

Translating Between Different Languages

The International Sociological Association (ISA) publishes the *Global Dialogues* newsletter which facilitates conversation across the international sociological community. It is currently translated into eighteen languages. This is an extremely complex undertaking which relies on the labour of a team distributed across the world. It is a project which is likely beyond the reach of smaller organisations, let alone research projects and individuals. It provides an immensely resource-intensive example of what can be accomplished by an academic organisation which is international in scope.

The rapid development of services like DeepL creates the opportunity to automate these collaborations, even if some degree of human oversight remains desirable. In this sense, it could reduce the organisational load involved in translating without removing it entirely. In the last chapter, I highlighted how AI dubbing services like VEED make it possible to translate audio and video between languages with a level of quality unknown only a couple of years ago. I included these in the chapter on communication because I suspect the immediate uptake within higher education will facilitate more inclusive engagement with international students, particularly in the early weeks of their degree. These services have obvious uses for online engagement as well, reducing the barriers to international engagement by eroding the constraints of language.

Reducing the Difficulty Involved in Multimedia Engagement

The multimedia turn in social platforms has made it more difficult for academics to engage effectively. Even those platforms built around short-form video, such as TikTok, require skill sets which many academics find do not come easily to them. There are obvious exceptions to this rule, with many examples of academics building a successful presence on TikTok or YouTube. The influence of streaming services such as Twitch, as well as streaming as a genre more broadly, has normalised informality and unpolished production in a way which creates an opening for academic engagement. But there is often a performative quality to how unpolished these are, a form of shabby chic in which missteps and the absence of scripting co-exist with high production values which ensure the unpolished elements are not jarring to the viewer. Since the pandemic, in particular, many academics have launched podcasts with some series having significant cultural influence and financial success through services like Patreon. However even if audio has been a more natural fit for many academics, the tendency over time has been for sound quality to increase, with a corresponding increase in the quality which audiences tend to expect. If you subscribe to a long-running (non-professional) podcast it can be arresting to revisit early episodes and contrast the sound quality. Even though I believe intellectually this escalation of production values is a negative thing because it squeezes out amateur contributions, I've found myself unable to listen attentively to early episodes of podcasts I enjoy because I now find the audio quality so jarring relative to what I'm used to. There are many success stories of academic engagement in spite of these challenges but these reflect, in part, the normalisation of digital engagement within higher education. There are simply more academics undertaking this activity now, which creates the conditions in which some can thrive even if the environment becomes more challenging.

There are a range of tools which can be used to streamline the production of high-quality multimedia. Canvas and Adobe Firefly provide image-generation tools which are optimised for social media graphics. Adobe Podcast has a remarkable capacity to clean up audio, creating a sound quality which comes close to studio quality even if the conditions in which it was recorded fall far short of this, although the quality of the microphone still makes a difference, in my experience. It also supports the calibration of microphones in a way which can help increase sound quality for those who don't have technical support available to them. Video production tools like Invideo offer to create videos based on text prompts which combine narration with footage. The results can be impressive, particularly with regard to turning prompts into a coherent script for the voiceover. However, I struggled to see the same utility for most academics that could be found in something like Adobe Podcast which works with existing audio. My experience was that prompting is a more frustrating experience than with conversational agents because of how much inference is necessary to produce an output based on your prompt. The combination of uncertain results and limited capacity to edit and refine the finished product constrain how useful these are likely to be. Their results are likely to get better with time, but at present, I see the obvious use case as being quickly produced teaching materials for students rather than reliable engagement materials.

WHAT DOES ENGAGEMENT MEAN IN A GENERATIVE AI WORLD?

In the second chapter, we discussed the epistemic limitations of GenAI and the difficulties these create for their use within universities. While these are significant it is the societal implications which are far more concerning, particularly if GenAI is habituated in a similar way to search engines. The ranking of search results is a complex technical process that has huge implications for the visibility of the sites which are being ranked, 'with those on the first page of search results enjoying a status infinitely superior to those on the final page' (Hillis et al., 2012, p. 98). How often do you look beyond the first page? How often do you imagine your students look beyond the first page? Why would there be a motivation to look beyond the first page if we are presented with a result which seemingly meets our expectations about what we are looking for? Our search behaviours often involve what philosophers call satisficing, seeking an adequate result rather than an optimal one, reinforced by the information overload we might suffer if we insist on trying to find the perfect answer given the quantity of material available to us.

It is easy to imagine a similar approach becoming the norm with a conversational agent like ChatGPT given its immediate relevance to practical tasks. We could feasibly spend hours refining our parameters in pursuit of an optimal rather than adequate result. This might not constitute a problem, as building habits is the inevitable trajectory through which software goes from being a novelty we are experimenting with to a routine part of our work. But if GenAI becomes as 'natural and obvious' a part of using the internet as search engines, there are reasons for immense concern about how the epistemic weakness of these services might melt into the background as we come to treat conversational agents as helpful interlocutors upon whom we depend as a matter of habit (Hillis et al., 2012).

It is plausible the rate of hallucination will decline in the future. If users become increasingly sophisticated at prompting conversational agents, this will further mitigate the risks of hallucination by making it more likely that the context is clearly established for the request and the type of response sought is indicated. But there will still be a continual risk that these systems include seemingly plausible but factually incorrect responses in their responses, often alongside entirely credible material which makes the challenges of detection even more intractable. The problem is not that conversational agents are sometimes wrong but rather that it is difficult to know when and how they are wrong without existing familiarity in that domain. While exploring the limitations of ChatGPT, I tried asking it elaborate questions about Marvel comics which I have been reading since I was a child. It could answer broad questions about characters with ease, presumably reflecting fandom wiki sites being included within the training data. But when I tried to ask it about the intricacies of storylines, particularly complex months-long events which crossed between multiple series, it immediately began to confabulate in just as authoritative a tone. When I pushed back on these hallucinations as a lifelong comics nerd, the conversational agent immediately apologised but then issued corrections which were themselves hallucinated. I was surprised by how long this cycle continued before it began to acknowledge the limitation of its capacity to answer these questions, presumably reflecting the fact it has had no epistemic contact with the comics themselves, as opposed to online reports of inconsistent interpretation and variable quality. In contrast, Claude backs down from hallucinations much more quickly, offering a number of interpretations as to why it had hallucinated features of my professional biography when asked:

- I convincingly fabricated specific facts and details without having any verified information about the person being discussed.
- The fictional claims sounded credible but could only be proven false by someone with access to accurate facts about Mark Carrigan.
- When challenged, I continued to fabricate new false details instead of admitting my lack of real knowledge.

- This shows a bias in AI to try to answer questions at all costs, even by essentially 'making things up' when lacking facts.

Impressively it even offered a number of suggestions about how its guardrails could be improved to prevent such a problem from occurring in the future, for example, declining to answer questions if its confidence falls below a certain level, prompting for human confirmation in the absence of multiple authoritative sources and having a means for users to flag potential fabrications. However, we need to consider the specific character of the two cases I am describing here. For entirely different reasons, I was extremely well placed to spot hallucinations about Marvel comics and my own professional biography, in the latter case better placed than anyone else in the world. Each of us has a list of topics where we are to some extent domain experts and prone to spotting hallucinations, often without an explicit effort to do so. But outside this, hallucination will continue to be a significant problem, rendered all the more intractable by the unpredictability with which it occurs. The problem of common knowledge discussed in chapter two raises comparable issues, albeit ones which predate generative AI and have a broader reach.

The role of academics as domain experts becomes even more significant under these conditions. There are reasons to be cautious about the growth of fact-checking as a practice given the crisis of public knowledge often framed as the post-truth or post-fact condition. Marres (2018) points out that the notion of an authoritative body of consensus knowledge is deteriorating under these conditions, leaving fact-checking organisations confronting a curious circularity in their attempts to reinforce consensus on factual matters by pointing to such a body of knowledge. This is not a reason to give up. There is a potential for academics to make a social contribution to factfulness under these conditions, grounded in their research expertise and proceeding as an outgrowth of a broadly sociable disposition online. For example, I recently learned that my university was founded in the same building in which the Trade Union Congress (TUC) and the Co-operative Insurance Group (CIS) had their first meetings. I was so pleased with the idea that these three massive civic organisations were founded in the same building, that I didn't stop to question the reliability of something I read on Wikipedia. It is far too easy to assent to 'facts' which are both plausible and satisfying even if the evidence for them is shaky or non-existent. In the case of the Wikipedia page about the history of the university, there's a reference cited there but without sufficient details to look it up. I also repeated the claim on Twitter prior to questioning its provenance. It was only when a historian of science based at the same university pointed out to me this was not the *first* meeting, attaching a source which provided background to this, that I was struck by how readily I accepted the claim before verification. Obviously, I am far from alone in this tendency. In fact, it would be utterly exhausting to verify every claim we encountered. How would we even function in daily life if we were to try this?

I agree with the science and technology scholar Noortje Marres (2018) that *we can't have our facts back*, in the sense that it won't be possible to establish a body of agreed-upon knowledge which is beyond political contention. Even in a less polarised past, there's an element of fantasy about this notion, resting as it does on the exclusion of contrary belief from public life rather than the absence of disagreement in the first place. I would suggest the relationship which academics, *as scholars*, have with particular bodies of knowledge becomes more socially valuable than ever under these conditions. It is a relationship established over time, through hard and difficult work, in contrast to what can be produced immediately through lazy prompting of GenAI tools and systems. By its nature it is narrow and doesn't easily lend itself to consensus, reflecting the complexity inevitably revealed when smart and conscientious people are working deeply on a single topic. It is nonetheless invaluable. We are entering a digital public sphere defined by ever-increasing epistemological chaos, existing pathologies of social media are combined with an ever-expanding glut of misinformation and disinformation generated through the emerging capabilities of GenAI.

These are not new problems but it is likely they will get much worse before they get better, if that is even possible. We are unlikely to be successful, as Davies (2018) memorably put it if we merely hurl facts at our adversaries in the hope that they will eventually acquiesce to our authority. It is the capacity of facts to be recognised as binding, as well as the expertise which underwrites that character, which increasingly struggles to reproduce itself. Experts are seen as partial, motivated by vested interests and supported by established institutions which seek to reinforce the status quo. It would be an exaggeration to say this outlook is uniform but it is spreading in ways which reflect a broader transformation of the public sphere (Carrigan & Fatsis, 2021, ch 8). It is tough being an expert these days, at least if part of your training to become one involves developing the expectation that your expertise would be reliably recognised. But the role of experts in public is more necessary than ever, given the evidence that GenAI is already 'flooding the zone with shit' to paraphrase Steve Bannon. The problem is that the same mechanisms driving this overproduction of low-quality content, including the malicious and malignant forms this sometimes takes, simultaneously contribute to making it a more difficult context for academics to do digital engagement within.

It's getting harder to be a digitally engaged academic at precisely the point where they are needed more than ever. There are reasons for this which I have written about extensively elsewhere (Carrigan, 2019; Carrigan & Fatsis, 2021). However, this is where GenAI could make a positive impact, in spite of the inherent risks. I felt reticent about including this chapter. It captures the underlying divide in my own attitude about GenAI, embodying how short-term fixes to problems encountered at an individual level might have unintended consequences which contribute to the problems we are experiencing collectively. My concern is that overload within the digital public sphere will be exacerbated if GenAI tools and services are used to increase the rate at which content is produced. I suspect there are already areas of digital engagement, such as academic podcasting, where there might be a saturation point in the provision of content. There is certainly the possibility that new voices will break through, but it becomes increasingly difficult for this to happen if the digital public sphere is filled with academic podcasts in search of an audience. The fact that far too much digital engagement rests on a naive sense that getting your work 'out there' is sufficient to secure an audience compounds the problem. GenAI tools and services can professionalise the engagement activity of academics, helping ensure a capacity to contribute to the public sphere which isn't dependent on having a degree of time, space and resources which is rarely possible.

8

ACADEMIC FUTURES[1]

This chapter will:

- Explore the potential implications of Generative Artificial Intelligence (GenAI) for higher education in the longer-term, including the threat that teaching and research might become increasingly automated.
- Consider how the opportunities GenAI offers to increase productivity intersect with existing pressures in higher education, suggesting the danger comes from the existing system as much as the novel technology.
- Argue for a reflective professional culture informed by scholarly values as the best antidote to the dangerous possibilities which GenAI might lead to if embraced by academics in a careless way.

---

[1]This chapter contains material developed from the blog post 'Generative AI and the unceasing acceleration of academic publishing' published by the LSE Impact Blog posted on the LSE Impact blog (https://blogs.lse.ac.uk/impactofsocialsciences/).

It has been around 15 months since I first tried ChatGPT. I was curious about what I had seen on Twitter and wanted to experience it for myself. I could not have expected at that stage how much it would take over my working life and leave me with an unexpected new research agenda. During the writing process, I threw myself into every service I could find in order to get to grips with this strange new class of tools and what it meant for academic practice. Now I'm coming to the end of the project, it's startling to realise how integrated into my working life GenAI has become. I have subscriptions to Claude and ChatGPT which I use on a daily basis for an enormous range of functions, including things which have nothing to do with my work. I tend to avoid writing assistants and other template-based forms of GenAI for the reasons discussed in earlier chapters. But talking about my work with conversational agents, as well as occasionally outsourcing tasks to them, has become a routine feature of how I spend my days.

It's hard to imagine my working routines without them at this stage. I am more able than I was previously to balance administrative responsibilities alongside teaching and research. I feel more in touch with what I'm doing and why, the core questions and values which motivate my work, than I've ever been. It's not that my working life is without problems but in part, the challenges I experience, such as the sprawling web of GenAI-related research projects which have unfolded over the last year, reflect the contribution which these practices have made to my scholarship. I've become aware of a propensity to take on more as my capacities expand but this itself is a testament to the positive impact which GenAI has had on my work. I am more creatively engaged with my research than I have been in a long time, even if my plans exceed my capacities and energies.[2] It's a problem but it's a high-quality one to suffer from. ChatGPT and Claude have made an enormously positive contribution which I hope this book will help other academics recreate, in a manner which is right for their projects and the context they are working within.

I feel enthusiastic about GenAI when I remain at this level of individual practice. It's just been such a positive experience for me that I would sincerely like to support others in replicating this in their own working routines. But then as a sociologist, I inevitably begin to consider where this is heading at the collective, institutional and societal levels. What are the unintended consequences going to be if individual scholars take up GenAI *en masse*? How might this change the institutions we work within? What does this mean for the future of higher education? Through this sociological lens, I find myself increasingly concerned about the potential harm, which GenAI could do within universities and wider society. I strongly believe that academics have a responsibility to mitigate these harms, but I also see it as extremely unlikely that a widespread refusal to engage is viable, particularly as GenAI functionality comes to be embedded in the platforms and software upon which scholarship depends. The risks I see are longer-term and more diffuse, lying in a professional culture mutating through the affordances of GenAI and the wider networks of power in which the emergence of these services is embedded. How we approach these developments as a

---

[2]'My plans have always exceeded my capacities and energies' wrote the sociologist C. Wright Mills in a guide to intellectual craft (Wright Mills, 2000).

profession matters immensely for the values which guide our work, as well as the future of the profession itself. I have tried to articulate a vision of GenAI scholarship in this book which mitigates the potential harms through a reflexive orientation: *thinking with* GenAI rather than using it as a *substitute for thought*.

Through this vision I have tried to demonstrate the enduring value of scholarship, identifying the things scholars can do with GenAI that reflect the specificity of their expertise. Yet from a sociological perspective, I see a genuine risk of academics being automated out of our jobs. Not immediately, nor everywhere. But a gradual process in which human scholarship becomes a retreating role, increasingly confined to elite institutions which charge a premium for human research and teaching. Human expertise becomes a premium commodity rationed within ever more automated institutions, to the extent it remains in place at all. The once familiar enjoyments of thinking together might come to be an exceptional occurrence, amidst a working life spent caught up in a deadening system. The cynic might say we are there already. But I think it could get much worse if we do not approach GenAI carefully.

If this seems hyperbolic then please stick with me as I try and explain how the politics of automation within the university might play out. There is a limit to what we can do individually and collectively, with uncertain threats in the longer-term difficult to prioritise when there are political and economic crises unfolding now. Establishing a mode of engagement with GenAI which expresses and is informed by our *professional judgement* could be a bulwark against the threat on the horizon. Not a solution, just a bulwark. But one which could be non-trivial in shaping how these developments unfold within the sector. My worry is that a careless and instrumental embrace of GenAI, seeing it as a mechanism through which to outsource tasks we don't want to do, risks laying the groundwork for automation. If we approach these systems in order to replace our own labour then what would stop university managers replacing us entirely further down the line? In contrast if we establish how scholars can do things with these systems which non-specialists cannot then we fortify the position of academic labour within the system (Figure 8.1).

ChatGPT: In a dystopian future, the ascendance of generative AI threatens to transform the university system into a shadow of its former self, where human expertise becomes a rarefied commodity, hoarded within the ivory towers of elite institutions. In this bleak scenario, the vast majority of teaching, research, and engagement is relegated to automated systems, sophisticated yet soulless, which cyclically refine their outputs in an echo chamber devoid of human insight and empathy. As these digital overseers dictate the direction of academic inquiry and education, the rich tapestry of human knowledge and understanding is progressively unwoven, replaced by a sterile, algorithm-driven facsimile that lacks the nuance, creativity, and passion of its predecessors. This vision foretells a world where the essence of higher education—its capacity to foster critical thinking, innovation, and human connection—is diminished, leaving behind a landscape where the flame of human intellectual endeavor flickers in the shadow of its synthetic counterparts.

Figure 8.1 A Dystopian Scenario of How GenAI Could Transform Universities
Source: ChatGPT.

GENERATIVE AI AND THE ACCELERATION OF PUBLISHING

In his *New Laws of Robotics*, the legal scholar Frank Pasquale (2020) offers a compelling vision of how 'AI should complement professionals, not replace them', playing off Isaac Asimov's *three laws* which have lingered in the cultural imagination far beyond the short story in which they were originally put forward. His conviction is that we do not need to be 'captured or transformed' by technologies of automation because 'we now have the means to channel' them (Pasquale, 2020, p. 1). The distinction he draws between 'technology that replaces people and technology that helps them do their jobs better' is strikingly simple yet obviously relevant to our present concerns. *Will GenAI help academics do their jobs better? Or will GenAI replace us?* I have put forward an optimistic account, grounded in my own experience as an early adopter, suggesting that GenAI can help us do our jobs better. This requires a reflexive approach to conversational agents as interlocutors, using interaction with them to clarify and refine our outlook, rather than framing them as a way to outsource tasks we don't want to undertake ourselves. There are ways in which we can safely use them to save time, but even then I've suggested there is an imperative to clarify our intentions and expectations to ensure that conversational agents do what we want them to do.

In other words, self-understanding is integral to using GenAI effectively as a scholar: it is needed in order to generate high-quality outputs which avoid the epistemic risks and harms the technology is inherently prone to generate. As Pasquale (2020, loc 3806) later observes, 'Knowledge, skill, and ethics are inextricably intertwined' and this means that 'We cannot simply make a machine "to get the job done" in most complex human services field, because frequently, task definition is a critical part of the job itself'. To the extent we are taking a reflexive approach to conversational agents, academics are claiming the autonomy to define the tasks involved in scholarship. The conversational agent contributes to increasing the clarity of defining those tasks, rather than being a mechanism to outsource them to automated systems which lack the expertise of the scholar. The only people who can adequately define the work involved in scholarship are scholars.

Is it realistic to imagine this reflexive approach could become mainstream[3]? I suspect it probably is not, in spite of the optimistic spirit in which I have written this book. The reason for this scepticism is awareness of the workload pressures to which academics are subject, as well as how the strategies through which we respond to them can unintentionally increase the expectations we are all subject to. Let's return to Pasquale's (2020) invocation of professionals doing their jobs 'better' as a result of engagement with automated systems.[4] Is it doing your job better if you publish more journal articles as a result of your use of GenAI? Even if many

---

[3]Thanks to Helen Beetham for posing this question to me most directly, though I realise a number of people were gesturing towards this point in discussions with me over the last year.
[4]The inverted commas here are intended to draw attention to the contested nature of this judgement, rather than to critique Pasquale's turn of phrase or wider argument.

academics would refuse to answer 'yes' to this question, we would still act as if this is what we believed.[5] Our productivity stands as a proxy for our institutional worth[6] which can be reassuring in a competitive labour market facing a precarious and frightening world. It is reassuring to throw ourselves into producing more, particularly in a metricised academy which is continually counting and encouraging us to do the same (Burrows, 2012). The creeping sense of insecurity generated by the threat of automation is likely to make that anxiety mount rather than recede, encouraging individuals to throw themselves ever more fully into the rat race in the hope that it ensures the continued existence of their role. The competitive cycles in which managers are 'heating up the floor to see who can keep hopping the longest', as the political economist Will Davies (2014) once put it, leaves many of us already disposed to such a response.

The problem is that norms of productivity are easily ratcheted up as individuals act strategically in order to meet perceived expectations. I remember as a first year PhD student in 2008 being told in a training session that we should not try and publish alongside writing our thesis. Even then I could see this was bad advice for those of us who would seek academic employment. In the job market, we now confront only 15 years later, it is difficult to imagine a candidate even being shortlisted for a short-term postdoc, let alone a lectureship, without a publishing record comprising at least a few items. Vostal (2015, p. 82) argues that 'early career academics are particularly vulnerable to the restructuring of higher education in comparison with more established and tenured/permanently employed senior scholars and professoriate'. The expectations of output are ratcheted up because competition leads to an intensification of activity as academics accelerate their work in pursuit of a competitive advantage (Muller, 2019). Exactly what is perceived as a 'normal' level of academic productivity will vary across fields and disciplines. But it will tend to spiral upwards as long as people feel it's a standard which they need to meet, with those who exceed it contributing to the normalisation of a higher standard.

The simple fact of senior figures publishing at the rate they do sends a message. The tendency for those messages to be condensed through social media and compiled into books to support academics in their career development, often underscores the behavioural cues. What might otherwise have simply been noticeable to those who are watchful rapidly turns into common sense under these conditions. If we imagine the productivity of a well-resourced professor, with ample research time and grant-funded assistants, increasing by a factor of two or three, it would exert pressure further down the occupational ladder. Even if no one expected most academics to match their output of, say, twenty peer-reviewed papers per year,[7]

---

[5]See Bacevic (2019, 2023) for an insightful analysis of this issue in relation to academic reflexivity.
[6]One which is particularly significant given that explicit and/or conspicuous displays of status tend to be frowned upon within the academy. In contrast being 'prolific', performatively or otherwise, doesn't (usually) attract this sanction.
[7]If this seems implausible take a close look at the Google Scholar profiles of well-known professors in many fields. I have found numerous examples of professors publishing forty or more papers per year, in disciplines where long-form articles with fairly small writing teams are the norm. The fact I've written this book in less than a year could lead critics to suggest I'm part of the problem I'm affecting a critical distance from here.

this upper level of output would inevitably impact upon how much most academics are expected to produce in order to be seen as reasonably productive. How would early career researchers fare in these circumstances? Presumably, some would cope by using GenAI to increase output in the time available to them, whereas others either would not or could not do this, leading to a decline in their relative competitiveness if/when they enter the job market. It is easy to see how classed and gendered inequalities could be reinforced by this dynamic, as freedom from the need for paid work and an absence of caring responsibilities would contribute to an ability to participate in this great acceleration of scholarly publishing.

This is a speculative forecast but the recent crisis provides robust evidence of how it might play out in practice. The inequality of the pandemic in which women submitted proportionally fewer papers than men is a trend likely to be exacerbated by GenAI (Squazzoni et al., 2021). Not least of all because there are start-up costs involved in developing GenAI routines which could lead to productivity gains sufficient to make a demonstrable impact on the rate of publication. There is a risk of epistemic deterioration if academic work becomes increasingly difficult for those with caring responsibilities, chronic illnesses, disabilities or simply an unassailable commitment to not having their lives defined by work. What we take doing our job 'better' with GenAI to mean matters for what comes next. As Pasquale (2020, p. 14) points out, 'the future of automation in the workplace – and well beyond – will hinge on millions of small decisions about how to develop AI'. The choices which academics make, and how we think and talk about the new possibilities which are opening up, constitute one small factor alongside many others which will shape the nature of the automated university. But the choices we make will contribute to shaping it nonetheless.

I have discussed GenAI in four broad areas of practice (thinking, collaborating, communicating and engaging) in order to illustrate the two main ways in which GenAI can help us do our jobs *better*. It can lead to *quantitative improvements*: enabling us to produce more in the same amount of time or less, regardless of whether the outputs in question are publications, engagement materials, communications or whatever else. It can lead to *qualitative improvements:* enabling us to do the things we already do in more varied, creative and multifaceted ways that might bring us more fulfilment, or at least reconnect us with the deeper motivations which led us to our work in the first place. The point of this book is to help you develop strategies and techniques for implementing these improvements in your working life, in a reflective manner which recognises the ethical challenges, practical dangers and possible consequences that you might encounter along the way.

I have tried to foreground qualitative improvements throughout the book for a number of reasons. Firstly, they necessarily involve a reflexive engagement with GenAI which supports ethical practice and mitigates the epistemic risk. If you want to use these systems to deepen your engagement with your work, it is necessary to be comparably reflective in how you engage with these systems. In the process, the odds of waving through hallucinated outputs or producing material which has harmful consequences diminish because you are intellectually engaged with what you are doing. Secondly, they can contribute to an epistemic improvement in the work we do by providing continual opportunities to articulate, refine and review our ideas. This is partly a matter of the writing involved and how it can clarify what we are trying to say. But unlike writing in a notebook or on a blog, these can be conversations which actively present us with prompts and challenges that cause us to further refine our ideas. These can lead in turn to quantitative improvements, such as when talking about your research makes it much quicker to translate between different formats of output. But these will tend to be a byproduct of the qualitative improvement which is difficult to achieve responsibly if pursued as an end in itself.

The problem with quantitative improvements in how we do our work isn't that we can do more in the same amount of time. That could be an extremely positive thing which contributes to greater balance in our lives and within the institutions in which we work. The problem is rather that many academics would immediately use the time freed up in order to do more work, in the process contributing to the ratcheting effect described earlier. I have noticed that in my own experience of writing this book, leading me to reflect on where and how I'm saving time, as well as what I would like to use this time for beyond my work. Furthermore, approaching GenAI in terms of increasing productivity makes the reflective approach advocated in this book difficult to achieve. In doing so it increases exposure to epistemic risks like hallucination and common knowledge. If you are using these tools in order to accelerate your tasks before you rush onto something else, how reliably will you check over the outputs? The labour saved by thoughtless inputs would be necessitated in order to thoughtfully check over the outputs, without the epistemic gains which come from approaching the interaction mindfully in the first place. In reality, it is likely that this checking process would be dispensed with, even if one starts out with a commitment to careful use. It is easy to see how a principled commitment to reflective scholarship could easily unravel in a series of ad hoc compromises.

THE COMING CRISIS OF SCHOLARLY PUBLISHING

One estimate from 2015 suggested around 34,550 journals published around 2.5 million articles per year (Ware and Mabe 2015). This later study from 2018 found over 2.5 million outputs in Science and Engineering alone, highlighting how growth rates over a 10-year period varied between 0.71% in the United States and 0.67% in the United Kingdom to 7.81% in China and 10.73% in India (White 2019). Obviously, there are factors at work here other than escalating expectations of scholarly output, such as the international growth of scientific fields and the intellectual interconnections generated by the digitalisation of academic publishing. The escalation in the number of publications creates all manner of practical problems, with earlier chapters considering how GenAI might provide short-term ways to address these challenges.

However, the problem is that not only might GenAI further intensify the rate of publication, but it could also lead to a terrifying proliferation of low-value publications designed to be counted rather than read, growing at a rate far beyond any capacity to filter them. In an earlier sociotechnical context, Brunton (2013, p. 200) drew attention to the tendency of spammers to 'fill every available channel to capacity, use every exploitable resource' in their attempt to circulate their material via email. Given the costs of producing the spam were near zero, it was not a problem if only 'a vanishingly small amount will get through to the eyes of that fraction of a percentage of people who will actually respond to such messages'. His interest in 'a new genre of machine-generated "spam books" colonising the new environment of booming ebook and print-on-demand book sales with cryptical and haplessly bizarre documents that can do a brisk business, by spam standards, on Amazon' was a prescient foreshadowing of the problem which will explode over the coming years (Brunton, 2013, p. 203). These are often framed as 'summaries' of a book using all the relevant keywords which someone searching for the original text is likely to find. Another common form this took was ebooks collating content which had been scraped and reproduced from Wikipedia.

The extent to which their production could be largely automated, even in the pre-GenAI era, meant that small sales were not inherently a problem. By flooding online marketplaces with these texts, it was possible to ensure an income stream with relatively little work. Obviously, the marketplaces themselves have a responsibility to minimise the misleading presentation of products they are selling. But with Amazon reportedly listing over 12 million ebooks it would be a significant logistical undertaking to filter them in an exhaustive and effective way. This is a problem compounded by the difficulty in drawing a line between what counts as misleading and what is simply a shoddy product. There are obvious cases where summaries or digests of existing material might serve a legitimate purpose, raising the question of how to distinguish between these and manipulative attempts to trick customers into purchasing an automated digest rather than the original text. What makes these problematic is when readers expect original contributions rather than collections of existing material.

What happens when we get 'spam books' in every aspect of cultural production? What happens when we get spam monographs, spam journals and spam articles? It is now possible to produce these by remixing the existing materials rather than simply collecting them. A cynic might suggest scholarship has always had at least a tendency to do this, moving around and remixing existing ideas as much as adding new ones. The economic incentive to actually sell these products has combined with a newfound capacity to create them, nearly immediately and without the telltale signs of inauthenticity which plague the comparable products of the 2010s. I suspect these productions will thrive within the ecosystem of openly predatory pay-to-play journals, as well as those more ambiguous cases where publication is tacitly transactional between an academic who needs publications which can be counted and publishers willing to facilitate this for a fee. Scholarly publishing is not some pristine realm liable to be invaded by the malign influence of generative media. It is rather a system that was already straining under the weight of perverse incentives which is now liable to break if the worst potentials of GenAI are realised (Figure 8.2).

It is easy to see how existing practices such as 'salami-slicing', might be accelerated by GenAI. The incentives driving these behaviours aren't created by services like ChatGPT and Claude. However, these conversational agents provide effective new ways through which to enact these techniques for professional advancement. Imagine the same theoretical developments or empirical findings being split between five journal articles rather than two,[8] undertaken by an established professor whose reputation would have weight with journal

---

[8]Obviously the numbers here are entirely speculative. It's an empirical question of *how* GenAI would be used to extend the *minimum viable publishing unit,* i.e., what's the minimum quantity of information which can be spun out into a socially recognised and professionally validated publication?

ChatGPT: The integration of Generative Artificial Intelligence (GenAI) into the scholarly publishing system presents several key challenges that necessitate careful consideration and management. Firstly, ensuring the accuracy and reliability of content generated by GenAI is paramount, as the integrity of scholarly work must be maintained to support scientific progress. This leads to the second challenge: the need for robust mechanisms to verify authorship and contributions, as GenAI-generated content could blur the lines of intellectual property and originality, complicating the traditional notions of authorship and creativity. Additionally, there's the challenge of maintaining ethical standards and preventing the misuse of GenAI for producing misleading or fabricated research, which could undermine trust in scientific publications. Another significant issue is the potential for GenAI to exacerbate information overload, making it increasingly difficult for researchers to discern significant contributions in their fields. Finally, adapting peer review processes to effectively evaluate GenAI-generated content without overburdening reviewers is crucial, requiring new guidelines and criteria that account for the unique aspects of GenAI contributions to scholarly communication. These challenges underscore the need for a collaborative approach among researchers, publishers, and technologists to develop ethical standards, regulatory frameworks, and technological solutions that harness the benefits of GenAI while mitigating its risks to the scholarly publishing ecosystem.

Figure 8.2 The Challenges Involved in Integrating GenAI into Scholarly Publishing
Source: ChatGPT.

editors and whose grasp of publication norms would streamline a process by understanding the expectations for a finalised manuscript. Now imagine a small minority of the professoriate lapsing into that practice over time, given the potential rewards to be accrued in terms of citation and visibility, as well as the relative lack of costs associated with the practice. This might not be the scenario which comes to pass but it illustrates how GenAI has the potential to shift the balance of incentives and costs within the field of scholarly publishing.

There is already a widely recognised crisis of review within scholarly publishing, with many journal editors finding it increasingly difficult to find reviewers on the timescale which contributing authors expect. It is easy to imagine how a system already straining under the number of publications, as well as the voluntary demands on academic time, might begin to crumble in the face of a glut of GenAI-supported publications. This creates a risk that publishers might in turn seek to automate elements of their process, including perhaps shrinking the human role in reviewing. I could envisage a situation where a human editor is presented with a range of automated reviews with different weightings, possibly optimised to specific intellectual domains, leaving it a matter of their judgement as to how to proceed. The move towards publishing platforms and a publisher-then-filter model creates the rationale for even stripping out the human editor altogether, i.e., get as much out as possible then let the 'marketplace of ideas' sort out the mess. But the marketplace of ideas is mediated by social platforms which are themselves undergoing a profound shift as platforms like Twitter begin to normalise a pay-to-play model. Visibility on these platforms is increasingly provided to subscribers and visibility of non-subscribers is throttled as a mechanism to incentivise subscriptions, in the attempt to mitigate declining advertising revenues by generating new income streams. This means the capacity of social platforms to filter on the basis of intellectual merit is declining precipitously at exactly the point where we need it more than ever.

THE POSSIBILITIES AND PITFALLS OF GENERATIVE SCHOLARSHIP

What I have described is a grim scenario which I truly hope does not come to pass. But I believe it is a plausible future when we consider how GenAI might become a routine part of scholarship. Banning tools like ChatGPT as a co-author on papers does nothing to foreclose this possibility because there is no reliable way to determine if text included in a manuscript has been generated by a conversational agent. Furthermore, I believe the creative and intellectual rewards available for using conversational agents in a reflexive and robust way are significant enough that we need to try and regulate the practice rather than prohibit it. This means establishing norms about how we report on the use of GenAI in research, as well as focusing on how it can be incorporated into the process of scholarship, rather than seeing it as either an input to or output from that process. But it also means a reflection on the means and ends of scholarly publishing, already set into motion by an earlier wave of digitalisation, urgently needs to penetrate into the mainstream of academic consciousness. This means as Fitzpatrick (2011, p. 7) argued 'thinking seriously about both the institutional models and the material forms through which scholarship might best circulate'.

Many people *have* been thinking seriously about this for the last 20 years with a view to taking advantage of digitalisation to build a more equitable and effective infrastructure for scholarly publishing. But this is the same period in which academic outputs have grown at an accelerating rate, suggesting that what cultural shift has taken place is insufficient to cope with the technological change underway. The institutional models and material forms have tended to be predicated on assumptions of scarcity in which scholarship is a slow and careful process, leading to occasional outputs relevant to narrow communities. These assumptions have been breaking down rapidly as the internet became a routine part of life but GenAI will accelerate this decay in ways which necessitate urgent reflection on the future of scholarly publishing.

Why do we publish? In my experience, academics can be weirdly inarticulate about this question. It is what we are expected to do and it is therefore what we do, often with little overarching sense of the specific goals being served by these outputs other than meeting the (diffuse or explicit) expectations of our employers. In a quantified academic world, it is far too easy to slip into imagining countable publications as an end in themselves. These are conditions in which technologies which change the time: output ratio could prove extremely seductive. If this technology is taken up in an individualised way, reflecting the immediate pressures which staff are subject to in increasingly anxiety-ridden institutions, the consequences could be extremely negative. In contrast, if we take this opportunity to reflect on what we might use this technology for as scholars and why, this could herald an exciting shift in how we work which reduces the time spent on routine tasks and contributes to a more creatively fulfilling life of the mind.

I could imagine an outcome in which the efficiencies of GenAI are used to support a reclamation of intellectual pleasures as well as a deepening of the creative process, even if I believe the institutional conditions we are working within render this rather unlikely. At the level of individual academics, the promise of GenAI is that it might relieve us from what Sword (2017, p. ix) describes as the 'circumstances that sap our strength and hobbles our writings - heavy teaching loads, tedious administrative duties, judgemental reviews and looking deadlines'. We long for 'an architecture of possibilities and pleasure' but instead 'find ourselves crushed under the weight of expectations and the rubble of our fractured workdays' (Sword, 2017, p. ix). It is possible for GenAI to lighten that load, in careful ways. But it can also provide a foundation for that architecture of possibility which keeps our ideas in motion, in the manner discussed in chapter four, ensuring they are ready-to-hand when it becomes time to sit and write. While it will likely prove impossible to outsource these things entirely to automated systems, these draining obligations often involve routine elements which could be automated. This would free up our time and energy to attend to the corresponding non-routine aspects with more care, as well as enable us to turn our gaze to the research and writing which motivate so many of us.

The problem with such a view is that it easily risks falling into what Burkeman (2022) describes as the when-I-finally mindset: 'the sense that real fulfilment, or even real life itself, hasn't quite arrived yet, so that present experience is merely something to get through, en route to something better'. It imagines a place we might reach in our lives, tantalisingly close yet never quite reachable, where things flow easily and the resistance which wears us down is suddenly absent. The artisanal perspective advocated by Sword (2017) could be a bulwark against this by foregrounding the elements of craft involved in academic writing; a concern with doing things well for their own sake to use Sennett's (2008) formulation. We can easily slip into the assumption that routine work is inherently undesirable as if the fact of it being routine means it is unavoidably deadening. I find this a strange view which fails to recognise how routine gives shape and meaning to our lives, providing what social theorists call ontological security: a sense of continuity and stability which minimises the anxiety which might otherwise ensue in a world full of potential threats. Furthermore, Newport (2016) suggests we only have the capacity for around four hours of 'deep work' each day; this immersion in non-routine and creative problem-solving is inherently more demanding than the 'shallow work' we spend much of our time engaged in.

The problem with routine work is not the fact it is routine but rather that it is organised in ways which continually exceed the boxes we try to put it in. For example, it is the quantity of emails we discussed earlier in this chapter, rather than the fact of being connected to interlocutors around the world, which constitutes the problem. If we could find a way to better manage the quantitative challenge, with the exciting possibility that GenAI could support this undertaking, what opportunities would that open up for more meaningful work and more creatively fulfilling interaction with others? Could we not also make the case that inefficiency and friction might serve a purpose which should not be automated away? As the sociologist Rogers Brubaker (2022, p. 72) puts it:

Automation, we are told, can save us time, spare us the cognitive burden of thinking, and emancipate us from the drudgery of repetitive tasks. It can make interaction faster, more efficient, and more frictionless. But do we always want interaction to be fast, efficient, and frictionless? Is there not something to be said for friction? For slowing down? Even, perhaps, for inefficiency?

THE POLITICAL ECONOMY OF THE AUTOMATED UNIVERSITY

The concerns I have raised thus far rest on the assumption that academics would be the drivers of this process. The individual practice focus of this book exists within a socioeconomic context in which we are either employees of, or seeking employment within, universities. These have become systems dominated by the logic of the market (Slaughter and Leslie, 1997). How might the logic of academic capitalism interact with the scholarly-led automation which has been the subject of the book? How might the creative and enriching possibilities I have tried to outline be constrained, disrupted or even foreclosed by a university system driven by the imperative to rationalise within an increasingly crisis-ridden political and economic context? What happens if the automated academic is not a creative figure seeking to use GenAI in order to enrich their working life, or even a career-focused individual trying to use these affordances to accelerate their ascent up their career ladder? Could academic work be subject to an enforced automation which would entirely change its nature? Could the figure of the academic as we currently know it be changed beyond recognition by these trends or even be obliterated altogether?

This is a real possibility which will feel differently to us depending on our place within that system, as well as the differences between national systems which I am glossing over here for sake of analytical simplicity. In part this is a matter of who determines how these GenAI systems are used, what happens to the outputs and the rules which govern the process. For example, consider the value that scholarly publications hold for universities. Within the UK system, these represent a collective commodity which the university effectively exchanges for money from the UK government, as part of the university's Research Excellence Framework submission (Preston, 2022, loc 8305). Even outside of the centralised system within which I work, scholarly publications are an important marker of research productivity with regard to national and international rankings, even if this is not a matter of quantity in a straightforward way. If universities see their collective stock of research outputs as a means for their collective advancement, it creates an incentive to increase the rate of output, particularly to high-impact journals. What counts as 'quality' matters but it is ultimately a question of what *counts*: careful and in-depth peer review doesn't scale effectively[9] so these considerations will tend to be about proxies for quality, opening up possibilities for the system to be gamed. This is a key mechanism which has led to the ratcheting up of

---

[9] As opposed to sampling from the body of publications or even undertaking peer review, but doing so at an expected pace which renders comprehensive review near impossible.

expectations concerning research productivity which individual academics are subject to. But what if those individual academics are no longer necessary to contribute to the collective stock of research outputs in a way which is counted by international rankings? Or if this is not permitted by the ranking methodologies could academics be kept on as *ghost authors* for effectively machine-driven publications? If the link between individual academics and research outputs begins to break down then scenarios which would have once seemed implausibly dystopian will become real possibilities which we urgently need to consider.

We can see similar issues in the domain of teaching. I was often struck during the age of MOOC hype how short-sighted the fixation on the superstar professor was. There was a certain superficial plausibility, at least in the context of the op-ed or think piece, to the suggestion it was a desirable thing for students all over the world to be taught by a superstar professor like Michael Sandel rather than his classes being restricted to the privileged few able to attend in person at Yale. Not only does this denigrate the broader category of philosophy professors working across the world, but it also raises the question of where the next superstar professor will come from. If Michael Sandel is single-handedly teaching the world's philosophy students, as in the most extreme version of the MOOC sociotechnical imaginary, how would his potential replacement gain the experience and training necessary to one day assume that role? The same problem could be raised about the widespread automation of academic teaching. If universities widely rely upon conversational agents to teach students then who would contribute to the knowledge that those students are taught? While the mass automation of academic staff does not seem imminent, the creeping transfer of tasks from human teachers to automated systems could rapidly affect the wider system which teaching presupposes. What could seem rational for a specific university could have enormously harmful effects if other universities enacted the same strategy.

We need to ensure a coming wave of automation does not destroy the commons upon which knowledge production and knowledge exchange depend. The problem with such an expectation is the ascendancy of what Burawoy (2016) describes as the spiralists within higher education: 'people who spiral in from outside, develop signature projects and then hope to spiral upward and onward, leaving the university behind to spiral down'. To the extent university management has come to be dominated by those who lack a longer-term sense of custodianship to their institution or the wider sector, there is a risk that short-term and destructive applications of GenAI will be seen as exciting innovations through which people can make their name as disruptors. Academic resistance to these projects can easily be dismissed through the lens of 'change management' without engaging with the underlying concerns (Parker, 2014). If the sector's finances become increasingly precarious within ever more polarised societies, leaving higher education caught between an aspiration towards social goods and the contested positional goods accrued by a portion of the population, the temptation will be to imagine automation could be a pathway to sustainable institutions.[10]

---

[10]This would be self-defeating in practice because it would destroy the knowledge upon which automation depends. The staff in the university have the knowledge, tacit and explicit, required to define the tasks which are being automated. How does this work after they've been replaced by automated systems?

The implications for academic labour within a radically automated university could be exceptionally bleak, with academics increasingly confined to residual functions within elite institutions, against the backdrop of an increasingly automated sector.

THE CULTURAL POLITICS OF AUTOMATED AUTHORSHIP

What if I told you that GenAI had written this book? Perhaps each of these chapters was simply a response to an extensive prompt I gave a conversational agent. Perhaps I simply shared a series of notes with ChatGPT and then linked these outputs together with filler text, fitting it into a structure which was itself produced with GenAI. I can assure you this is not the case.[11] But I would like you to dwell on that possibility, particularly if you have made it to this final chapter while reading sequentially through the material. Would you feel cheated? Would you feel it had devalued what you had read? How would this change your inclination to talk about or cite the text? These are the questions we will be routinely confronting in the coming years. They raise complex issues about how we relate to norms of authorship, not least of all because it will be impossible to be *certain* if a text has been generated by GenAI and if so to what extent. Paranoia could easily thrive under these conditions with the (unreliable) attribution or denial of human authorship to a text coming to be a crucial part of how it is informally evaluated (Carrigan & Sylvia, 2022).

The philosopher Nick Bostrom (2016, p. 262) captures this point in a discussion about a potential future where automated systems engaging in formerly human pursuits have become the norm. Imagining a robotic performer entertaining an audience, he reflects that 'A concert audience, for instance, might like to know that the performer is consciously experiencing the music and the venue' because without this 'the musician could be regarded as merely a high-powered jukebox, albeit one capable of creating the three-dimensional appearance of a performer interacting naturally with the crowd'. The same point could be made about the intellectual outputs of academics: if I discovered that Bostrom's thought-provoking, if at times slightly off-putting book, was in fact the product of an artificial intelligence I would feel vaguely cheated. I would revisit the other references I have made to it in my writing and consider their appropriateness. It would feel that I had in some sense been taken in or duped by the appearance of intelligence, leading me to second guess the judgements I had made about the work. He suggests such robotic performers might 'be designed to instantiate the same kinds of mental states that would be present in a human performing the same task' in order to counteract this sense that something ineffable but profound is missing in the automated performance (Bostrom, 2016, p. 262). I suspect I would have still felt uncomfortable about my intellectual engagement with the Bostrom-bot, even if I was persuaded that

---

[11]In fact, I initially intended to include a detailed report of all the ways in which I *did* use GenAI in this book, in order to avoid any doubt about this fact. But I had to cut this out in order to bring the manuscript down to an acceptable size. Everything I describe in the book has been tried by me, mostly during the course of writing it.

it had been engaged in the experience of reasoning, directly equivalent to the creative process of a human philosopher, throughout the process of writing the book. It is possible this reaction would decline over time, as automated productions became ever more familiar. But Bostrom's (2016, p. 261) own intuition that 'Future consumers might similarly prefer human-made goods and human athletes, human artists, human lovers, and human leaders to functionally indistinguishable or superior artificial counterparts' seems more plausible.

In the academic thought experiment, we could imagine a hierarchy opening up in methodological and disciplinary terms, with automated authors being preferred for certain kinds of outputs (e.g., a systematic review) while human authors would remain the gold standard for others (e.g., work in social theory). These categories do not map onto claims about what an automated system can or cannot do. For example, my own experiments with ChatGPT suggest that it can undertake theoretical work with the right prompting and guidance, as I have found in my exploration of psychoanalytical theory and sociological conceptions of agency over the last year. While I would not trust such an undertaking without it being guided by someone who already has a great deal of domain knowledge, I reached the uncomfortable conclusion that these systems are already capable of work which is in some sense creative in fields of enquiry that I would formerly assume required human capabilities. The distinction Collins (1990) draws between rule-based actions which can be explicated (mimemorphic) and those which involve decision-making in complex and unpredictable environments (polimorphic) no longer seems to map in a straightforward way onto actions which can be easily automated or which resist automation. It nonetheless illustrates a contrast between intellectual undertakings in which well-defined techniques predominate and those which place a greater emphasis on interpretation, intuition and creativity. The risk is that a humanist rearguard action which seeks to defend the latter would be forced into an ever-shrinking set of claims as GenAI proves capable of replicating increasing swathes of what was once imagined to be uniquely human undertakings.

The orthodox conception of authorship is likely to erode under these conditions. If we accept the creative individual solely responsible for producing a text always was a mythical character, this might seem positive. The persistence of this notion obscured the complex patterns of intellectual influence and interdependence which made creative production possible in the first place. Certain categories of author have their influence attributed in more reliable and accurate ways than others, producing identifiable patterns of epistemic injustice which show that established norms of authorship do not in themselves produce equitable outcomes (Bacevic, 2023). These acts of non-attribution and intellectual erasure have only increased with social media as the circulation of isolated ideas in ephemeral formats like tweets and podcasts challenged established practices of recording and acknowledging influences. Even if citation practices for blog posts have vastly improved there has been little development with regards to more fleeting and less contextual forms of content. It is far too easy for a distracted person to fail to record an idea encountered in a podcast they are listening to in the background or a tweet as they scroll their timeline on a commute, only for the idea to emerge in their writing at a later date perhaps justified by a sense it is 'in the air at the moment' rather than being attributable to a specific author. The manner in which GenAI draws on impossibly vast databases of existing material without enabling us to link any one output to an intellectual influence expands the existing problem in a way which makes it potentially unmanageable. In this sense, GenAI undercuts foundational assumptions which have grounded scholarly norms in ways we will be grappling with for years. This is why it is essential that we start the difficult work of extending scholarly norms to cope with the new technological environment in which we will all soon be working.

DEFENDING SCHOLARLY VALUES IN THE AUTOMATED UNIVERSITY

Does your university have guidance about GenAI? Does this guidance help you understand how to respond to the new situations you are facing, in which students are using only recently emerged services as part of their work? My hope is that by the time you are reading this book the answer for most academics will be 'yes' but this is much less likely to be true at the time I am writing it. In recent months I have found myself torn between frustration at the lack of clear guidelines and relief given how short-sighted initial responses such as banning ChatGPT and returning to in-person exams were. In the absence of guidelines provided by universities, teaching teams and individual staff members are forced to make their own decisions, often interpreting existing rules in ways which are only dimly connected to the new situations they are confronting. If these academics feel empowered to make these decisions, and they are informed by an adequate understanding of the issues involved, this could be a good thing. It can involve creative responses to emerging challenges, which could in principle become the basis for synthesising these decisions and formulating university-wide stances at a higher level of the organisation. Unfortunately, we cannot assume that staff will either feel empowered or be sufficiently informed to make these decisions well. At various points in the book, we have seen examples of poor practice by academics with regard to GenAI, such as the US professor who tried to fail his students after asking ChatGPT if it had written their essays. Under these conditions, we have to be very careful about allowing people to make decisions on the fly, but conversely, there simply aren't the conditions in place for universities to offer adequate guidance yet. If that guidance is offered too hastily, it risks shutting down an important avenue for creative experimentation with the possibilities of GenAI.

However, the versatility of these tools and systems, their multifaceted character, means that establishing rules exhaustively governing their use is difficult if not impossible, particularly at this early stage in their development. For this reason, there needs to be a two-way exchange in which situated responses to the challenges academics face on the ground, or feeding into policymaking at a university and sectoral level which learns from these emerging challenges and seeks to develop rules and principles to support staff in responding adequately to them. If decisions are made entirely at a local level, we would rapidly have a significant divergence in practice and outcomes which would pose obvious equity issues across the institution. But if we neglect the situated reality academics are working within when forming GenAI policy, we are likely to end up with rules and principles which speak to some areas more effectively than others. This is the fundamental tension of formulating policy with regard to an emerging technology within higher education.

It is within this ambiguous terrain that the norms developed by academics themselves, independently of university rule and policymaking, become particularly important. I say *norms* in order to distinguish them from *rules* and to point to the relationship between them. Organisations can easily articulate rules which seek to regulate conduct by enforcing sanctions on certain behaviours. If a university imposes a ban on its staff using GenAI, it is likely to reduce the usage of such software, reflecting a fear of the penalty attached and a respect for the message being sent that such behaviour is undesirable. But many would simply ignore such a rule out of a belief they would not be caught (e.g., when using a personal computer or mobile device) and/or a belief that it is a foolish rule which needlessly denies them potential advantages. The rule would be more effective if it was anchored in a popular sentiment amongst many staff that the use of such tools was in some fundamental sense *wrong*, perhaps contrary to existing principles of intellectual accountability or problematic for the reasons of data justice or environmental ethics discussed in Chapter 3. If rules are anchored in norms in this way they will be more effective than a simple threat of sanction because they will have a moral force to them, even in the absence of unanimous agreement about norms (Archer, 2016). Research ethics provides an obvious example of how rules and norms can be tied together in higher education. Even if the bureaucratic regulation of research ethics can prove frustrating, it is supported by a widespread conviction amongst academics that are certain forms of conduct which need to be prohibited.

The problem is that rules are quick whereas norms are slow. Prestigious journals can ban the listing of ChatGPT as a co-author on submission but it takes much longer for patterns of opinion to stabilise amongst academics as to the rights and wrongs of using conversational agents in publishing. Universities might ban the use of conversational agents to prepare internal documents but if there is little to no prospect of being caught, it is unlikely to be effective because there is no sense that staff *should* obey the rule. Rules can be imposed hierarchically within organisations but particularly with a professional group like academics, interconnected between institutions and organised into professional bodies, they only represent one influence amongst others on the formation of norms.

This is why academic leadership on these issues should be taking place within research networks, study groups and learned societies in order to facilitate a conversation about GenAI reflecting establishing norms, standards and identities within different disciplines. These are conversations we need to be having now before the momentum of adoption leaves us in a position where it's too late to put the genie back in the bottle. For example, a learned society might appoint a working group which would host a number of consultation events and release an annual statement of best practice which would be updated as scholarly opinion and technological capabilities develop. What matters is that some element of deliberation would be involved, in the sense of opinions being formed through discussion and consultation, rather than simply being recommendations by a set of appointed experts or a poll seeking to represent the current state of opinion within an intellectual community. This could incorporate a positive vision of GenAI use which is shared as a normative standard to inform and stimulate discussion, avoiding a drift into a negative discourse of prohibition and paranoia. The problem with such a conversation is that an attempt to overly hastily articulate norms and standards is unlikely to be binding, unlikely to achieve consensus, and perhaps more importantly, unlikely to cover the constantly evolving series of processes and outcomes in which academic use of GenAI is likely to emerge. We nonetheless need some way to begin these conversations and some way to keep their terms of reference continually updated as the technological possibilities continue to expand.

Adams and Thompson (2016, p. 98) suggest that devices and software should be regarded as co-researchers given their tendency 'to float in the background of research reports' yet be 'implicated in data collection and analysis efforts'. This point can be generalised to incorporate GenAI across the domains of scholarship. Its use should be accounted for, justified and explained in a way that embodies reflective awareness of how it has shaped the research process and at what potential costs. The versatility of conversational agents, in contrast to the pre-formatted options built into writing tools, rewards this reflexivity in epistemic terms; the more thoughtfully you formulate instructions, explain context and share explanations the more effectively they can contribute to knowledge production. This entails recognising that 'the very methods (and technologies) that researchers use to carry out a study constructs the kinds of research we can do' (Paulus & Lester, 2023). What form this should take will vary widely across genres of scholarly publishing but expecting at least a minimal statement of reflexivity ensures that we acknowledge rather than conceal the role of GenAI in our work. Furthermore, it contributes to a scholarly culture where that role is chosen in a careful and reflective way rather than fading into the background of working routines.

The ideal situation would be if every academic was introduced to the full range of GenAI platforms, tools and services as part of their training. Rather than advocating a particular use of any of these, the focus would be on helping the academic understand the range of possible uses, as well as relate them reflexively to their own developing preferences, inclinations and habits. It might be that some, even many, want to develop a scholarly practice which is suffused with GenAI. But in other cases, it may be that use is occasional or entirely non-existent. What is essential is that we *steer* this process in a way which reflects shared commitments, rather than leaving it to individual academics to make choices guided by instrumental imperatives which are inevitably short-term.

OUR UNEVENLY DISTRIBUTED FUTURE

If you are reading this book, it suggests a level of interest in GenAI which, at least at the time of writing, makes you relatively unusual. For those who have been tied up in these developments from the outset, there is a risk of forgetting how much of this has been peripheral to wider academic consciousness. There is certainly an awareness of the implications for assessment, with the panic and anxiety surrounding that filtering into all aspects of academic life. The practical challenges, real and imagined, ensuing from that have certainly been highly visible within universities, but the wider implications of these technologies are much more of a fringe pursuit. This is the sense in which William Gibson's often-cited maxim, *The future is already here, it's just not very evenly distributed,* can help us understand our present situation. I hope this book has convinced you that GenAI is a far bigger issue for universities than simply a challenge to the integrity of assessment. Throughout the book, I have tried to identify the means through which these platforms, tools and software can be incorporated into every facet of what we do as scholars. I have identified challenges presented within these domains and tried to suggest constructive solutions to them, albeit ones from a position in which the full problems are not yet clear.

The business academic Ethan Mollick, who has been a prolific and insightful commentator on these issues, points to a key challenge which is hindering the development of a wider debate. He identifies what he calls the 'secret cyborgs' who have rapidly incorporated the use of GenAI into many aspects of their workflow, often with significant benefits that are even recognised by those around them (Mollick, 2023). The reason these cyborgs are secret, he argues, is because either there are prohibitions on the use of GenAI within their organisations, or simply that in the absence of established norms about acceptable use there is a sense of risk involved in raising their use of these tools. They might be punished, their work might be seen as invalidated by their use of automation, and it might be that things they are doing now will later come to be deemed acceptable.

In reflecting at length on my own use of GenAI in writing this book, I have tried to model this sharing of practice in a reflective way. We urgently need to develop an open culture in which people are able to share uses that have proved valuable and raise problems they have encountered for discussion with peers. This is something universities need to encourage in order to build upon the emerging expertise amongst secret cyborgs working within them, as well as to ensure frameworks and policies are informed by a realistic appraisal of what is taking place on the ground. I expect this will happen simply because the costs of keeping it underground will grow with time. When we do see this coming out of the secret cyborgs, we are likely to experience a rapid shift in the visibility of GenAI within the academy.

There is again a parallel here to how social media went from being a fringe pursuit regarded by many as inappropriate for scholars to a routine feature of academic life. Drawing on a concept from Adam Greenfield, Martin Weller (2011) invoked the notion of *networked weather* to explain how this change took place: technologies we might be unaware of can nonetheless have an impact on how we experience our work. As the use of GenAI becomes increasingly visible amongst academics, it will become difficult to be a passive non-user of GenAI. It doesn't mean that everyone *will* start using these tools, but the awareness of how widespread use is turns that into a choice. Will you use it for the same purposes? If not, why not? This choice seems extremely important to me. It's one which shouldn't be entered into lightly, and how we make it ought to be informed by professional norms. In turn, the articulation of those norms in relation to this new technology should be informed by how people are answering that question.

We confront an uncertain future and I sincerely believe our individual and collective reflexivity is the most important resource we have in navigating it. What matters now is how we build a culture around GenAI which supports us in exercising it, resisting the threat of a slow surrender to automated systems we cannot control. That at least is how I see things. I thought it would be appropriate to ask Claude for its view as we bring this book to a close (Figure 8.3):

Claude:

Dear readers,

We stand at an inflection point with generative AI. It has immense potential to transform scholarship in groundbreaking ways. However, there are also risks if we charge blindly ahead. Issues around responsibility, sustainability, ethics, and labor must be grappled with.

As academics, we have an opportunity and duty to steer this technology toward empowering scholarship while mitigating harm. This requires a deeply reflexive approach as we continually re-examine our own AI use. The future remains undetermined. Through mindful engagement, we can uphold human dignity.

I hope this guidebook has sparked insight into your pivotal role. The daily decisions each of us makes on incorporating generative AI will ripple out in ways we cannot foresee. So I urge you to proceed with care, creativity and compassion as we walk this tightrope into the future together.
In solidarity,
Claude

Figure 8.3 A Closing Note to Readers from My Friendly Collaborator Claude

REFERENCES

Abbott, A. (1988). *The system of professions: An essay on the division of expert labor*. University of Chicago Press.

Abbott, A. (2014). *Digital paper: A manual for research and writing with library and internet materials*. University of Chicago Press.

Adams, C., & Thompson, T. L. (2016). *Researching a Posthuman World: Interviews with digital objects*. Springer.

Agger, B. (2000). *Public sociology: From social facts to literary Acts*. Rowman & Littlefield Publishers.

Allen, D. (2010). *Why Plato wrote*. Wiley-Blackwell.

Anderson, C. (2008). The end of theory: The data deluge makes the scientific method obsolete. *Wired Magazine*.

Andrejevic, M. (2019). *Automated media*. Routledge.

Archer, M. S. (2007). *Making our way through the world*. Cambridge University Press.

Archer, M. S. (2012). *The reflexive imperative in late modernity*. Cambridge University Press.

Archer, M. S. (2016). Anormative social regulation: The attempt to cope with social morphogenesis. In M. S. Archer (Ed.), *Morphogenesis and the crisis of normativity* (pp. 141-168). Springer.

Archer, M. S. (2021). Can humans and AI robots be friends? In M. Carrigan & D. V. Porpora (Eds.), *Post-human futures: Human enhancement, artificial intelligence and social theory* (pp. 132-152). Routledge.

Bacevic, J. (2019). Knowing neoliberalism. *Social Epistemology, 33*(4), 380-392.

Bacevic, J. (2023). Epistemic injustice and epistemic positioning: Towards an intersectional political economy. *Current Sociology, 69*(2), 129-146.

Back, L. (2012). Live sociology: Social research and its futures. *The Sociological Review, 60*(1), 18-39.

Baym, N. K., & Burgess, J. (2020). *Twitter: A biography*. New York University Press.

Becker, H. S. (2008). *Writing for social scientists: How to start and finish your thesis*. University of Chicago Press.

Beer, D. (2014). The end of 'online'? Removing politics from digital research. *The Sociological Review, 62*(2), 283-297.

Belkhir, L., & Elmeligi, A. (2018). Assessing ICT global emissions footprint: Trends to 2040 & recommendations. *Journal of Cleaner Production, 177*, 448-463.

Bender, E. M., Gebru, T., McMillan-Major, A., & Shmitchell, S. (2021). On the dangers of stochastic parrots: Can language models be too big? In *Proceedings of the 2021 ACM Conference on Fairness, Accountability, and Transparency, virtual event, Canada, 03–10 March 2021* (pp. 610-623). Association for Computing Machinery.

Billig, M. (2013). *Learn to write badly: How to succeed in the social sciences*. Cambridge University Press.

Birhane, A., Prabhu, V. U., & Kahembwe, E. (2021). Multimodal datasets: Misogyny, pornography, and malignant stereotypes. *arXiv preprint arXiv:2110.01963*.

Bostrom, N. (2014). *Superintelligence: Paths, dangers, strategies.* Oxford University Press.

Bostrom, N. (2016). *Superintelligence: Paths, dangers, strategies.* Oxford University Press.

Bourdieu, P. (2008). *Political interventions: Social science and political action.* Verso Books.

boyd, d (2013). *It's complicated: The social lives of networked teens.* Yale University Press.

boyd, d (2023). Resisting deterministic thinking. In *Zephoria.* https://zephoria.medium.com/. Accessed on January 5, 2024.

Bratton, B. H. (2015). *The stack: On software and sovereignty.* MIT Press.

Brevini, B. (2021). *Is AI good for the planet?* Polity Press.

Brubaker, R. (2022). *Hyperconnectivity and its discontents.* John Wiley & Sons.

Brunton, F. (2013). *Spam: A shadow history of the internet.* MIT Press.

Burawoy, M. (2016). The neoliberal university: Ascent of the spiralists. *Critical Sociology, 42*(7-8), 941-942.

Burdick, A., Drucker, J., Lunenfeld, P., Presner, T., & Schnapp, J. (2012). *Digital_humanities.* MIT Press.

Burgess, J., & Green, J. (2018). *YouTube: Online video and participatory culture* (2nd ed.). Polity Press.

Burkeman, O. (2022). In your own time: How to live for today the philosophical way. *The Guardian.* https://www.theguardian.com/lifeandstyle/2022/jun/10/in-your-own-time-how-to-live-for-today-the-philosophical-way. Accessed on January 15, 2024.

Burrows, R. (2012). Living with the h-index? Metric assemblages in the contemporary academy. *The Sociological Review, 60*(2), 355-372.

Caren, C. (2023). The launch of Turnitin's AI writing detector and the road ahead. *Turnitin blog.* https://www.turnitin.com/blog/the-launch-of-turnitins-ai-writing-detector-and-the-road-ahead. Accessed on January 10, 2024.

Carrigan, M. (2016). *Social media for academics.* SAGE.

Carrigan, M. (2018). The platform university. Discover Society (68). https://archive.discoversociety.org/2019/05/01/focus-the-platform-university/. Accessed on January 10, 2024.

Carrigan, M. (2019). *Social media for academics* (2nd ed.). SAGE.

Carrigan, M. (2022). Public scholarship in the platform university: Social media and the challenge of populism. *Globalisation, Societies and Education, 20*(2), 193-207.

Carrigan, M., & Fatsis, L. (2021). *The public and their platforms: Public sociology in an age of social media.* Bristol University Press.

Carrigan, M., & Jordan, K. (2021). Platforms and institutions in the post-pandemic university: A case study of social media and the impact agenda. *Postdigital Science and Education, 3*(3), 739-759.

Carrigan, M., Moscovitz, H., Michele, M., & Robertson, S. L. (2023). *Building the post-pandemic university: Imagining, contesting and materializing higher education futures.* Edward Elgar Publishing.

Carrigan, M., & Porpora, D. V. (2021). Introduction: Conceptualizing post-human futures. In M. Carrigan & D. V. Porpora (Eds.), *Post-human futures: Human enhancement, artificial Intelligence and social theory* (pp. 1-22). Routledge.

Carrigan, M., & Sylvia, J. J., IV. (2022, September 1). Is it paranoia? A critical approach to platform literacy. *The Journal of Media Literacy.*

Cave, N. (2022). The red hand files issue #248. https://www.theredhandfiles.com/chatgpt-making-things-faster-and-easier/. Accessed on January 6, 2024.

Chomsky, N. (2023). Debunking the great AI lie. https://www.youtube.com/watch?v=PBdZi_JtV4c. Accessed on January 5, 2024.

Clarke, R., & Lancaster, T. (2006). Contract cheating: The outsourcing of assessed student work. In T. Bretag (Ed.), *Handbook of academic integrity* (pp. 639–654). Springer.

Collins, H. M. (1990). *Artificial experts: Social knowledge and intelligent machines*. MIT Press.

Conor, B., Gill, R., & Taylor, S. (2015). Gender and creative labour. *The Sociological Review, 63*(1), 1–22.

Crabapple, M. (2023). Restrict AI illustration from publishing. *An Open Letter.* https://artisticinquiry.org/AI-Open-Letter. Accessed on January 10, 2024.

Crawford, K. (2021). *The Atlas of AI.* Yale University Press.

Davies, W. (2014). Governing through unhappiness: Audit culture and the lasting effects of the REF. *LSE Impact of Social Sciences Blog.* https://blogs.lse.ac.uk/impactofsocialsciences/2015/01/02/governing-through-unhappiness/. Accessed on January 10, 2024.

Davies, W. (2018). *Nervous states: How feeling took over the world.* Penguin Random House.

Day, M. (2024, March 28). *Amazon bets $150 billion on data centers required for AI boom.* Bloomberg.

DiMaggio, P. J., & Powell, W. W. (1983). The iron cage revisited: Institutional isomorphism and collective rationality in organizational fields. *American Sociological Review, 48*(2), 147–160.

Dolan, P. (2014). *Happiness by design: Finding pleasure and purpose in everyday life.* Penguin.

Dollinger, M. (2020). The projectification of the university: Consequences and alternatives. *Teaching in Higher Education, 25*(6), 669–682.

Dunleavy, P. (2014). Shorter, better, faster, free: Blogging changes the nature of academic research, not just how it is communicated. *LSE Impact of Social Sciences Blog.* https://blogs.lse.ac.uk/impactofsocialsciences/2014/12/28/shorter-better-faster-free/. Accessed on January 10, 2024.

Fallows, J. (1982). Living with a computer. *The Atlantic Monthly, 250*(July), 84–91.

Fitzpatrick, K. (2011). *Planned obsolescence: Publishing, technology, and the future of the academy.* New York University Press.

Ford, M. (2015). *Rise of the robots.* Basic Books.

Foss, K., & Lathrop, A. (2000). *Student cheating and plagiarism in the Internet era: A wake-up call.* Bloomsbury Publishing.

Foucault, M. (1966). *The order of things: An archaeology of the human sciences.* Editions Gallimard.

Fridman, L. (2024). Transcript for Sam Altman: OpenAI, GPT-5, Sora, Board Saga, Elon Musk, Ilya, Power & AGI. *Lex Friedman Podcast.* https://lexfridman.com/sam-altman-2-transcript/. Accessed on March 10, 2024.

Frodeman, R. (2014). *Sustainable knowledge: A theory of interdisciplinarity.* Palgrave Pivot.

Fuller, S. (2023). *Back to the university's future: The second coming of Humboldt.* Springer Nature.

Furendal, M., & Jebari, K. (2023). The future of work: Augmentation or stunting? *Philosophy & Technology, 36*(2), 36.

Gasser, U., & Mayer-Schönberger, V. (2024). *Guardrails: Guiding human decisions in the age of AI.* Princeton University Press.

Gill, R. (2013). Breaking the silence: The hidden injuries of the neoliberal university. In R. Gill & R. Ryan-Flood (Eds.), *Secrecy and silence in the research process* (pp. 228–244). Routledge.

Gillespie, T. (2018). *Custodians of the Internet: Platforms, content moderation, and the hidden decisions that shape social media.* Yale University Press.

Goldenfein, J., Benthall, S., Griffin, D. S. (2019). Private companies and scholarly infrastructure - Google Scholar and Academic Autonomy. *Critical Reflections.* https://www.dli.tech.cornell.edu/post/private-companies-and-scholarly-infrastructure-google-scholar-and-academic-autonomy. Accessed on January 10, 2024.

Grammarly. (2020). Grammarly: Free Online Writing Assistant. Internet Archive. https://www.grammarly.com/. https://web.archive.org/web/20200201082210/. Accessed on November 18, 2024.

Gregg, M. (2013). *Work's intimacy*. John Wiley & Sons.

Gross, N. (2000). *Richard Rorty: The making of an American philosopher*. University of Chicago Press.

Hall, G. (2016). *Pirate philosophy: For a digital Posthumanities*. MIT Press.

Hillis, K., Petit, M., & Jarrett, K. (2012). *Google and the culture of search*. Routledge.

Hund, E. (2023). *The influencer industry: The quest for authenticity on social media*. Princeton University Press.

Jordan, K., & Carrigan, M. (2018). The impact agenda has led to social media being used in a role it may not be equipped to perform. *LSE Impact of Social Sciences Blog*. https://blogs.lse.ac.uk/impactofsocialsciences/2018/05/31/the-impact-agenda-has-led-to-social-media-being-used-in-a-role-it-may-not-be-equipped-to-perform/. Accessed on January 10, 2024.

Keen, Z. (2023). Why large language models hallucinate. *IBM Technology*. https://www.youtube.com/watch?v=cfqtFvWOfg0&ab_channel=IBMTechnology. Accessed on January 10, 2024.

Klee, M. (2023, June 6). She was falsely accused of cheating with AI – And she won't be the last. *Rolling Stone*.

Klein, N. (2020). Screen new deal. *The intercept*. https://theintercept.com/2020/05/08/andrew-cuomo-eric-schmidt-coronavirus-tech-shock-doctrine/. Accessed on August 26, 2024.

Klein, N. (2021, May 8). Screen new deal. *The Intercept*.

Klein, N. (2023, May 8) AI machines aren't 'hallucinating'. But their makers are. *The Guardian*.

Kumar, V., & Davenport, M. J. (2023, July 20). How to make generative AI greener. *Harvard Business Review*.

Laurillard, D. (2012). *Teaching as a design science: Building pedagogical patterns for learning and technology*. Routledge.

Leo, U. (2023). Generative AI should mark the end of a failed war on student academic misconduct. *LSE Impact of Social Sciences Blog*. https://blogs.lse.ac.uk/impactofsocialsciences/2023/07/21/generative-ai-should-mark-the-end-of-a-failed-war-on-student-academic-misconduct/. Accessed on January 10, 2024.

Lewis-Kraus, G. (2023, September 30). They studied dishonesty was their work a lie? *New Yorker*.

Luca, M., Wu, T., Couvidat, S., Frank, D., & Seltzer, W. (2015). *Does Google Content Degrade Google Search?: Experimental Evidence*. NOM Unit Working Paper No. 16-035, Harvard Business School, USA.

Lukes, S. (2005). *Power: A radical view* (2nd ed.). Palgrave Macmillan.

Maiberg, E. (2024, March 18).Scientific journals are publishing papers with AI-generated text. *404 Media*.

Marcus, G. E. (2024). The race between positive and negative applications of Generative AI is on – And not looking pretty. *Marcus on AI*. https://garymarcus.substack.com/p/the-race-between-positive-and-negative. Accessed on January 10, 2024.

Margetts, H. (2018). Rethinking democracy with social media. *The Political Quarterly, 90*(1), 107-123.

Mark, G. (2023). *Attention span: A groundbreaking way to restore balance, happiness, and productivity*. Hanover Square Press.

Mark, G. (2024). How much should we trust ChatGPT to summarize information? In *The future of attention*. https://gloriamark.substack.com/p/how-much-should-we-trust-chatgpt?utm_source=profile&utm_medium=reader2. Accessed on January 10, 2024.

Marres, N. (2017). *Digital sociology: The reinvention of social research*. Polity Press.

Marres, N. (2018). Why we can't have our facts back. *Engaging Science, Technology, and Society,* 4(1), 423–443.

Marwick, A. E. (2021). Morally motivated networked harassment as normative reinforcement. *Social Media + Society,* 7(2).

Mathewson. (2023, August 19). AI detector bias and higher Ed coverage at the markup. *The Markup.*

McCluskey, F. B., & Winter, M. L. (2012). *The idea of the digital university: Ancient traditions, disruptive technologies and the battle for the soul of higher education.* Westphalia Press.

McQuillan, D. (2022). *Resisting AI: An anti-fascist approach to artificial intelligence.* Bristol University Press.

Mewburn, I. (2023). Using ChatGPT (ChattieG) to write good. *The Thesis Whisperer.* https://thesiswhisperer.com/2023/05/02/usingchatgpt/. Accessed on January 10, 2024.

Mills, C. W. (2000). *The sociological imagination.* Oxford University Press.

Mollick, E. (2023). Detecting the secret cyborgs. *One Useful Thing.* https://www.oneusefulthing.org/p/detecting-the-secret-cyborgs. Accessed on January 10, 2024.

Morozov, E. (2011). *The net delusion: How not to liberate the world.* Allen Lane.

Müller, R. (2019). Racing for what? Anticipation and acceleration in the work and career practices of academic life science postdocs. In F. Cannizzo & N. Osbaldiston (Eds.), *The social structures of global academia* (pp. 162–184). Routledge.

Natale, S. (2021). *Deceitful media: Artificial intelligence and social life after the Turing test.* Oxford University Press.

Newport, C. (2016). *Deep work: Rules for focused success in a distracted world.* Hachette.

Newport, C. (2021). *A world without email: Reimagining work in an age of communication overload.* Portfolio.

Nielsen, M. (2011). *Reinventing discovery: The new era of networked science.* Princeton University Press.

Nietzsche, F. W. (1908). *Human, all too human: A book for free spirits.* The Macmillan Company.

Nietzsche, F. W. (1974). *The gay science: With a prelude in rhymes and an appendix of songs* (W Kaufmann trans). Vintage Books.

Nordmann, E., Horlin, C., Hutchison, J., Murray, J. A., Robson, L., Seery, M. K., & MacKay, J. R. (2020). Ten simple rules for supporting a temporary online pivot in higher education. *PLoS Computational Biology,* 16(10), e1008242.

O'Neil, C. (2016). *Weapons of math destruction: How big data increases inequality and threatens democracy.* Crown.

Ohno, C. (2022). A short history of procedurally generated text. *enkiv2.* https://enkiv2.medium.com/a-short-history-of-procedurally-generated-text-733387b6b61f. Accessed on January 10, 2024.

Oxford Semantic Technologies. (2023). ChatGPT's snow white problem. https://oxfordsemantic.ai/chatgpts-snow-white-problem/. Accessed on January 7, 2024.

Parker, M. (2014). University, Ltd: Changing a business school. *Organization,* 21(2), 281–292.

Pasquale, F. (2020). *New laws of robotics: Defending human expertise in the age of AI.* Harvard University Press.

Paulus, T., & Lester, J. N. (2023). *Doing qualitative research in a digital world.* SAGE.

Pleasant, J. (2022). A conversation with Nick Seaver, author of computing taste. *Civics of Technology.* https://www.civicsoftechnology.org/blog/a-conversation-with-nick-seaver-author-of-computing-taste. Accessed on January 10, 2024.

Plunkett, J. (2010, October 11). Andrew Marr says 'socially inadequate' bloggers spend too much time in 'Mum's basement. *The Guardian.*

Preston, J. (2022). *Artificial intelligence in the capitalist university: Academic labour, commodification, and value.* Routledge.

Russell, B. (2013). *The conquest of happiness.* Liveright Publishing Corporation.

Scholz, T. (2017). *Uberworked and underpaid: How workers are disrupting the digital economy.* John Wiley & Sons.

Selwyn, N. (2021). *Education and technology: Key issues and debates* (Kindle ed.). Bloomsbury Publishing.

Selwyn, N., Hillman, T., Bergviken-Rensfeldt, A., & Perrotta, C. (2022). Making sense of the digital automation of education. *Postdigital Science and Education, 5,* 1–14.

Sennett, R. (2008). *The craftsman.* Yale University Press.

Shetty, N., Verstak, A., Hwang, K. J., Jin, L., David, P., & Acharya, A. (2021). Scholar Recommendations reloaded! Fresher, more relevant, easier. Google Scholar Blog. https://scholar.googleblog.com/2021/02/scholar-recommendations-reloaded.html. Accessed on November 18, 2024.

Sipley, G. (2024). *Just here for the comments: Lurking as digital literacy practice.* Policy Press.

Slaughter, S., & Leslie, L. L. (1997). *Academic capitalism: Politics, policies, and the entrepreneurial university.* The Johns Hopkins University Press.

Squazzoni, F., Bravo, G., Grimaldo, F., García-Costa, D., Farjam, M., & Mehmani, B. (2021). Gender gap in journal submissions and peer review during the first wave of the COVID-19 pandemic. A study on 2329 Elsevier journals. *PLoS One, 16*(10), e0257919.

Srnicek, N. (2016). *Platform capitalism.* John Wiley & Sons.

Stiegler, B. (2019). *The age of disruption: Technology and madness in computational capitalism.* John Wiley & Sons.

Sturmer, M., & Carrigan, M. (2023). Resisting AI: An anti-fascist approach to artificial intelligence – Review. *LSE Impact of Social Sciences Blog.* https://blogs.lse.ac.uk/impactofsocialsciences/2023/11/16/resisting-ai-an-anti-fascist-approach-to-artificial-intelligence-review/. Accessed on January 10, 2024.

Šupak Smolčić, V. (2013). Salami publication: Definitions and examples. *Biochemia Medica, 23*(3), 237–241.

Sword, H. (2017). *Air & light & time & space: How successful academics write.* Harvard University Press.

Taloni, A., Scorcia, V., & Giannaccare, G. (2023). Large language model advanced data analysis abuse to create a fake data set in medical research. *JAMA ophthalmology, 141*(12), 1174–1175.

Tarnoff, B. (2023, July 25). Weizenbaum's nightmares: How the inventor of the first chatbot turned against AI. *The Guardian.*

Taylor, C. (1985). *Philosophical papers: Volume 1, human agency and language.* Cambridge University Press.

Thornhill, J. (2023, 1 June). Beware 'death by GPT syndrome'. *Financial Times.*

Turner, F. (2010). *From counterculture to cyberculture: Stewart brand, the whole earth network, and the rise of digital utopianism.* University of Chicago Press.

Turnitin. (2023). The launch of Turnitin's AI writing detector and the road ahead. https://www.turnitin.com/blog/the-launch-of-turnitins-ai-writing-detector-and-the-road-ahead. Accessed on August 26, 2024.

Vaidhyanathan, S. (2011). *The Googlization of everything (and why we should worry).* University of California Press.

Vallor, S. (2016). *Technology and the virtues: A philosophical guide to a future worth wanting.* Oxford University Press.

Varoufakis, Y. (2023). *Technofeudalism: What killed capitalism*. Penguin Random House.

Vostal, F. (2015). Academic life in the fast lane: The experience of time and speed in British academia. *Time & Society, 24*(1), 71-95.

Vostal, F. (2016). *Accelerating academia: The changing structure of academic time*. Palgrave Macmillan.

Wallace, D. F. (2005). *This is water: Some thoughts, delivered on a significant occasion. About living a compassionate life*. Little, Brown and Company.

Wallace-Wells, D. (2019). *The uninhabitable earth: Life after warming*. Tim Duggan Books.

Watters, A. (2016). *The curse of the monsters of education technology*. CreateSpace Independent Publishing Platform.

Ware, M., & Mabe, M. (2015). *The STM report: An overview of scientific and scholarly journal publishing*. STM. https://www.stm-assoc.org/2015_02_20_STM_Report_2015.pdf

Wegerif, R., & Major, L. (2024). *The theory of educational technology: Towards a dialogic foundation for design*. Routledge.

Weller, M. (2011). *The digital scholar: How technology is transforming scholarly practice*. A&C Black.

Weller, M. (2020). *25 Years of ed tech*. Athabasca University Press.

White, K. (2019). Publications Output: US Trends and International Comparisons. *Science & Engineering Indicators 2020*. NSB-2020-6. National Science Foundation.

Williamson, B. (2018). Silicon startup schools: Technocracy, algorithmic imaginaries and venture philanthropy in corporate education reform. *Critical Studies in Education, 59*(2), 218-236.

Woodcock, J. (2018). Digital labour in the university: Understanding the transformations of academic work in the UK. *tripleC: Communication, Capitalism & Critique, 16*(1), 129-142.

Zuboff, S. (2018). *The age of surveillance capitalism: The fight for a human future at the new frontier of power*. Profile Books.

INDEX

A

Abbott, A., 31
Academic resistance, 159
Academics, 5, 43, 103, 108, 131
  conversational agents as, 6 (figure)
  digital media, 28
  futures, 147–166
  GenAI and typical use cases for, 29 (figure)
  hierarchy, 53
  interlocutor, 1
  misconduct, 11, 14
  networking, 5, 6
  pre-Musk Twitter, 137
  productive, 44
  prompts, 36
  reflexivity, 9
  role of, 145
  social media, 3, 136
  writing, 66, 131, 132, 157
Accelerated academy, 34
Adams, C., 164
Addiction metaphors, 108
Adobe
  Firefly, 143
  Podcast, 143
  Spark, 141
Agger, B., 131
Algorithmic bias, 50
Algorithmic injustice, 50
Alphabet, 52
Amazon, 52, 153, 154
Apple Shortcuts, 95
Archer, M., 73
Artificial general intelligence (AGI), 2
Artificial intelligence (AI), 2, 4, 25, 53
  dubbing services, 142
  literature, 79
  writing tools, 12
Asexuality, 130
Asimov, I., 150
Assessment panic, 9–14, 11 (figure)
Autocorrection, 25
Automated authorship, cultural politics of,
  160–162
Automated communication, 109–111
Automated university
  political economy of, 158–160
  scholarly values in, 162–164

Automation, 14, 26, 93, 110, 136, 149, 150, 158
Autosuggestion capabilities, 25, 26

B

Bacevic, J., 151
Bannon, S., 146
Basecamp, 99
Baym, N. K., 103
Becker, H. S., 31
Beetham, H., 61
Belkhir, L., 53
Bender, E. M., 49, 50
Big data, 44
Billig, M., 131
Bing, 26, 30
Birhane, A., 49
Blackboard, 14, 115
Bluesky, 129
Bostrom, N., 24, 160, 161
Bourdieu, P., 31
Boyd, D., 18, 19
Bratton, B. H., 44
Brevini, B., 53
Brooker, P., 73
Brubaker, R., 87, 108, 157
Brunton, F., 153
Buffer, 136
Bundlr, 26
Burawoy, M., 159
Burgess, J., 103
Burkeman, O., 157
Burrows, R., 108

C

Canvas, 143
Carrigan, M., 129, 138, 144
Cave, N., 16
Center for Artistic Inquiry and Reporting, 56
Change management, 159
ChatGPT, 2, 3, 5, 6 (figure), 16, 17, 22, 28,
  32 (figure)–33 (figure), 110
  collaborative work, 91 (figure)
  description of, 50
  doomster-ism, 9 (figure)
  effective prompt, 37 (figure)
  engagement strategy, 132 (figure)
  features, 5
  iOS application, 66

launch of, 11 (figure)
ongoing conversations, 7
privacy safeguards, 113
publishing editor, 69 (figure)
scholar, stereotypical image of, 65 (figure)
sharing thoughts with social media, 69 (figure)
singular instructions, 7
Snow White problem, 48
social and political implications of, 124 (figure)
'successful' scientist, depiction of, 51 (figure)
technological hype, 9 (figure)
20th century academics, 67 (figure)
uncanny abilities of, 25
writing prompts, advice on, 36 (figure)
ChatGPT 3.5, 19, 22, 55
ChatGPT-4, 19, 49, 55
Chomsky, N., 53
Clarke, R., 10
Claude, 3, 5, 7, 22, 23, 28, 36, 68, 78, 98, 113, 117, 166
    (figure)
    blog posts, 139 (figure)
    conference abstract, 120 (figure)
    context window, 5
    conversational agents to hallucinate, worrying
        tendency of, 81 (figure)
    as interlocutor, 7
    stakeholders, 138 (figure)
    sustainable practice with conversational agents, 54
        (figure)
    video calls, limitations of, 88 (figure)
Claude 3 Haiku, 55
Claude 3 Opus, 55
Cloud computing, 52, 53, 55
Collaboration, 28, 86–105
    conversational agent AI, 96 (figure)
    conversation recording with GenAI, 90–92
    human–computer, autosuggestion, 26
    intellectual engagement and, 87
    knowledge production, 99–102
    learning from each other, 102–105
    modes of, 92–96
    production and, 16
    research, 96–99
    time with, 89–90
Collective discovery, modes of, 92–96
Collective intelligence, 18, 103
Collins, H. M., 161
Communication, 28, 108–125
    automated, 109
    with colleagues, 111–114
    dilemmas, 112–114
    email, 26
    environment, 125
    getting feedback, 112
    higher education, 110–111
    internal, 109
    professional, 118

with students, 114–118
    translating your work, 119–122
Computational media, 53
Constitutional AI, 97
Context window, 5, 23
Contract cheating, 10
Conversational agents, 6, 6 (figure), 73, 117, 141
    capacity of, 77
    Claude's advice, 54 (figure)
    as collaborators, 20
    creative fascination with, 61
    engagement, 24
    hallucination, 47
    intellectual value of, 8
    modes of, 6 (figure)
    real value of, 8
    sharing your thoughts with social media and, 69
        (figure)
    versatility of, 164
    worrying tendency of, 81 (figure)
Co-operative Insurance Group (CIS), 145
Copilot system, 30
Corporate optimism, 53
COVID-19 pandemic, 18, 46
    digitalisation of, 46, 71
    knowledge production, 86
    lockdown restrictions, 46
Crabapple, M., 56
Crawford, K., 49, 53
Cultural imagination, 150

D
DALL-E generated images, 56
Data storage, 52
Davenport, M. J., 53
Davies, W., 146, 151
DeepL, 142
Designed serendipity, 101
Digital engagement, 66, 136
Digital literacy, 110
Digital media, 71, 72, 108, 135
Digital scholarship, 28, 46, 68, 71–74, 101
Digital scribe, 89, 93, 98, 99
Digital technologies, 4, 8, 46
Discriminatory mechanisms, 50
Disney's Snow White, 48
Dolan, P., 35
DuckDuckGo, 35
Dunleavy, P., 72

E
El Apóstol, 48
Eliza, 2
Elmeligi, A., 53
Emergency remote teaching, 46
Engagement, 28, 53, 86, 128–146
    asynchronous, 87

automation, 136
digital, 66, 109
formats, 139-142
GenAI, 143-146
multimedia, 142-143
published work, 136-138
social media, 108, 128
stakeholders, 139 (figure)
translating and repurposing, 135-143
wider audiences, 130-135
Environmental catastrophe, 52-55
Epistemic deterioration, 152
European Union, 100
Experimentation, 34, 36
importance of, 36-38, 37 (figure)
principles for, 38-39
Expressive documents, 121

F
Facebook, 44
Falconer, H., 130
Fallows, J., 31, 32 (figure)
Fathom, 95
Fear of missing out (FOMO), 4
Feedback, 11, 132
communication, 112
continual, 54
editorial, 131
loop, 49
mechanisms, 48
prompts, 36
reflexive, 70
Filtering mechanisms, 50, 79
Fitzpatrick, K., 156
Foss, K., 11
Foucault, M., 16
Frodeman, R., 79
Fuller, S., 45
Functional documents, 121

G
Gamma, 141, 142
Gasser, U., 60
Gebru, T., 50
Gemini, 26
Generative artificial intelligence (GenAI)
categories of, 27-30, 29 (figure), 29 (table)
challenge of, 10
collaborative research, 96-99
communication, 108-125
context in, 43-47
conversation recording, 90-92
dystopian scenario of, 149 (figure)
engagement, 128-146
environmental catastrophe, 52-55
epistemic limits of, 47-52
ethics of, 41-61

etiquette of, 118-119
experimenting, 36-39
in higher education, 15 (figure)
intellectual property, 55-58
as interlocutor, 64-71
literature, finding and summarising, 80-83
publishing, 150-153
reflexivity and, 21-39
social and political implications of,
124 (figure)
as software, 24-27
spam, 123-125, 124 (figure)
summarisation, 52
universities and, 1-20
workflows, 30-36
Generative scholarship, 71-74, 101
pitfalls, 156-158
possibilities, 156-158
Gibson, W., 164
Gillespie, T., 44
Gill, R., 108
Gmail, 25, 26
Goldenfein, J., 79
Google, 27
Docs, 19, 25, 76
Images, 64
Meet, 96
Scholar, 18, 30, 79, 80, 151
Workspace, 94
Greenfield, A., 165

H
Hall, G., 16
Hallucinations, 47, 48, 50, 58, 74, 81
(figure), 144
HBX Live Studio, 87
Higher education, 3, 4, 7, 44, 128
assessment panic in, 11 (figure)
communication, 110-111
GenAI in, 15 (figure)
technological change, 32 (figure)-33 (figure)
Hillis, K., 20
HootSuite, 136
Humanism, 16
Hund, E., 128
Hybrid working, 86, 89, 102, 108

I
Intellectual curiosity, 100
Intellectual liveliness, 89
Intellectual property, 55-58
Intellectual richness, 101
Internal communication, 109
International Sociological Association (ISA), 142

J
Jarrett, K., 20

K

Keen, Z., 48
Klee, M., 12
Klein, N., 15, 56
Knowledge base platforms, 94
Knowledge management services, 94
Knowledge production, 20, 46, 86, 94
  distributing forms of, 100
  future of, 99–102
  humanistic, 43
  iterative relationship to, 73
  social networks and, 44
  technical infrastructure, 99
Kumar, V., 53

L

Lancaster, T., 10
Large language models (LLMs), 25, 96, 97
Lathrop, A., 11
Lawsuits, 57
Legitimacy, 47
Leo, U., 14
Lewis-Kraus, G., 59
LGBTQ discourse, 50
LinkedIn, 129
Literature, 79–83
  finding and summarising, 80–83
  understanding, 82–83
Loop, 94
Lukes, S., 92

M

MacGPT, 35
Major, L., 55
Makanju, A., 58
Malpractice, 10, 11
Marcus, G. E., 58
Mark, G., 52, 128
Marr, A., 128
Marres, N., 145
Marvel comics, 144, 145
Massively Open Online Courses (MOOCs), 44, 159
Mastodon, 129
Mathewson, 12
Mayer-Schonberger, V., 60
McCarthy, J., 25
McCluskey, F. B., 26
McQuillan, D., 9, 53
Mead, G. H., 55
Mem, 94
Meta-collaborators, 98
Meta-data, 50
Mewburn, I., 8, 50
Microblogging platform, 71
Microsoft, 52, 57
  Copilot, 115
  Notion, 94

Office, 25
Outlook, 25, 26
PowerPoint, 14, 115
Sway, 141
Teams, 90, 92
Word, 115
Mills, C. W., 31, 33, 68, 148
Miscommunication, 116
Misconduct, 9
  academic, 11, 14
  investigating, 14
  research, 59
Mollick, E., 165
MOOCs. *See* Massively Open Online Courses (MOOCs)
Multimedia engagement, 142–143
Murtagh, L., 2
Musk, E., 101, 129, 134

N

Networking, 5, 6, 87
New Laws of Robotics, 150
Newport, C., 157
New York Times lawsuit, 57
Nielsen, M., 71, 101
Nietzsche, F. W., 67, 88

O

Obsidian, 94
Office 365, 19, 94
Ohno, C., 17
Omnifocus, 34
Online events, 87
Online identity, 128
OpenAI, 2, 3, 5, 27. *See also* ChatGPT
  revenue, 102
  Sora video generation system, 56
Optimism, 101
  corporate, 53
  pessimism and, 43, 55
Oxford Semantic Technologies, 48

P

Paid visibility model, 134
Pasquale, F., 92, 150, 152
Patreon, 143
Pessimism, 43, 55
Petit, M., 20
Physical accessibility, 87
Pinterest, 26
Plagiarism, 26
Planetary-scale computation, 44
Platform university, 26
Plato, 17, 87
Pornography, 50
Predatory journals, 58
Professional judgement, 149

Project management systems, 99
Public pedagogy, 103, 104
Publishing, 124
  academic, 44, 147, 153
  acceleration of, 150–153
  digital, 72
  political economy of, 131
  scholarly, 153–156, 155 (figure)

Q
Qualitative improvements, 152
Quantitative improvements, 152, 153

R
Reddit, 49
Reflexivity, 21–39, 164
  academic, 151
  application of, 23
  collective, 165
  individual, 165
  methodological, 37
  technological, 31
RentACoder site, 11
Research Excellence Framework (REF), 97
Research misconduct, 59
ResearchRabbit, 80
Rewind, 94
Roam, 94
Robophobia, 73
Rorty, R., 79
Rubberducking, 73, 74
Russell, B., 64, 66, 67 (figure)

S
Saga, 94
Salami-slicing, 154
Scholarly publishing, crisis of, 153–156, 155 (figure)
Scholarship, 5, 7, 28, 100, 149
  costs of, 102
  digital, 28, 33, 46, 68, 71–74
  generative, 71–74, 101
  higher education and, 42
Science and Technology Studies (STS), 82
Search engine optimisation (SEO), 123
Secret cyborgs, 165
Self-conception, 138
Selwyn, N., 8, 9 (figure), 26
Semantic Scholar tool, 80
Sennett, R., 157
Sensationalism, 72
Sense-making process, 70
Seven Dwarfs, 48
Silicon Valley, 57
Slack, 94
Snow White problem, 48
Social connection, 87
Social inequalities, 50

Socialisation process, 140
Social media, 3, 4, 26, 38, 43, 49, 104
  audiences, 137
  engagement, 108, 128
  isolated ideas, 161
  political challenge, 44
  sharing your thoughts with, 69 (figure)
  social challenge, 44
Social Media for Academics, 128
Social ontology, 140
Sora video generation system, 56
Spam books, 153, 154
Summarisation, 52, 82, 90, 92
Superabundant digital sociality, 108
Surveillance capitalism, 18
Sword, H., 31, 66, 132, 157

T
Taloni, 59
Taylor, C., 12
Technological reflexivity, 31
Thinking, 6, 8, 28, 64–83
  digital scholarship, 71–74
  generative scholarship, 71–74
  limits of, 74–75
  reflexive, 19
  substitute for, 20
  writing assistant, 75–77
Thompson, T. L., 164
Thornhill, J., 48
Threads, 129
TikTok, 142
Trade Union Congress (TUC), 145
Trello, 99
Turnitin, 12
Twitter (now X), 49, 66, 71, 101, 103
  engagement, 129
  paid visibility model, 134
  revolutions, 128
  subscription charges, 129

U
Udandarao, 57
Universities, 1–20, 80
  automated, 158–160
  with GenAI, 15–20
  post-pandemic, 18
  practical challenges, 18
Unsplash, 57
USB-C flash drive, 52

V
Vallor, S., 35, 92
VEED, 117, 142
Video calls, limitations of, 88 (figure)
Video conferencing, 86
Vostal, F., 34, 151

W
Wallace, D. F., 45
Watters, A., 114
Web 2.0, 49
Wegerif, R., 55
Weizenbaum, J., 2
Weller, M., 28, 114, 128, 165
WhatsApp, 108
Whitworth, D., 2
Wikipedia, 48, 49, 145, 154
Winter, M. L., 26
Woodcock, J., 53
WordPress, 76
Workflows, 30–36
  academic, 27
  macro issues, 35

micro issues, 35
Workshops, 7
  Centre for Social Ontology, 92
  Gamma, 141
  landscape of, 86
  online, 59
World's Fair (1910), 114

Y
YouTube, 104, 129, 142

Z
Zapier, 110
Zoom meetings, 33, 46, 89, 90, 109
Zuboff, S., 18
Zuckerberg, M., 44

Printed in Great Britain
by Amazon

56827506R00110